# Out of the North

# Out of the North

## THE SUBARCTIC COLLECTION OF
## THE HAFFENREFFER MUSEUM OF ANTHROPOLOGY

BY BARBARA A. HAIL AND KATE C. DUNCAN

BRISTOL · RHODE ISLAND

HAFFENREFFER MUSEUM OF ANTHROPOLOGY

BROWN UNIVERSITY · 1989

BROWN UNIVERSITY

THE HAFFENREFFER MUSEUM OF ANTHROPOLOGY

STUDIES IN ANTHROPOLOGY AND MATERIAL CULTURE

VOLUME V

COPYRIGHT 1989 BY HAFFENREFFER MUSEUM OF ANTHROPOLOGY

COVER ILLUSTRATION

MITTENS, CREE-MÉTIS, CHIPEWYAN-MÉTIS

CIRCA 1860, COLLECTED BY EMMA SHAW COLCLEUGH

AT FORT McMURRAY IN 1894 (CAT. 21)

BIRCH BARK

COLLECTED BY FRANCIS BRIERE, LUNENBURG, VERMONT

DISTRIBUTED BY

HAFFENREFFER MUSEUM OF ANTHROPOLOGY, BROWN UNIVERSITY

MOUNT HOPE GRANT, BRISTOL, RHODE ISLAND 02809

AND

THE UNIVERSITY OF WASHINGTON PRESS

P.O. BOX C 50096

SEATTLE, WASHINGTON 98145

CIP 89–080594

ISBN 0–912089–07–5

# Contents

# Acknowledgements

Many people and many institutions have contributed to this work. For funding our research, we thank the National Endowment for the Arts; the Haffenreffer Family Fund; Brown University; the American Philosophical Society, Phillips Fund; the American Indian Studies Program, University of Washington; the Canadian Ethnology Service, National Museum of Civilization, National Museums of Canada, Ottawa; and Mr. and Mrs. Bruce M. Docherty.

We especially thank the individuals who most graciously contributed their time and knowledge in interviews; they include, in Winnipeg, Dorothy Garbutt, Sidney Keighley; in Selkirk, Victor Colcleugh, Barbara Johnstone, Jim Sinclair; in Norway House, Georgina Albert, Walter and Betsy Apetagon, Marian and Jemimah Bee, Esther Chubb, Myrtle Muskego, Geraldine, Audrey and Flora Simpson, Albert Ross, and Mildred and Stanley Sinclair of Cranberry Portage; at Cross Lake, Adelaide Blacksmith, Jane Harriet Mason, Frances M. Ross; at The Pas, Alex Bignell, Moses Bignell, Margaret Cartwright, Kathleen de la Ronde, Bishop DuBuchelle and Harry Sanderson. In Edmonton, Bella Boucher; in Fort Chipewyan, Maria Houle, Alice Marten, Snowbird Martin, Elsie and Lawrence Yanik; in Jackfish Camp in the Fort Chipewyan Reserve, Ben and Mary Marcel, Victoria Mercredi, John James and Mary Rose Waquan; in Fort Smith, Louis Mercredi; in Fort Simpson, Celine Lafferty, the Nets'enelu Society; in Hay River, Rosa Louttit, Irene Mongren and Germaine Page (West Channel); in Fort Providence, Mary Agnes Bonnetrouge, Rosa Lie Causa, Elsie La Corne, Christine Minoza, Dora Minoza, Sisters Anna Neumier and Flore Pierson; in Kakisa Lake, Margaret Leishman, Monique Providence, Madeline and Philip Simba; in Rae, Violet Camsell, Dora Migui; in Yellowknife, Judith Buggins, Agnes Mercredi Williams; in British Columbia, William Orlando Colcleugh; in Edinburgh, Scotland, Margaret Swain; in Thompson, Connecticut, Elmer White.

Assistance in archival and museum research was given by Edwina Hoganberg, Linda Lazorovich, David Ross, Lower Fort Garry; Conrad Grahame, McCord Museum; Douglas Leonard, Kathy Pettipas, Manitoba Museum of Man and Nature; Thora Cooke, Western Canada Pictorial Index, University of Winnipeg; Judith Beattie, Shirlee Anne

Smith, Hudson's Bay Company Archives, Winnipeg; Byron Apetagon and Raymond Beaumont, Norway House School; Henry La Tourneau, St. Boniface Museum; Paul Thistle, Little Northern Museum, The Pas; Pat McCormack, Alberta Provincial Museum; Michelle Currie, Debra Henry, Bill Robbins, Northern Life Museum, Fort Smith; D. Richard Valpy, Barbara Winter, Prince of Wales Northern Heritage Centre, Yellowknife; Father Serrault, Oblate Archives, Fort Smith; Sisters Germaine Gagnon, Georgine Leduc, Marie Lemire and Estelle Mitchell, Musée des Soeurs Grises de Montreal; Ted Brasser, Judy Hall, Judy Thompson, Canadian Museum of Civilization; Dorothy Kealey, Anglican Church of Canada Archives, Toronto; Gaston Montmigny, Archives Oblates, Saint Albert; Mary Jane Lenz, Nancy Rosoff, James G. E. Smith, Eulalie Wierdsma, Museum of the American Indian, Heye Foundation; Susan Bean, Peabody Museum of Salem; Ian Brown, Peabody Museum of Archaeology and Ethnology, Harvard University; Ives Goddard, Smithsonian Institution; Susan Giles, Jennifer Stewart, City of Bristol Museum and Art Gallery, United Kingdom; Dale Idiens, Royal Scottish Museum, Edinburgh; Jonathan H. C. King, Museum of Mankind, British Museum, London; Schuyler Jones, Pitt-Rivers Museum, Oxford; Christian Feest, Museum für Volkerkunde, Vienna.

For hospitality and assistance, we are indebted to John and Flo Chornabee and Kathy Fitzpatrick, Norway House; William and Michele Tracy, Edmonton; Ron Davies, Wood Buffalo National Park, Fort Smith; John Rigney, Fort Chipewyan; Irene Kudelik, Hay River; Ted Malewski, Memoree and Beth Philipp, Fort Providence; Mike Johnson, Walsall, England; June Bedford, London; Mr. and Mrs. James Wilson, Edinburgh. We especially thank the Science Institute of the Northwest Territories and native band councils for granting us permission to visit their communities.

For reading part or all of the manuscript, we thank Douglas Anderson, Richard Conn, Shepard Krech III, June Helm, Bill Holm and Andrew Hunter Whiteford. Additional readings of the text were of special value, and for this we thank Thierry Gentis, Ann McMullen, Margot Schevill and Joyce Smith. Many improvements were incorporated at the suggestion of our readers. Any remaining faults are, of course, our own. For laboratory analysis of beads and silk we thank Alexandra O'Donnell and Elizabeth Reid; for editorial assistance, Joy Murphy and Ruth Sanford; for word processing, Marilyn Fetterman and Ethel Rudy; for cartography, Lyn Malone; for photography, Danielle Toth and Richard Hurley. Our primary illustrator was Seth Ballou, with additional illustrations by Susan Aldworth. Finally, we thank Gavin Duncan and Edward Hail for their cheerful patience.

# Foreword

This volume, the fifth in the Haffenreffer Museum of Anthropology's series, *Studies in Anthropology and Material Culture*, was conceived from Barbara Hail's analytical interests in and musings on the Subarctic collection of Emma Shaw Colcleugh, a late-Victorian-era traveller, and took form in the subsequent creative collaboration between Hail, who is Curator and Associate Director of the Haffenreffer Museum and Kate Duncan, an art historian and specialist in Subarctic material culture at Seattle University. The result—this catalogue—is published to accompany a major exhibition of the Haffenreffer Museum's Subarctic collections and is a stellar addition to the publication series.

Early collections found today in many museums—the Haffenreffer is no exception—were acquired by Victorian travellers like Emma Shaw Colcleugh, a Rhode Island journalist and teacher who travelled widely in the 1880s and 1890s. One of Hail's priorities is to place Colcleugh's artifacts in a context more meaningful than one that simply lists, in catalogue entries, the name of the collector and date of the acquisition. Accordingly, following her introduction to the Subarctic region, its inhabitants, their languages, and their history, Hail provides a biographical sketch of Colcleugh, who was at the center of an active woman's movement in the waning years of the nineteenth century, and excerpts at some length from the travel letters—a typical period genre—she published for the vicarious pleasure of her readers as well as her own livelihood.

Emma Shaw Colcleugh's collection is used as a jumping-off point for discussion and analysis of historic and contemporary Subarctic collections. Duncan, in the tradition of art historians interested in the analysis of design and style, presents a probing analysis of regional and temporal differences in Subarctic geometric designs and floral styles and uses artifacts collected by Colcleugh and many others to investigate questions of design symmetry, internal detail, color and complexity to test various propositions derived from visual perception theory. Duncan's fine analysis of Algonquian firebag and shot pouch forms (panel and so-called octopus bags), which will be examined with interest by all who have seen these bags in museum storerooms or on exhibit, concludes the chapters for which she is primarily responsible.

One virtue of this catalogue is that it does not present traditional material culture in an ahistorical vacuum. Another is that it does not ignore the contemporary production of the visual arts. Both Hail and Duncan have gone into "the field" in the Subarctic to engage native consultants in discussions about the objects their ancestors made and travellers like Colcleugh collected, as well as to observe the contemporary scene of production of material culture. The interests of Hail and Duncan in the connections between present and past show throughout the sections for which they are responsible. This is especially true of the catalogue proper, where a large number of objects both "old" (nineteenth and early-twentieth centuries) and "new" (mid-twentieth century) are dissected. It is reflected as well in the contributions they requested from June Helm and William A. Tracy. In chapters by Tracy and Hail, an epilogue by Helm, and the catalogue entries, there are useful descriptions and discussions of contemporary quillwork, moose and caribou hair embroidery, beadwork, hareskin garments produced either for internal (native) or external (tourists, museums—the non-native world) consumption. Recent decades in the north have been marked by a revival of interest in "traditional" crafts. This has been due in part to the recognition that the production of what others might consider as collectible "folk art" could be an economically rewarding enterprise. It also stems from the resurgence of pride of native people in their own identity and past and from their understanding that these aesthetically pleasing objects of expressive culture constitute a widely admired and readily visible marker of ethnic identity.

In this as in so many of its efforts, the Haffenreffer Museum acknowledges the generosity and support of the Haffenreffer Family. In 1930, Rudolf F. Haffenreffer Sr. purchased the Colcleugh collection that Hail and Duncan so ably analyze here; it was in Mr. Haffenreffer's memory that the collections and the Haffenreffer Museum of Anthropology were donated to Brown University in 1955. The Haffenreffer Family Fund and the National Endowment for the Arts have provided the major funds in support of this publication; to both we are grateful. Mr. and Mrs. Carl W. Haffenreffer and Mr. and Mrs. Rudolf F. Haffenreffer 3rd have shown constant support for the Museum's acquisitions, exhibitions, publications and its research and educational programs; we can not do less than offer, to them, this catalogue in thanks.

*Shepard Krech III*
PROFESSOR OF ANTHROPOLOGY AND DIRECTOR
HAFFENREFFER MUSEUM OF ANTHROPOLOGY

# Introduction

The inspiration for this book was the recognition that there is, in the Haffenreffer Museum of Anthropology, a fine body of Subarctic materials, collected between 1888 and 1897 by Emma Shaw Colcleugh, a Rhode Island journalist and teacher. Colcleugh, one of a select group of nineteenth-century women who chose to venture into unknown lands for professional purposes of journalism and personal pursuit of adventure, was sponsored in her travels by New England newspapers to which she sent descriptive and anecdotal reports for publication. She became widely known and respected, both at home in New England and in Winnipeg, Manitoba, where she spent the years of her married life. Her major journalistic travels took place in successive trips "into the North": the Canadian and American Subarctic and Arctic regions. In later years she travelled to the Pacific, the Caribbean, Africa, and South America. In addition to recording her impressions of these regions little known to her readers, she gathered objects of both utility and beauty, made by native peoples, in most cases carefully noting where she acquired them. Her sixty-eight Subarctic objects are part of a larger group of 218 pieces collected by Colcleugh in the Americas, Oceania and Africa, and purchased by Rudolf F. Haffenreffer Sr. in 1930.

Colcleugh's original collection notebook, and an annotated list of the objects received from her by Mr. Haffenreffer, had accompanied the collection. Although no personal information existed in the Museum's records about the collector, research in local historical societies, the Providence Journal archives, the Provincial Archives of Manitoba and Alberta, and the Hudson's Bay Company archives, as well as interviews with former acquaintances and family members, provided additional information to amplify knowledge of her personality. Her two books and many published travel articles provided background information about the circumstances through which her collection was gathered. Both the collector and the collection seemed to present rich areas for research which would be of interest to specialists in Subarctic material culture, to those intrigued by the world-view of Victorian age travellers, and to those for whom women's studies are of special interest. With this catalogue, Colcleugh's Subarctic pieces are for the first time studied as a unit.

There are many different ways of viewing and analyzing a museum collection. Ethnographic collections in anthropology museums have often been described by concentrating on the function and meaning of artifacts within a given society. Attention has also been given to materials and techniques of construction, and to the importance of the object in context of subsistence, status and ceremony, thereby shedding light on the economic, social and ritual structure of the groups who made and used the objects.

Since one of the obvious strengths of the Colcleugh Subarctic collection is its ornately decorated objects embroidered with beads or silk in a variety of floral forms, it was considered important to look at this collection from a stylistic viewpoint in addition to that of its social and utilitarian functions. Therefore this book is a collaboration between Barbara Hail, a museum curator and ethnohistorian, and Kate Duncan, an art historian who has worked extensively with Athapaskan material. We believe that the Colcleugh material, already important for its specificity in time and point of collection, has thus been increased in scholarly value by serving as an illustration of regional styles of Central Subarctic Algonquian and Athapaskan bead and floss embroidery and of porcupine-quill weaving.

In the process of analyzing the Museum's Subarctic collection and planning its publication and exhibition, we determined that, with a few additions, it could include most of the major Algonquian and Athapaskan bead styles. In 1986 and 1987, through the Haffenreffer Family Fund, the Museum was able to obtain additional fine nineteenth-century pieces from private collectors. Among these, June Bedford's collection of bead and silk-decorated objects acquired in London between 1962 and 1986 is of special significance. As with most Subarctic material from this period, including non-Colcleugh examples acquired by Rudolf F. Haffenreffer Sr. between 1917 and 1954, documentation was weak or lacking. Through a combination of style analysis and comparison with the few known well-documented pieces, these have been placed within the Subarctic style continuum, filling out the Museum's Subarctic collection. In addition, the Museum has received several important Subarctic pieces from donors, including James Houston, an artist with a long and distinguished record of encouraging the work of native Canadian artists. He also assisted us with information on traditional techniques.

A vital aspect of museum research is to carry on fieldwork, both in order to update collections and to better understand the people whose work composes these collections. Both of the authors felt, after reviewing the Museum's nineteenth-century holdings, that it was essential to the interpretation of both past and present directions of central Subarctic arts to consult with twentieth-century native artisans. We carried out ethnographic field work jointly in the summer of 1985 and separately in 1987. In 1985, as much as possible, we followed in the footsteps of Emma Shaw Colcleugh, starting our journey in Winnipeg and Selkirk on the Red River, and proceeding north to the Cree communities of Cross Lake and Rossville near the Hudson's Bay Post of Norway House at the northern end of Lake Winnipeg. From there we travelled west to The Pas, a Cree community visited by Colcleugh, located on the Saskatchewan River, thence to Edmonton where we began our own journey "into the North," following by air Colcleugh's 1894 steamer journey on the Athabasca-Slave-Mackenzie river system. We visited Fort Chipewyan on Lake Athabasca, Fort Smith on the Slave River, Fort Resolution and Hay River on Great Slave Lake, and Fort Providence on the Mackenzie River. In 1982 Duncan had carried out related research in Hay River, and forts Simpson, Rae, Resolution, and McPherson. In 1987 Hail conducted interviews in Rae and Yellowknife, and Duncan continued research among far western Athapaskans in British Columbia.

We interviewed, using color enlargements and slides of nineteenth-century examples from the Colcleugh and other collections, to discover what earlier styles, forms, techniques and materials were remembered, particularly, but not exclusively, by older Cree, Ojibwa and Athapaskan people. We also wished to learn which of the earlier kinds of skilled handwork were still being practiced, one hundred years later, by Subarctic native people. Much valuable information was provided by native consultants during the course of these interviews and has been incorporated throughout the book.

While interviewing in the North, we added fifty-eight new objects to the Museum's collection. We looked particularly for (1) objects incorporating rare, older techniques, such as hare-skin looping, porcupine-quill weaving and bark biting; (2) objects similar in form and function to those in the older collection, for example, moccasins, baby belts, moss bags, gun cases, babiche bags and embroidered mitts; (3) any newer types of objects that native people make today, such as fur mukluks; (4) objects incorporating new techniques, such as moose hair tufting; and finally, (5) affordable objects that were available. A few rarer, more expensive objects were commissioned for later delivery to the Museum.

These new examples joined a small collection of objects purchased a few years earlier, between 1975 and 1980, from Chipewyan, Slavey and Cree people in Saskatchewan and Manitoba by William Tracy and his wife, Michelle, while he was a graduate student in the Department of Anthropology at Brown University. Tracy was subsequently asked to contribute to this catalogue.

In the catalogue we have used the objects gathered by Emma Shaw Colcleugh on her trips "into the North" to ask a number of important questions about Subarctic material culture in the nineteenth century and today. With other, smaller collections in the Museum, it provides the basis for a discussion of the nature and development of central Subarctic arts and culture, and the ways in which Subarctic materials now in museum collections reflect native life, particularly in two regions: that of the Athabasca, Slave and Mackenzie rivers, and Great Slave Lake; and the Lake Winnipeg and Interlake region of Manitoba and eastern Saskatchewan. Among the important issues addressed are the extent of outside influence on both materials and techniques used in native arts production; the role of the Hudson's Bay Company and other traders as suppliers of materials used by native craftspeople, and as an outlet for the sale of native-made goods; continuities in the role of traditional arts within society, despite the introduction of non-native trade materials; gender differentiation in artistic production and consumption; and the influence of outsiders: early collectors, visitors, resident missionaries, teachers, and Hudson's Bay Company and other traders, on the nature, quality, and quantity of objects made for use within, or sale outside the home.

The background of the Subarctic region and its people is discussed in the first chapter of this book. The second chapter provides an in-depth look at the major collector, Emma Shaw Colcleugh, and her experiences as a female Victorian-era journalist and traveller. It includes excerpts from a series of articles she wrote in 1932, at age eighty-six, entitled "I Saw These Things," recalling her journeys in the Subarctic.

The third chapter is composed of three essays focused on questions concerning style. The first and second essays utilize examples from the Haffenreffer Museum collections, first to illustrate the major Subarctic Algonquian and Athapaskan styles, then to demonstrate the role that visual perception factors play in the ways that designs change when reproduced. The third essay, citing examples from both the Haffenreffer collection and other sources, traces the evolution of the tabbed bag and the panel bag, two major bag forms that have spread across the northern part of North America.

The fourth chapter discusses traditional arts today. There follows a case study of craft production in the northern Manitoba community of Brochet, where William and Michelle Tracy lived from 1978 to 1980 while he wrote his dissertation and she taught in the native school.

In the epilogue, June Helm, from the vantage point of many years of ethnological research among the Athapaskan people of the Mackenzie

River region, offers some perspectives on women's work as it merges into women's art in the context of the traditional Indian world.

The catalogue proper follows, organized so that the nineteenth-century collections of Colcleugh and others appear first, followed by the contemporary collections made approximately one hundred years later. Within these major divisions, the organization is by technique and material, and within these sub-divisions, the entries are arranged by type of object and by point of collection, from southeast to northwest. This organization allows us to group design styles, thus following through in the catalogue proper the style discussion of Chapter III.

This book has been a collaborative project from its initial conception through the phases of research, fieldwork and writing. As indicated in the table of contents, both authors have contributed text chapters. In the catalogue section, Duncan prepared the entries for nineteenth-century silkwork, beadwork, quillwork, and babiche bags, and Hail the entries for early objects made of other materials and for the contemporary collection. All entries reflect continual discussion and exchange of information.

To summarize, in this book we have sought to expand the analysis of a traditional nineteenth century museum collection by the addition of contemporary comparative material and points of view, and the use of an interdisciplinary approach. We have combined methods of ethnohistory, anthropology and art history to enrich the understanding and appreciation of native Subarctic cultural expression.

*Barbara A. Hail*
ASSOCIATE DIRECTOR/CURATOR
HAFFENREFFER MUSEUM OF ANTHROPOLOGY
BROWN UNIVERSITY

*Kate C. Duncan*
ASSISTANT PROFESSOR OF ART HISTORY
SEATTLE UNIVERSITY

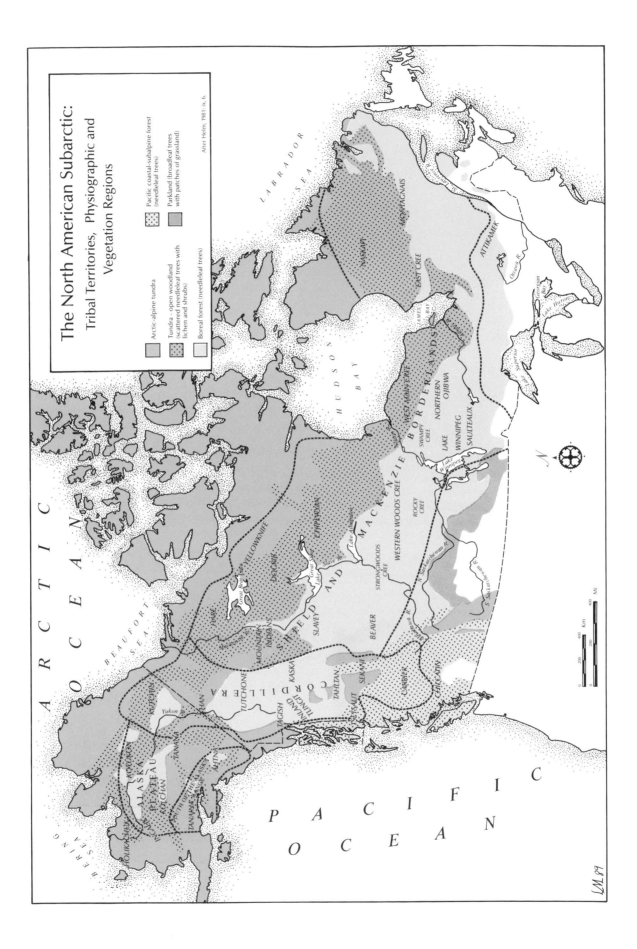

The North American Subarctic:
Tribal Territories, Physiographic and
Vegetation Regions

After Helm, 1981: ix, 6.

Arctic-alpine tundra

Tundra – open woodland
(scattered needleleaf trees with
lichen and shrubs)

Boreal forest (needleleaf trees)

Pacific coastal-subalpine forest
(needleleaf trees)

Parkland (broadleaf trees
with patches of grassland)

# I The Subarctic Region: People, History and Art

## THE SETTING AND THE PEOPLE

The North American Subarctic, a region of boreal forest and taiga, extends across northern Canada and into interior Alaska. It includes parts of Labrador and Quebec, northern portions of Ontario, Manitoba, Saskatchewan, Alberta, and British Columbia, most of the Yukon and Northwest Territories, and central Alaska. Beyond its northern boundary is the Arctic tundra. On the southwest it borders the high grass plains. Its southeastern boundary corresponds generally to the change from boreal, coniferous forest to mixed deciduous-coniferous woodland and divides Algonquian-speakers of the Subarctic from those of the Northeast.[1]

The Subarctic contains four major physiographic regions: from east to west, the Canadian Shield and associated Hudson Bay Lowlands and Mackenzie Borderlands, the Cordillera, the Alaska Plateau, and the region south of the Alaska Range. Throughout these northern lands, winters are long and cold, summers brief and mild. Lowlands and mountain flanks are covered with boreal forest, mountain heights with alpine tundra, and there is a multitude of lakes and rivers. The forests are largely spruce, pine, cedar, larch, white birch, alder and willow, the particular association of trees depending on the region. North of the forests is open woodland with scattered needleleaf trees, mosses, lichen and shrubs; north of this lies the tundra. The Hudson Bay lowlands include large areas of open bog or muskeg. Mosses and lichens, berries and colorful wildflowers thrive on the high water table and provide a luxuriant ground cover in the summer time.

As glaciers receded—about 10,000 to 8,000 years ago in the western regions and somewhat later in the east—the Subarctic became inhabited by small bands of hunting people, known to anthropologists as Paleo-Indians. They subsisted mainly on large animals, particularly caribou and moose (Clark 1981:108; VanStone 1974:5), but were also adventitious foragers, with an eclectic diet. As the climate warmed, forests advanced northward, and people honed their hunting and fishing skills. The ancestors of present-day Athapaskans and Algonquians developed a forest-based culture, which continued well after the first contact with

Fig. 1-1. Map of Subarctic region of North America showing vegetation regions, major physiographic zones, location of culturally affiliated groups. Drawn by Lyn Malone after Helm 1981.

Europeans. They were not numerous compared to Amerindians elsewhere on the continent because successful hunting and fishing strategies require large amounts of land for the support of small numbers of people.[2]

The languages spoken by these native Subarctic people belong to two major families—Algonquian and Athapaskan.[3] The two major branches of Algonquian are Cree and Ojibwa, and a number of groups speak these languages. Cree speakers include the Naskapi, Montagnais, East Cree, Attikamek (Tête de Boule), West Main Cree, and Western Woods Cree (including the Swampy Cree, Strongwoods Cree and Rocky Cree); Ojibwa speakers include the Northern Ojibwa and Lake Winnipeg Saulteaux.[4]

The Athapaskan speakers, who live to the northwest, are less numerous than the Algonquians. They include, in the Mackenzie borderlands, the Beaver, Slavey, Chipewyan, Dogrib, Yellowknife, Bearlake, Mountain, Hare, and Eastern Kutchin or Loucheux. Farther west, in the Cordillera, live other Athapaskans: the Chilcotin, Carrier, Sekani, Tahltan, Kaska, Inland Tlingit, Tagish, Tutchone, Han, and Western Kutchin.[5] Northwest on the Alaska Plateau are the Tanana, Koyukon, Holikachuk, Ingalik and Kolchan (Upper Kuskokwim). South of the Alaska range live the Tanaina and Ahtna. These group names are used today by non-Athapaskans, by one Athapaskan people to refer to members of a different group, or as self-designations, although today, in many groups, people are as likely to refer to themselves as "Dene," meaning "the people" (VanStone 1974:8–9) (fig. 1-1).

At the time of contact with Europeans, and some years after, the seasonal round of peoples in the central Subarctic region—that is, the Canadian Shield and associated Hudson's Bay lowlands and Mackenzie borderlands, particularly the area around Lake Winnipeg and the Great Slave Lake–Mackenzie River drainage, where most of the materials in this catalogue originated—was based on hunting large and small game animals and on fishing. Caribou and moose, hunted with spears and bows, were of primary importance; hare and other small animals such as beaver, squirrel and muskrat were trapped with snares and deadfalls. The rivers and lakes contained trout, sturgeon, whitefish, pike and pickerel caught with spears, hooks, nets, weirs and traps. Birds and waterfowl were significant sources of food, and included grouse, ptarmigans, gulls, ducks and geese. Numerous types of berries were gathered.

Food was prepared and preserved here as it was throughout the Subarctic. Meat was roasted or boiled in bark or hide containers using boiling stones, or dried and cached for later use. In summer, fish was split thin and preserved by sun-drying on racks and, among many

Fig. 1-2. Spruce-bark lodge. Eastern Cree, Rupert's House. James Bay, Ontario. Bark- and hide-covered lodges served as shelters throughout the Subarctic. Photo by Alanson Skinner, 1910–1913. Courtesy Museum of American Indian, Heye Foundation.

groups, was then smoked; in winter it was often freeze-dried in the open air. Dried meat, berries and fat were pounded together in a paste and stored as pemmican.

Small bands of extended families moved within limited hunting ranges during most of the year, following the movements of the principal game animals. Because of the demands of the environment and cyclical possibility of food shortage, a strong sense of mutual dependence and cooperation was developed between individuals, families and bands. Ties were strengthened during the summer when people gathered in larger groups of a hundred or more at favorite fishing camps. Leadership in Subarctic groups was loosely organized, vested in a trusted individual who was usually a good hunter, possibly charismatic, who often had shamanistic powers, and who could allocate hunting territories and guide his band with the help of other elder men (Helm and Leacock 1971: 347; Wilson 1982: 7). The mobile existence demanded shelters easily erected or carried, and resulted in a variety of structures, both conical and dome-shaped, of bark, brush, hide and earth (fig. 1-2).

Fig. 1-3. Athapaskan Indians, Northern Alaska. Sketch by Alexander Hunter Murray in his *Fort Yukon Journal*, 1847–50. After Richardson, J., Vol. I, opp. p. 377. London 1851 (1969 Greenwood). HMA Spinden coll.

The quantity of material possessions of people who must constantly move in order to harvest resources cannot be great. Clothing was of caribou or moose hide, scraped and smoked, with the hair often left on winter garments for warmth, or of twined hareskin. Clothes were tailored, and consisted of a shirt or tunic, parka or dress with fitted or separately attached sleeves, and often a skin cap and mitts. Some Algonquians wore leggings, breechcloths and moccasins. Among most Athapaskans, foot coverings were attached to trousers. Considerable ingenuity was shown in devising clothing tailored to protect the body from cold (fig. 1-3). Decoration of clothing and personal gear was imaginatively carried out with porcupine quills, seeds, dentalia shell, painted designs and occasionally bird quills. The body might be ornamented with jewelry, painting or tattooing. Tools and weapons were made of the bones and antlers of caribou, moose and deer. Copper was also worked into weapons. With knives and shavers of stone, bone, antler and beaver teeth, split lengths of wood were whittled into snowshoe frames, bows, arrows and spear shafts. Wood was used to form the framework for bark-covered canoes, and for the planks of toboggans. Throughout the Subarctic birch bark was used to fill a wide range of needs, from containers and cooking vessels to canoes and shelters (Helm and Leacock 1971: 346).

PEOPLE IN CONTACT

The arrival of Europeans in the North altered the aboriginal Subarctic hunting and gathering way of life.[6] It was fur that attracted Europeans to this cold, forested land. Regular trading contacts had begun to develop between Europeans and Indians during the early sixteenth century, mostly along the eastern coast of the continent, but it was not until the late sixteenth century that the growing popularity of the beaver felt hat created a strong market for beaver pelts in Europe (Ray 1978: 19). Gradually a new emphasis on intensive trapping of small fur-bearing animals for trade to outside markets changed the traditional seasonal round of the hunter-gatherers. As trading companies grew, interdependence developed between outside traders who provided a primary source of income and supplies and natives who provided furs and food provisions. Locations of summer band gatherings were changed from favorite fishing spots to favorable trading posts, and some families changed the pattern of their seasonal rounds, staying longer near the posts to serve as hunters for the fur traders. Survival for Subarctic peoples had always meant continuous adaptation to ever-changing environmental, cultural and physical stresses. The fur trade was one more in a series of stresses, and the Indians adapted their skills to suit this new circumstance.[7] They began to rely on an outside market where furs could be traded for the Euro-Canadian manufactured goods that came to be considered necessary: firearms, iron tools, traps, iron and copper kettles, steel needles, cloth, tea, flour, tobacco and, in many cases, liquor.

The Subarctic people who made their livelihood by river portering provided a market for specialized goods such as tumplines and Assumption sashes. New materials such as glass beads, velvets, felted wools, and gold or silver braid became part of a repertoire of materials that inspired artistic innovation in the decoration of native and métis clothing and accessories.

Naturally, since their first contact, intermingling and intermarriage between native North Americans and Europeans has occurred, particularly among those who worked together in the fur trade. The descendents of Indians and Europeans have been referred to variously as métis, mixed-blood, michif, half-breed, bois brûlé and non-status Indians. They developed varying life-styles in the Northeast, Great Lakes, Northern Plains, and Subarctic (Brown 1980; Slobodin 1966; Peterson and Brown 1985). In the southern Subarctic, descendents of French-Canadian workers in the fur trade and their Cree or Ojibwa wives emerged in the early nineteenth century as a distinctive ethnic group at Red River and later on the Saskatchewan River, and were largely Roman Catholic and bilingual in French and Cree. Those living north and west of Fort Simpson in the Mackenzie District, the Yukon, and Alaska, generally known as Northern Métis, are descendants of more recent unions (post 1850) and northern European (especially Scottish) paternal descent, and are generally Protestant in religion and bilingual in English and an Athapaskan language (Slobodin 1981: 362; Helm, Rogers, Smith 1981: 150). The métis played a major role in the development of the Subarctic fur trade, have served as cultural intermediaries, and have contributed significantly to Subarctic cultural life and arts.[8]

## THE IMPACT OF EUROPEAN ECONOMICS AND POLITICS

The economic policies of sixteenth- and seventeenth-century European nations had a direct effect on North America. In order to build up home industries, in both manufactures and agriculture, and to secure a favorable balance of trade, foreign trading monopolies were sought. It was especially desirable to find raw materials to exchange for finished products. Merchants joined together in monopolistic trading companies to achieve these ideals, benefitting both individuals and the home nation.

"The Governor and Company of Adventurers trading into Hudson's Bay," better known as the "Hudson's Bay Company," was chartered by King Charles II of England in 1670 as a joint-stock company. Through it the King gave title to a broad area of northwestern Canada, that became known as Rupert's Land, to his cousin, Prince Rupert, and his trading partners. The charter granted the partners a monopoly of the fur trade in the area drained by streams flowing into Hudson Bay. The right of the English Crown to give away such lands was, in European eyes, clear, as Englishmen had been the first Europeans to explore and claim the lands. The ownership claims of native people already living on these lands were considered easily reconciled by treaty. The company's primary objective was economic, to make a sustained profit for its share-holders, but since it was given the powers of a sovereign state

Fig. 1-4. Residents in front of Hudson's Bay Company Post, Garden Hill, Island Lake, Manitoba, c. 1940. Photo by Rev. Chapin. Courtesy Western Canada Pictorial Index, UWP.

subject only to the authority of the Crown, it was expected to govern within its territories, negotiate treaties with native inhabitants, and pay the costs of defending its lands against rival interests. It was also charged with seeing to certain broad interests of the Crown, such as exploration and territorial expansion (Ray 1978: 12).

In the seventeenth and eighteenth centuries the Hudson's Bay Company co-existed in the Subarctic with independent French traders and a major rival, the North West Company of Montreal. At first the Hudson's Bay Company confined its activities to large trading posts on the shores of the Bay, to which it encouraged native trappers to bring their furs. This usually entailed a long journey by land and through the river-lake chains. When their competitors began intercepting furs by travelling inland and westward to the Indian camps, the Hudson's Bay Company also began setting up more westerly posts. In 1821 this bitter rivalry ended in a merger, under the name of the Hudson's Bay Company. Between 1867 and 1870 the Company's political sovereignty over Rupert's Land came to an end with the birth of the Canadian nation. Throughout the nineteenth century the Company remained a singularly successful economic monopoly, operating solely on the basis of the profit motive, and it is still today an important force as a major supplier of outside goods to the North[9] (fig. 1-4).

European nationalism was another force which served to fire desires to explore and claim the yet uncharted areas of the world. One of the first Englishmen to explore the interior was Henry Kelsey, an apprentice with the Hudson's Bay Company, who was sent west from Hudson Bay to open up trade with Plains tribesmen near the present-day settlement of The Pas on the Saskatchewan River in 1690. Samuel Hearne, also of the company, journeyed to the Coppermine River in 1770 in search of both copper deposits and the elusive "northwest passage" to the Pacific. He was the first white man to reach the Arctic Sea from the interior. In 1731 Pierre Gaultier de Varennes de la Vérendrye started from Montreal and established French trading posts as far west as the Saskatchewan River. Alexander Mackenzie, a trader with the North West Company, was interested in finding a shorter route to the northwest. He left Fort Chipewyan on Lake Athabasca in 1789 and descended the river that later bore his name 1,600 miles to the Arctic Ocean. A few years later he ascended the Peace River, crossed the Rockies and reached the Pacific Ocean. Many explorers and fur traders followed, and, with typical European ethnocentrism, many posts and rivers were given European names.

A central figure who served as a stimulus and a symbol for much of the exploration that followed him was the Englishman Sir John Franklin, who made several attempts to find a northwest passage through the Arctic between 1816 and 1843, using both overland and sea routes. When his last expedition failed to return after two years, other Englishmen carried out a series of searches that continued for many years. Sir John Richardson led one of the search parties between 1847 and 1849 and his lengthy report of 1851 became an important source for ethnographers of the North. Another who added to geographic and ethnographic knowledge as a result of participation in the search for Franklin was Dr. John Rae, whose detailed observations were published in 1882. Slowly, over the course of the nineteenth century, a fairly complete map of the central and western Subarctic was constructed by Europeans, laying the groundwork for their increasing interest in and eventual settlement in some of the area.

## EUROPEAN SETTLEMENT, RED RIVER, AND THE MÉTIS

Other outsiders came to the North as a reaction to European political and economic events. The first permanent settlement of Europeans in the western Subarctic was organized by Thomas Douglas, fifth Earl of Selkirk, in 1811. His purpose was humanitarian—to resettle displaced Scottish "crofters," farmers who had been forced from their small farms by large landowners eager to increase sheep herds in order to take part in the growing English woollen manufacturing industry. Lord Selkirk obtained a large tract of land along the Red and Assiniboine rivers by becoming a major stockholder in the Hudson's Bay Company which had received the land by charter from the King of England in 1670.

The Company favored the settlement, as it would supply fresh produce to their trappers and traders, provide a small market close at hand for furs, and act as a buffer with the nearby post of the rival North West Company, thus inhibiting the latter's trade with native people. In fact, the Red River land was already occupied. Chief Peguis had led the Saulteaux people to the Nemis River flats south of Lake Winnipeg about 1795, joining and partially displacing Cree and Assiniboine residents. In 1817 Selkirk negotiated a treaty with the Saulteaux, Cree and Assiniboine peoples, promising delivery of certain goods on an annual basis in return for the lands. By the late nineteenth century, the government of Canada had established a series of such land treaties with native groups; goods were delivered at annual treaty days, which became gathering times of social and political importance to native people. Emma Shaw Colcleugh experienced a treaty day at St. Peter's Reserve on the Red River in the late 1880s (see Chapter II).

In 1821, the two rival fur companies merged, and many employees of both, including French, English and Scottish traders with their native wives and mixed-blood children, stayed on at Red River permanently. In the same year a community of Swiss joined the settlement for a brief time, followed by Germans and other Europeans from the "de Meurons," a regiment of mercenary soldiers who had been hired by Lord Selkirk during the fur company troubles. With the Cree, Saulteaux, Scots, English and French inhabitants, they formed an ethnically mixed population.

Trappers, traders and missionaries had been the first Europeans to penetrate the North. Alliances with native women developed naturally among the early trappers and traders, for both personal and practical reasons: shared companionship, as well as women's skills in making and repairing the hide and fur clothing so necessary for survival. Trading relationships among native groups were traditionally based on family ties, and marriage to the daughter of an influential family could be instrumental to a European or Euro-Canadian in gaining access to the trade of an area. Early nineteenth century reports of David Thompson, geographer for the North West Company, record that the advantages of mixed unions worked equally well for the family of the native wife, who received preferential trading arrangements (Coues 1897).

Policies of both the North West Company and the Hudson's Bay Company at first discouraged marriage with native women, but as it became clear that few non-native women were able to endure the severe climate and isolated lives of traders' wives, company policies changed. Although many men and women lived "a la façon du pays," without formal marriage, fathers often accepted responsibility for their ethnically mixed children, considered them their legal heirs and, in the mid-nineteenth century, sent them to Red River or Upper Canada (Quebec), or even to Scotland or England for schooling.

As the progeny of mixed marriages increased to form a significant portion of the population, sons were taken into the trading companies and daughters were looked on favorably as suitable wives for Company men. Children of unions between native women and English and Scottish men, especially if they were Company officers, were more likely to receive education and career advancement than children of native women and French traders, who were more frequently independent and mobile, and for whom a settled life and formal schooling were often impossible. Many of the sons of this latter group found employment as voyageurs and porters, providing the water transport service upon which the fur trade depended; some became buffalo hunters on the plains of southern Manitoba and Saskatchewan, and across the border in the northern United States, supplying buffalo hides, tongues, and pemmican to the Hudson's Bay Company.

By the early nineteenth century, both church and company officials were beginning to look favorably upon marriages between Europeans and native women and even more so upon those with half-breed women. By the mid-nineteenth century, in Selkirk's colony of Red River in southern Manitoba, Alexander Ross, a retired Hudson's Bay Company factor who had married an Okanagan woman and had thirteen children, wrote that half-breeds made up nearly half of the settlement (Ross 1856: 242).

In 1867 when the new nation of Canada was born, the West was opened to settlers from the East, and suddenly people from Upper Canada began to arrive in Red River seeking farm land. New and complex regulations for land ownership were instituted, and many Red River families of mixed ancestry were not able to establish legal claims to the lands they had long occupied. This was especially true for those of French-Cree/Ojibwa (Saulteaux) descent whose livelihoods as trappers, buffalo hunters, and voyageurs had resulted in a mobile life style. Many Métis, finding themselves homeless, left Red River at this time, dispersing in many directions. Some moved north; others moved west and south to form permanent settlements among relatives on the Plains. With actual and threatened displacement, there developed among many a desire for a "new nation" of their own. Unified by a charismatic Métis leader, Louis Riel, the Red River Métis sought unsuccessfully for in-

Fig. 1-5. Packing supplies from the dock at Fort Resolution on Great Slave Lake to the Hudson's Bay Company post. Note the fish-drying rack. Many métis were employed in such river portering jobs. Photo by C. E. Mathers, Edmonton. Courtesy Northwest Territories Archives, PWNHC.

dependent status, first in the courts and finally on the battlefield. After the final defeat of Riel and his followers in 1885, there was a further dispersal of Red River Métis. Some families who had been dispossessed of their lands moved north to the Slave and Athapasca and Mackenzie River regions. There, along with descendents of mixed Athapaskan-EuroCanadian unions, they continued to play an important role as trappers and as boatmen and porters in the river transport system vital to both fur trade and mission life (Slobodin 1966) (fig. 1-5).

## CHRISTIANITY IN THE NORTH

European religious convictions added another outside influence in the North. Both Catholic and Protestant churchmen believed in the need for missions wherein native people could be converted to Christianity and their children educated in western knowledge and practical trades. The Jesuits had established missions in the Eastern Subarctic in the seventeenth century. Early in the nineteenth century, priests of the Roman Catholic Oblate Order, and Protestant Anglicans, Presbyte-

Fig. 1-6. Rev. John West stopping for the night at an encampment of Indians, between Qu'appelle and Red River Colony, January 1821. Rev. West recruited this "fine looking little boy" for the Church of England mission school in Red River. Adapted from an engraving used as frontispiece in West 1824. Courtesy Manitoba Provincial Archives.

rians, Baptists and Methodists arrived in the central Subarctic. In 1820 the first Anglican clergyman, Reverend John West, was sent from England by the Church Missionary Society to reside at the Red River Settlement, and to "seek the instruction, and endeavour to meliorate the condition of the native Indians" (West 1966: 2). When West attempted to persuade Chief Peguis of the Saulteaux to place children in a mission school, Peguis asked him, as West told it, "what I would do with the children after they were taught what I wished them to know." West replied that "they might return to their parents if they wished it, but my hope was that they would see the advantage of making gardens, and cultivating the soil, so as not to be exposed to hunger and starvation, as the Indians generally were, who had to wander and hunt for their provisions. The little girls. . . . would be taught to knit, and make articles of clothing to wear, like those white people wore; and all would be led to read the Book that the Great Spirit had given them. . . . which would teach them to live well and to die happy" (West 1966: 103; and fig. 1-6). Building on West's work, a successor, William Cockran, established the first permanent Protestant church and school buildings in the central Subarctic in 1824 at St. Andrews on the Red River in Manitoba, to serve

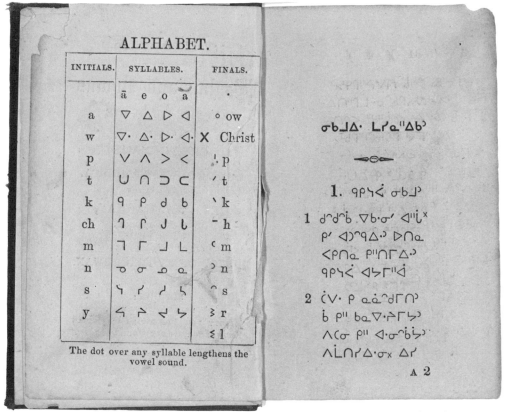

**ALPHABET.**

| INITIALS. | SYLLABLES. | | | | FINALS. |
|---|---|---|---|---|---|
| | ā | e | o | a | · |
| a | ▽ | △ | ▷ | ◁ | ° ow |
| w | ▽· | △· | ▷· | ◁· | X Christ |
| p | ∨ | ∧ | > | < | ¦· p |
| t | ∪ | ∩ | ⊃ | ⊏ | ' t |
| k | ٩ | ρ | ḃ | ḅ | ` k |
| ch | ⸜ | ⸝ | ⌣ | ⌣ | - h |
| m | ⅂ | Γ | ⅃ | L | ᶜ m |
| n | ⱷ | ơ | ⱶ | ⱹ | ⊃ n |
| s | ⸜ | ⸝ | ⸝ | ⸝ | ⌒ s |
| y | ⸜ | ⸝ | ⸝ | ⸝ | ⸝ r |
| | | | | | ≤ l |

The dot over any syllable lengthens the
vowel sound.

ᓂᑲᒐᐅᐧ ᒪᕆᐊᐦᐊᐸᐤ

1. ᖃᑭᓴᐸᐠ ᓂᑲᒧᐤ

(actual size)

Fig. 1-7. Cree syllabic hymnal collected by Emma Shaw Colcleugh at The Pas, Manitoba in the 1880s. Rev. James Evans, an Anglican minister, invented this way of writing for the Ojibwa language in the 1830s, and it was modified for use among various Cree and Ojibwa dialects. It became the means by which many Cree and Ojibwa people learned to read and write. Each character represents a consonant and its orientation indicates the following vowel. HMA 67–431.

a population of largely Hudson's Bay Company and former North West Company traders, their native wives, and mixed-blood families. In 1837 Cockran established a similar church and school at St. Peters, thirteen miles north of St. Andrews, within the settlement of Saulteaux under Chief Peguis, and in 1847 yet another among the mixed-blood population at Portage La Prairie . Anglican missions were later established in the Great Slave Lake and Mackenzie River area, at forts Chipewyan and Simpson and at Hay River (fig.1-7).

Members of the Oblate Order had come west to Red River (now Winnipeg) in 1818. A cathedral was erected at St. Boniface. In 1844 Grey Nuns joined the Oblate Fathers in Red River to staff a school and hospital (fig. 1-8). Gradually missions and schools were established farther north at Hudson's Bay Company posts on the Athabasca-Slave-Mackenzie chain of rivers. The Grey Nuns arrived in Fort Chipewyan on Lake Athabasca in 1849 to establish a mission station and a residential school, and at other Mackenzie River posts during the 1860s, '70s and '80s (fig. 1-9).

Fig. 1-8. St. Boniface Cathedral, built in 1839, and Grey Nun's Residence, Red River, 1857–8. Photo by Hine. Courtesy Smithsonian Institution, National Anthropological Archives.

Fig. 1-9. Fort Resolution Roman Catholic mission, boarding school and residence. Alma Guest collection. Courtesy Northwest Territories Archives, PWNHC.

## FLORAL EMBROIDERY IN THE SUBARCTIC

Both Christian mission schools and the métis population had an impact on decorative arts. Near the middle of the nineteenth century native and métis women in the Subarctic began to produce floral embroidery in silk thread and beads. The new floral forms supplemented an earlier decorative style, reaching into the pre-contact period, in which geometric forms were executed in paint, woven porcupine quills and birch-bark

Fig. 1-10. Swampy Cree girls doing embroidery, probably at Norway House. Note sinew thread, thimble, cloth, and papers of either beads or porcupine quills. Courtesy Pitt Rivers Museum.

incisings. It is not possible to document all of the avenues through which native women were exposed to the new designs and media, but direct teaching of embroidery techniques and designs and exposure to floral designs on goods used by Europeans were both important.

In the numerous fur trade posts where missions had been established during the nineteenth century, both native and métis children attended church and were taught European codes of dress and behavior. Young women learned the elements of good housekeeping, including stitching and embroidery, as part of their general education. The art of silk-floss and bead embroidery, applied to both cloth and hide, became an important Subarctic artistic expression. Working with introduced materials of silk and beads and an introduced floral style, to which they added their own individual interpretations, Subarctic women of native and mixed ancestry developed, in the nineteenth century, a unique and luxurious artistic tradition (fig. 1-10). Both native and métis took to the art and loved it. Those residing in the posts seem to have produced more of it.

Anglican missions as well as Catholic missions included residential schools, and likely similar training in embroidery was offered. In Red River, a series of schools for young ladies operated, beginning in 1824, and in 1832 the Red River Academy was formed, to serve families of Hudson's Bay Company men, many of them married to native or mixed-blood women. Several English women presided as school mistresses, and education was provided in the "ornamental arts" deemed necessary to turn girls into young ladies.

Another source of European design ideas in the first half of the nineteenth century may have been provided by English and Scots wives of Company officers. Following the example of Governor (of the Hudson's Bay Company) George Simpson, who married his cousin Francis in 1830 and brought her to reside in Red River, Chief Factors Connolly, Logan, Finlayson, and Chief Trader Hargrave, among others, married English or Scots brides (Van Kirk 1980: 185–191). These gentlewomen would have brought fairly extensive wardrobes with them to their new homes. It is likely that the floral prints on their dress fabrics and lace accoutrements and possibly embroidery they themselves were working on would have been admired by native and métis women, and may have been reproduced in silk or beads.

It is established that, in the first half of the twentieth century, Grey Nuns were teaching floral embroidery at residential mission schools such as that in Fort Providence. A large collection of finely executed silk-thread embroideries on hide exists in the Musée des Soeurs Grises, Mère de la Maison, Montreal. According to the conservateur, Marie Lemire, S.G.M., the collection was acquired through gifts to the Superior General during periodic trips to the Northern missions (pers. comm. 1986). Some pieces also accompanied retiring teacher Sister Beatrice Leduc when she returned to Montreal in the 1960s . Leduc and others taught floral embroidery to both native and métis students at Fort Providence. It appears that similar teaching was going on in the second half of the nineteenth century in the Mackenzie River area, and even earlier in Saint Boniface at Red River, where many girls of mixed French and Cree or Saulteaux heritage attended the church school founded in 1844.[10]

The French influence was early, probably originating in mission education, first in the Saint Lawrence River valley and Great Lakes, and later in Red River and the Mackenzie region, spreading throughout the Subarctic with the movements of people. Old journals indicate that French-métis, in particular, had a love for bright colors and ornately decorated clothing. A group of French-Indian voyageurs observed at Norway House in 1856 were described as "dressed in the costume of the country: most of them wore light-blue cloth capotes, girded tightly round them by scarlet or crimson worsted belts. Some of them had blue and others scarlet cloth leggings, ornamented more or less with stained porcupine quills, coloured silk, or variegated beads" (Ballantyne 1856: 446–447 in Doherty 1984).

Design ideas could be as varied as the ethnic groups who arrived in the Subarctic. For instance, a Norwegian presence was established as early as 1814 at the northern end of Lake Winnipeg. Other settlers were French, English, Scottish, Swiss, Germans, Scandinavians, and later East Europeans and Russians. A wealth of ideas may have been available to native and métis people for experimentation. Added to this was the opportunity to copy from nature, since choke-cherries, blueberries, wild roses and many other flowers bloomed abundantly during the brief northern summers and could have provided floral inspiration, although usually the conventions used for composing flowers are those established in European embroidery.

Because of the dispersal of people in the North—with much intermingling of different groups due to employment in portering for the fur trade, along with the movement of Hudson's Bay Company traders and their native or métis wives among several different posts—and because of training in mission schools, wherever floral work was being produced in a community it was much the same, whether executed by métis women or native women.[11] The women all knew one another, and ideas were exchanged, as with artists and artisans everywhere. Because of the movement of people, intermarriage, and the loss of many native women's tribal identities through marriage to non-natives, it is often not clear who produced particular pieces of art. Present-day craftswomen maintain that both native and métis women deserve credit for the floral embroidery arts of the Subarctic. As Maria Houle of Fort Chipewyan said, "It's the same—Cree, Chip, half-breed—the same." Agnes Mercredi Williams, Chipewyan-Métis, agreed: "Everybody did it. If there was a difference, perhaps the métis took a little more pains, perhaps because they were usually living in more comfortable places, where they were warm. It is easier to sew and do handwork when you are warm" (Hail and Duncan 1985; Hail 1987).

Because of their remoteness from centers of trade, Athapaskan women maintained a continuity of traditional methods of ornamenting objects during the nineteenth century and even well into the twentieth century. In the more accessible Lake Winnipeg country, a ready market influenced styles toward objects of "Victoriana."

In conclusion, it is impossible to overstate the impact of historical circumstances on the native people of the Subarctic as they affected traditional lifestyles and the production of native material culture (fig.

Fig. 1-11. "Indian families, Hay River". Northwest Territories, circa 1910. Sophie Rusler album. Sophie Rusler was the daughter of the Anglican minister at the Hay River mission in 1910. This picture was taken by Mr. Jones, a photographer, whose family is shown in figure 1-12. Athapaskan and métis families of mixed ethnic backgrounds make up most of the population of the northwestern Subarctic. Courtesy Sophie Rusler.

1-11). New materials, new techniques, and new functions for native arts, combined with a changing subsistence pattern, the introduction of European religious and social mores, and a growing ethnically mixed population, created constantly changing conditions, both social and economic, during most of the historic period (fig. 1-12). The elaborate floral embroidery arts that developed during the nineteenth century in the central Subarctic can be viewed as a result of this ethnic interchange. They were a product of both native and métis women, and they represent a high point of Subarctic artistic development.        BAH

NOTES TO THE SUBARCTIC REGION

1 This catalogue follows the *Handbook of North American Indians*, volume six, *Subarctic*, (Helm 1981) in orthography, tribal locations, and physiographic regions.

2 Kroeber (1939: 141) based on Mooney (1928) estimated about 60,000 people at the time of arrival of the first Europeans. Based on more recent research involving studies of disease, it seems likely that the number of people was much greater than

Fig. 1-12. The family of Mr. Jones, a photographer in Hay River, Northwest Territories, circa 1910, evidences mixed ethnic heritage. Compare beaded moss bag to cat. 74. Sophie Rusler album. Courtesy Sophie Rusler.

this before contact with Europeans introduced widespread epidemics to the North (Hurlich 1983, Krech 1978, 1984).

3 See Rhodes and Todd (1981) for discussion of language groups in the Subarctic. In 1980, Cree-speaking peoples in Canada numbered (rounded) 93,000, Ojibwa-speakers 63,000, Montagnais 7,000, Naskapi 400, and Ottawa-speakers 1,900, while Athapaskan-speakers in Canada numbered only 28,000 (*Linguistic and Cultural Affiliations of Canadian Indian Bands*. Dept. Indian Affairs & Northern Development, Ottawa 1980).

4 By the late-eighteenth century the Ojibwa had spread from their homeland around Sault Sainte Marie into three geographical areas: in the Subarctic, to northern Manitoba and Ontario (Northern Ojibwa), and Lake Winnipeg (Saulteaux); in the Woodlands, to southern Ontario, northern Minnesota, Wisconsin and Michigan (Ojibwa, in the United States called Chippewa). In the nineteenth century, some Ojibwa and Cree moved onto the grasslands of North Dakota, Montana, southern Saskatchewan and Alberta, adopting many aspects of the buffalo-hunting Plains cultures, and became known as Plains Ojibwa and Plains Cree.

5 In this instance the authors do not follow Helm (1981) in treating the Kutchin as a single Cordilleran group. Because of differences in material culture we suggest two groups: the Eastern Kutchin or Loucheux people of the Arctic Red and Peel rivers, who traded into Fort McPherson, and the Western Kutchin of the Yukon and Alaska whose trade focused on Fort Yukon.

6 Various chronological frameworks delineating major influences and periods of demarcation for the Subarctic have been suggested. Krech (1988: xvi) suggests five eras: Protohistoric, Early Fur Trade, Fur and Mission, Welfare Commercial, and Government Industrial. Previously, Helm (1975) had proposed, for Athapaskans only, a three-stage development: Incipient-Early Contact, Contact-Traditional, and Modern or Governmental-Commerical. Even earlier Helm and Leacock (in Leacock and Lurie 1971) had proposed, for the entire Subarctic, three periods: the Era of Early Contacts, the Stabilized Fur and Mission Stage, and the Government-Industrial Stage.

7 The relative impact of the fur trade on native life and the degree of native "dependency" has been the subject of scholarly debate (see Krech 1988: 62–70, and xvi).

8 Until recently, the term métis (meaning mixed) was applied most specifically to the French- and Cree-speaking descendants of the nineteenth century Red River Métis community (the term mixed-blood was used by members of this community in referring to those of mixed native and English or Scottish ancestry). Since the 1970s métis has come to signify to many "any person of mixed Indian-white ancestry who identified him- or herself and was identified by others as neither Indian nor white, even though he or she had no link to the historic Red River métis" (Peterson and Brown 1985: 5). According to the Métis National Council, "Written with a small 'm', métis is a racial term for anyone of mixed Indian and European ancestry. Written with a capital 'M', Métis is a socio-cultural or political term for those originally of mixed ancestry who evolved into a distinct indigenous people during a certain historical period in a certain region in Canada" (Peterson and Brown 1985: 6). Because of the evolving nature of the debate about who should be called "métis," as compared with "Métis," and because it is not always known whether the makers of specific objects within the collection came from Red River or elsewhere, in this book we are following Peterson and Brown (1985), and using lower-case except in headings or when a specific person or historical group is cited.

9 In 1987 the Hudson's Bay Company sold their fur, wholesale, and small northern stores divisions, retaining the medium-size "zellers" and large city department stores. They still own part-interest in the independently run stores, which are known as HBC Northern Stores, Inc.

10 Brasser, based on Thayer (1942) has brought attention to the important role of the métis, particularly those of Red River, in the production of objects with bead, quill and silk floral decoration in the Subarctic. For in-depth discussions of the role of the métis in floral embroidery, see Brasser (1975, 1976, 1985); Morier (1979); Duncan (1981, 1984, 1989); Nicks (1982, 1985).

11 Because native women usually took on the ethnicity of their husbands, much information has been lost as to their identity. In order to maintain the identity of the native mother as well as the existence of a European father, both ethnicities will be given where possible in attributions for objects in the catalogue: for example, Cree-Métis or Slavey-Métis.

# II Emma Shaw Colcleugh: Victorian Collector

It was a time when most women kept to the home, when men sought adventure in the fellowship of other men and returned to tell their wives of it, when travel outside of well-settled areas was always challenging, usually uncomfortable, and often dangerous. It was 1875, and a young Rhode Island schoolteacher with journalistic ambitions was about to depart on her first major trip away from quiet and well-ordered New England society. Emma Shaw, at the age of 29, had been advised for health reasons to spend the school vacation out-of-doors. Invited to Minnesota by relatives, she first inquired about direct rail routes from Boston to Minneapolis. Then, exhibiting the sense of adventure and curiosity which characterized her later wanderings, she decided to book passage on a steamer whose route followed the northern shore of Lake Superior, with stops at small villages to deliver supplies and pick up passengers. With an initiative based on financial need as well as long-held ambitions, she contacted both Providence and Boston newspapers and asked them if they would consider publishing articles about her trip. She did not ask to be paid for these first articles; only that, if satisfactory, they would appear in print. In this way, Emma Shaw formed the basis of her later journalistic career, specializing in travel to little-known places (fig. II-I).

Emma reached Toronto to find that an accident to the lake steamer would delay her sailing. She took the opportunity, at the invitation of the shipping company, to go on a trip through the Muskoka Lake country (in southern Ontario, east of Georgian Bay), which stretches northward nearly two hundred miles from Toronto through interlocking lakes and rivers—past "quaint villages and picturesque lumber camps" (ESC I).[1]

Rejoining the steamer at Collingwood wharf at the head of Georgian Bay, she began her voyage along the interior route, winding beween the hundreds of bay and channel islands along Lake Superior's northern shore. Although the seas were high, Emma was undaunted:

Nowhere upon the Great Lakes did we find such rough water as here. Its effect was noticeable, first, in a slight pallor on the faces of some of the passengers, soon others were, "Not at all sick, you know, only too tired to

Fig. II-I. Emma Shaw Colcleugh as a young woman, at the time she took her trips into the North. Courtesy Victor Colcleugh, Selkirk.

(a)

(b)

(c)

(d)

stay on deck." So, reeling and pitching, they found their way to their staterooms. I, fortunately, was one of the few who remained outside to enjoy the changing scene, and the perfect afternoon of one of June's rarest days (ESC I).

Occasional stops, "to wood up," gave opportunity to visit interesting Indian villages where could be obtained such a wealth of Indian canoes, fancy boxes ornamented with porcupine quills, sweet grass baskets, etc., as would make the "Indians" at Niagara turn pale with envy (ESC I) (fig. II-2a).

The route to the St. Marie River (the "Soo" in local parlance) was a perfect maze of islands. Among them, Great Manitoulin claimed special notice, because of its large Indian reservation. Between this island and the "Soo," save for an occasional hamlet, or the frail canoe of some lone fisher, no signs of life were visible. It was an endless panorama of wild beauty. . . .

After Lake Superior was entered, picturesque Indian villages—at which the big steamers of today make no stop—lent interest as did the accounts given of the mines on the North Shore. As the "painted rocks" were passed we ran close in shore to see plainly the Indian pictures (ESC I).

In the Ojibwa and Ottawa villages along the northern shores of Georgian Bay and Lake Superior in southern Ontario, Emma began to make purchases—the beginning of a lifelong habit of collecting native artifacts. She eventually gathered objects which represented the expressive arts of native people of the Americas, Oceania and Africa. Her appreciation for the aesthetics of these cultures and her interest in techniques of manufacture is evident from the consistently high quality and the variety of materials in her collection (fig. II-2 b–g).

For the next nine years Emma Shaw continued to teach school in the winter and enjoy travel each summer. She financed her trips by selling accounts of her travels to a number of newspapers, and by obtaining free passes for transportation and lodging: "At that time passes were easily obtainable by any one at all successful in bringing summer resorts to the attention of tourists" (ESC III). In 1884, Emma was invited by the President of the National Educational Association, Thomas W. Bicknell, to be a member of a party of educators who journeyed from Boston to Madison, Wisconsin, for the annual meeting. Post-meeting excursions had been planned for Yellowstone Park, Oregon and Alaska.

As I could not afford to take the trip, my only chance was to secure a pass. . . . Fortune favored me. At Chicago I met Charles S. Fee, the general passenger agent of the just-finished Northern Pacific Railroad. . . . A short conversation and the opportunity to show some of my work. . . secured for me a pass to Portland, and over the Northern Pacific and its branches as long as passes were legitimate. . . . When the members of the party started west, to their special train was added a car just arrived from the east in which was a party of notables bound for Alaska. In charge of this, the first eastern party to visit Seward's much maligned purchase, was the Rev. Sheldon Jackson.

(e)

(f)

(g)

Fig. II-2 a–g. Objects in the Haffenreffer Museum collected by Colcleugh on successive trips to the West and to Alaska: (a) quilled birch-bark box, coll. north shore Lake Superior 1875; (b) bottle, twined spruce root, coll. Wrangell, Alaska 1884–85; (c) bowl, Tlingit or Haida, coll. 1884–85; (d) basketry hat, Haida, coll. Masset 1885; (e) spoon, mountain goat horn, Haida, coll. Masset 1884–85; (f) soapberry spoons, Haida, coll. Alaska 1884–85; (g) frog effigy bowl, Tlingit, coll. Sitka 1884.

It grew to be quite the custom to gather each evening in Dr. Jackson's car to hear him talk about the territory in which, having spent some time as School Commissioner, he had become so much interested that, planning to make a home there, he was accompanied by his wife and daughters. . . . The more I heard of the Alaskan trip, the more enthusiastic I became, until, finally, I decided I must take it and, just before we reached Portland, I told Dr. Jackson he could secure a berth for me (ESC III).

After extensive sightseeing which included the mission station at Metlakatla, and the totem poles in the old Russian settlement of Fort Wrangell, she was invited by Dr. and Mrs. Jackson to remain with them as their guest until the next steamer called—more than a month away—but Emma was a working girl and "the Glenwood school bell called and there was no time to secure leave of absence" (ESC III).

Emma Shaw later gave illustrated lectures about her adventures as a member of this first excursion party from the East to travel over the newly completed Northern Pacific Railway to the Pacific Coast and on to Alaska, accompanying her descriptions with her own photographs.

Three years later, in 1887, she travelled over the summit of the not yet completed Stampede Tunnel in the Cascade Mountains. By then, she was submitting travel articles to papers in Springfield, Massachusetts, and New York City, as well as to the *Providence Journal*. Her summer trips took her to Canada several times, the first in 1888, on assignment in Winnipeg.

Shortly before my first visit to Winnipeg, Manitoba had for a brief time figured in the world's news as the scene of the Riel Rebellion. Talking one day with the editor of a Boston paper, he suggested that I "run up there and see what Winnipeg is like.". . . The first entry made in my notebook reads, "A great surprise awaits those who come to this, the capital of the Prairie Province, with the idea that it is the jumping-off place of civilization and refinement. Located at the junction of the Assiniboine and the Red Rivers, it has, as Fort Garry, long ago been made known to the world by the Hudson's Bay Company—always alert for the best centers of trade. But a short stay convinced me that those who failed to predict a great future for Winnipeg were as blind to its possibilities as were those who long ago applied the term 'Great American Desert' to some of the most fertile sections of the United States" (ESC VI; fig. II-3).

## THE VICTORIAN TRAVELLER

In this era, before the turbulence and world wars of the twentieth century, it was possible, for the first time, for ordinary people of middle income to travel literally around the world by steamer and train. A small group of intrepid adventurers became dedicated to world travel. They vied with one another for the most unusual adventure, the most distant

Fig. II-3. "I Saw These Things," one in a series of articles by Colcleugh, Providence *Evening Bulletin*, Winnipeg trip.

spot, the most difficult physical barrier to overcome, and they revelled, as they ran into one another in far away cities and seaports, in exchanging anecdotes. Emma Shaw Colcleugh relates that on her steamer trip to South America in 1910 on the *S.S. Bluecher*, "most of the passengers were seasoned globe trotters. As one of the tourists expressed it, wherever you went you'd find people swapping yarns from Timbucto to Sitka or Zanzibar to Santiago. That this added to the interest of the trip goes without saying" (ESC XIX).

Perhaps life at home in the industrializing late nineteenth century lacked excitement. Possibly the tight strictures of Victorian society created a desire to explore and romanticize the spectacular landscapes of far lands and the unfamiliar social customs of other people. For whatever reasons, Emma, like many other Victorian travellers, seemed intent upon experiencing every sensation that a country could offer her, and responded to the thrill of possible, yet not too fearsome, dangers that could be retold to delight her readers. While in Hawaii, Emma rode on horseback, alone save for her guide, through pouring rains up to the 10,000-foot summit of Haleakala, the world's largest extinct volcano, in order to peer into the ten-mile wide crater. In Australia she accepted the invitation of the curator to explore by lantern-light, at night and un-chaperoned, a series of tortuously narrow, unlit, underground crystal caverns that were soon to be opened in honor of Queen Victoria's Diamond Jubilee year. In Samoa, she climbed the long dusty road to the home of the recently deceased Robert Louis Stevenson and sat on his porch reminiscing about him with his step-daughter. In Labrador she spent weeks tramping rugged byways, talking with the inhabitants of isolated fishing villages, between scheduled stops of the Hudson's Bay Company steamers on which she was traveling; once she had to race the two miles from her lodgings in a fisherman's home to the dock, carrying her bags, at four o'clock in the morning, when she heard the ship's horn signalling both arrival and imminent departure.

In those days, when tourists were few, enthusiastic reception within a host country at the highest levels was almost assured. In Hawaii, Colcleugh was received by King Kalalaua and his sister who later be-came Queen Liliuokalani. Colcleugh presented the king with a Sioux "peace pipe"; he, in turn, remarking on the strange American interest in collecting curios, brought out for her viewing pleasure the magnifi-cent royal feather cloaks. In Tonga, she interviewed the young king, George Tabon 1. In Fiji she was the guest of Princess Andithakamban at a royal feast.

The indigenous peoples encountered in these journeys were consid-ered by most Victorians enthusiastically but distantly as "natives." Col-lections of their handiwork (which soon began to be produced in larger quantities and in a different manner than previously, specifically for the new tourist buyer), were destined for exhibit in private "cabinets of curiosities," many of which later became the bases of today's museum collections of non-Western art. Native arts, however, were considered largely as curios,[2] and represented the individual interests of the collec-tor more than an overview of the material culture of any society. An important exception to this was the serious collecting for world expo-sitions undertaken by museums and individuals, and the ethnographic collecting trips sponsored by major museums of anthropology and uni-versities (see Stocking 1985: 6–13).

One effect of Victorian travellers' reports and displays of their collec-tions of native arts was to stimulate the curiosity of other Westerners about faraway places and people. At a time when most people only dreamed of distant lands, the travelogues written by the fortunate few who did go provided vicarious adventure. Colcleugh told the editor of the *Edmonton Bulletin* that the object of her Mackenzie River trip to the Arctic Circle was "to visit wild and unknown regions, that she may delight 'stay-at-homes' with descriptions thereof" (*Edm. Bull.* 5: 28: 94). The travel letters of Colcleugh, written with a sense of joyous immediacy, were part of a genre developed by sprightly nineteenth-century lady adventuresses and later made more widely popular by authors such as Richard Halliburton, to delight "armchair" travellers.[3]

## EMMA SHAW COLCLEUGH AND THE WOMEN'S MOVEMENT

Emma Shaw Colcleugh was one of a relatively small group of very active women who pushed the frontiers of personal fulfillment and adventure. Born in 1846, she was descended from distinguished New England ancestors, among them Stukely Westcote, one of the original purchasers of Providence Plantations, and Thomas Hooker, founder of Hartford, Connecticut. She grew up in the small town of Thompson, Connecticut, where her father owned a jewelry store and was known for his skill in crafting combs and ornaments of tortoise shell. She attended local schools, and at age 18 began teaching in primary school. From then on until her retirement at age 84 she was a working woman. Teaching was a career that educated Victorian women of good family could properly enter, and journalism was just beginning to open its doors to women. By the fourth quarter of the nineteenth century, women journalists had formed their own New England Women's Press Association, and Emma was a member.

Women's rights were a much publicized political and social issue. At the Chicago World Exposition in 1893, the arts and achievements of women were recognized in a separate Women's Building which became one of the most popular centers of activity at the fair. In 1894 an international conference on women's issues was held in Europe, attended— by 10,000 delegates.[4]

As women's organizations became politicized, women's clubs across the nation became a forum for the expression of the female viewpoint. Emma Shaw Colcleugh, in becoming the Club Editor of the *Providence Journal*, was at the center of the active women's movement. She covered club meetings throughout Rhode Island in her column "Among Women's Clubs," kept her readers informed of the activities of the General Federation of Women's Clubs, and during her travels, always made it a point to visit other clubs. While in Australia in 1897, Colcleugh was made an honorary member of the Victoria Women's Club of Sydney, and she noted the great interest among Australian women in the organized activities of women in the United States (ESC xv). While her career as a travel journalist developed, so did her reputation on the lecture circuit. Her most popular lectures—"Through Hawaii with a Kodak," "Up the Saskatchewan" and "Inside the Arctic Circle under the Hudson's Bay Company's Flag"—were presented both in the United States and in Canada, at women's clubs, the YMCA and YWCA, teachers' meetings, church meetings, and occasionally in academic settings.

A forceful personality with many interests, good health, high spirits and a sense of humor, Emma seemed able to make friends wherever she went. She was told by a young admirer in Australia that she reminded her of Jo in *Little Women*. With self-confidence, she called upon heads of state and business leaders. Among her good friends were Sir Donald Smith, Lord Strathcona, Governor of the Hudson's Bay Company; John Muir, naturalist who became well known for his writings on the Alaskan wilderness; Dr. George Grenfell, founder of the Labrador missions; the Reverend Sheldon Jackson, Commissioner of Education for Alaska; and Capt. Hack Bartlett, skipper of the *Kite* when it sailed on the Peary Relief Expedition of 1895. She enjoyed her role as an adventurous woman treated as an equal by adventurous men. Emma's feminist principles clearly show in her pride at besting her male newspaper colleagues in daring the rapids of the Saskatchewan River with a Cree chief in a birch-bark canoe in 1888:

Upon my return to Winnipeg after several weeks' absence, I found, quite to my surprise, that people had been teasing the local newspaper men for letting, not only an American, but an American woman, take a trip that no Winnipeg correspondent had taken (ESC VI).

In fact, she met her future husband when he, as Mayor of Selkirk, Manitoba, was deputized "to do the honors to the American woman who had preceded Manitoba newspaper men in voyaging the Saskatchewan River, the first white woman to shoot the Grand Rapids in a canoe" (ESC VI). She was then forty-two years old.

Having supported herself as a professional for nearly a quarter century, Emma left her teaching and newspaper work in 1893 to live in Winnipeg as the wife of Frederick William Colcleugh, a widower with four grown children. He was a merchant and active politician, serving variously as Indian Agent at Selkirk, Mayor of Selkirk, and Member of the Manitoba Provincial Parliament. Through him she had entree at Government House and soon became good friends of the incumbent, Sir John Schultz and his wife, Lady Schultz. Before long she was giving lantern-slide lectures on her three Alaskan trips to the most distinguished audiences of Winnipeg society. Also recognized as a poet, she was frequently called on to present original poetry at special occasions. When Lord Aberdeen, Governor General of Canada, and his wife visited

Winnipeg, her poem in his honor was published in the *Manitoba Free Press*.[5] Prominent among the gentlemen she met were the officers of the "Honorable Hudson's Bay Company," whose headquarters were in Winnipeg. Through her acquaintance with the chief officer of the company, Mr. C. C. Chipman, Emma was invited to undertake one of her most interesting trips. In 1894, only a year after her marriage, she set off, unaccompanied by her husband, for a three-month journey as a passenger on one of the Hudson's Bay Company supply trips, visiting posts on the Athabasca, Peace, Slave, and Mackenzie rivers. Upon her return she was interviewed by the *Edmonton [Alberta] Bulletin*, which described her as an "adventuress and lecturer" who had made the trip "for pleasure and profit." They quoted her recommendation that the Mackenzie River trip was not one for others to take "if they only seek for pleasure." She had taken passage on three steamers, the *Athabasca*, the *Grahame* and the *Wrigley*, and had made a side trip of 300 miles up the Peace River to the "shoots," planning to use her experiences for illustrating lectures and magazine articles. "She had taken over two hundred photos with her Kodak and returned with a booty of ivory ornaments" (*Edm. Bull.* 9: 3: 94). See fig. II-4.

She was only the second woman tourist to enter the North and travel the steamer route to the delta of the Mackenzie. The first had been Miss Elizabeth Taylor, daughter of the American consul at Winnipeg, who had made a similar journey in 1892.[6] The few other prominent tourists who had preceded her on the Mackenzie water system were, for the most part, sportsmen or naturalists who were seeking the excitement of observing or hunting wood bison and musk-ox.[7] Among them were Hugh Lowther, Earl of Lonsdale, a British sportsman-aristocrat, who made the trip in 1888; followed by Warburton Pike, an Englishman who shot over thirty musk-ox, in 1889; the Count de Sainville, an explorer who spent the years from 1889 to 1893 in the lower Mackenzie region; naturalists J. B. and J. W. Tyrrell, in 1893; and Frank Russell, natural scientist whose expedition of 1893 was sponsored by the University of Iowa: its purpose, to collect natural specimens as well as anything he thought was of ethnographic interest.[8]

After the Mackenzie River trip Colcleugh returned to Rhode Island via a lecture circuit that included Toronto, Montreal and Boston, and the following summer again accompanied a Hudson's Bay Company steamer supplying posts in Labrador. She had learned of the work of Dr. George Grenfell in providing medical services to the native population there, and her travel letters carried detailed and enthusiastic descriptions of the work of the missions at Hopedale and Nain (ESC XV).

In 1897, her brief interlude of married life ended; she and Frederick

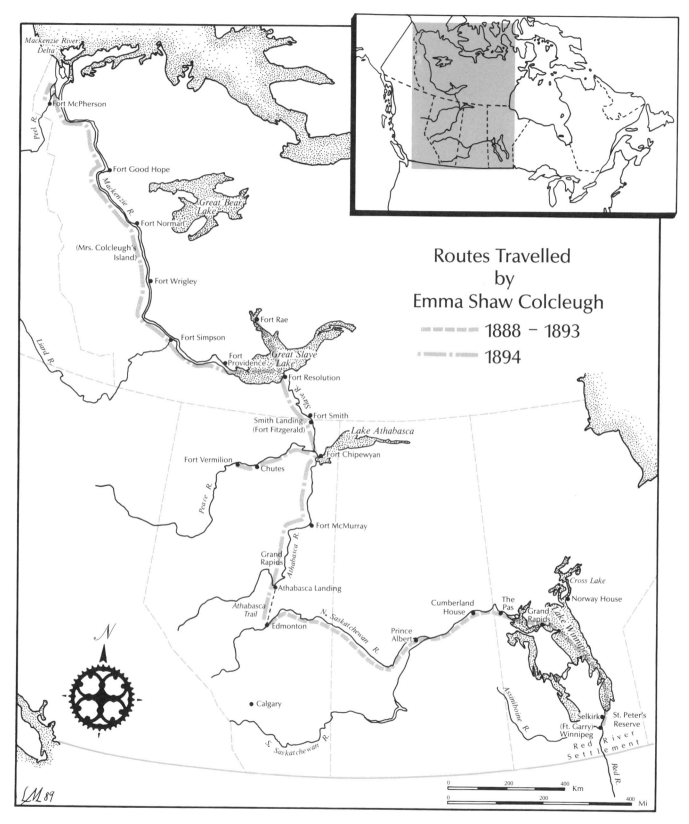

Routes Travelled
by
Emma Shaw Colcleugh

▬ ▬ ▬ 1888 – 1893
▬·▬·▬ 1894

Mackenzie River Delta

Peel R.

Fort McPherson

Fort Good Hope

Mackenzie R.

Great Bear Lake

Fort Norman

(Mrs. Colcleugh's Island)

Fort Wrigley

Liard R.

Fort Rae

Fort Simpson

Fort Providence

Great Slave Lake

Fort Resolution

Slave R.

Fort Smith

Smith Landing (Fort Fitzgerald)

Lake Athabasca

Fort Vermilion

Fort Chipewyan

Chutes

Peace R.

Fort McMurray

Grand Rapids

Athabasca R.

Athabasca Landing

Athabasca Trail

Edmonton

N. Saskatchewan R.

Cumberland House

The Pas

Cross Lake

Norway House

Grand Rapids

Lake Winnipeg

Prince Albert

Calgary

Assiniboine R.

S. Saskatchewan R.

Selkirk (Ft. Garry) Winnipeg

St. Peter's Reserve

Red River Settlement

Red R.

N

LM 89

| 0 | 200 | 400 | Km |
| 0 | 200 | 400 | Mi |

Fig. II-4. Map of route of travels: Saskatchewan River trips, 1888–1893; Winnipeg to Ft. McPherson 1894.

William Colcleugh separated, and she returned to Boston and Providence. Nevertheless, she always spoke with pleasure of the "cordial welcome and many courtesies extended to me" during the Winnipeg years, and when she took up her new post as Club Editor of the *Providence Journal*, she retained her married name, using the byline "Emma Shaw Colcleugh."

## EXCERPTS FROM "I SAW THESE THINGS"

In 1932, Emma Shaw Colcleugh described her life of travels in a series of articles written for the *Evening Bulletin* of Providence, entitled "I Saw These Things." Culling reminiscences from earlier notebooks and letters, she recalled highlights of her adventures. Her own words best describe her experiences. Clearly some of her attitudes and language, especially when referring to native people, reflect her times rather than ours, and are typical of Victorian-era travellers (Stocking 1985). The following excerpt is from the *Evening Bulletin*, September 6, 1932.

*Winnipeg and St. Peter's Reserve, 1888*

The broad streets and the buildings were a great surprise to me but as Winnipeg has long since loomed large on the tourist map no space need be given to description. Visitors today would, however, find lacking much that interested me at my first visit. The streets presented a great variety. Up-to-the-minute exquisites were jostled by half-breeds shod with moccasins; daintily-dressed ladies were side by side with Indian mothers who carried their infants on their backs in braided pockets with wooden backs. A sort of wooden yoke fastened these cradles to the necks of the mothers. The mounted police with scarlet coats and white helmet hats contributed bright color to the picture, but it was the Red River carts that, while I came to know them well in later years, struck me with astonishment. I have a distinct recollection of coming to an abrupt stop in the middle of a muddy cross-walk and staring—entirely oblivious to ought else—until I had gratified my curiosity respecting the non-descript vehicle.

A wooden cart on two wheels is the simplest description of these "Pembina buggies." They are built entirely of wood. The wheels are immense fellows, wide and never tired; the hub is sometimes encircled with a girdle of rawhide nailed on when wet and shrinking tight. The body of the cart is surmounted by a rail-fence which builds it up as high as the wheels.

Another, still more primitive method of conveyance was the "travois." This consisted of a pair of rude wheels from which depended two poles, their ends dragging on the ground. The space between them was filled by a sort of pocket formed by a network of strips of hide. In this the Indians were used to stow away their families as well as various belongings. The steed used with this as well as with the Red River carts, was a lone ox with a harness of rawhide; primitive enough but of infinite endurance, I was told.

[Winnipeg], centering about the old-time Fort Garry was headquarters for the "Honourable Hudson Bay Company." I met several of the high officials and to them I was indebted for much interesting information. . . .

Fig. II-5. Norway House, Treaty Day. Courtesy Pitt Rivers Museum.

Always interested in primitive people, I also learned much from the Indian agent. He told of a treaty made, nearly 20 years previous by which the Indians settled on the various reservations in the Canadian Dominion ceded to the government a portion of their right to the vast tracts occupied by them. In consideration of this the Government promised to pay them, "as long as the sun shines and the river runs," the sum of $5 annually to each individual of the tribe. The chiefs were to receive $25 and the councillors $15. . . . special days were set apart as "Treaty Days" (fig. II-5).

In 1888 Colcleugh was a guest at an annual Treaty Day at St. Peter's Reserve, home of the Saulteaux from whom Lord Selkirk had purchased land on the Red River near Fort Garry, headquarters of the Hudson's Bay Company. This Red River Colony eventually became the city of Winnipeg.

As the band at St. Peter's is quite a large one and as Treaty Day had grown to be a grand tribal reunion or visiting day, we found upward of 200 Indians assembled. During the two or three days occupied in the payment, the Indians are, in a way, considered as guests of the Government, and rations are dealt out to them at the grand "pow-wow" that inaugurates the affair. Each man, woman and child, I was told, received eight pounds of flour, two pounds of bacon, one quarter pound of tea and one eighth pound of tobacco, the tiniest papoose receiving its share of each. . . . (fig. II-6).

Flour was carried off in hats, handkerchiefs or any possible receptacle; small boys puffed away at their pipes with a vehemence indicating a speedy

Fig. II-6. Treaty No. 5 payment card, The Pas, Saskatchewan, 1885–87. Coll. ESC NB 213, 1888. HMA 87–238.

consumption of their share of the weed, baby-hands clutched chunks of bacon with an exceedingly satisfied air, and old crones lost no time in getting together material for a fire, that they might "boil the kettle," for no almond-eyed Celestial is more devoted to his tea than are all the Indians of the "Great Lone Land." Red River carts, travois, and a long line of birch canoes on the river bank, indicated the methods of transportation for the visiting Indians.

About the little log school house where the payments were to be made, lemonade booths were arranged, and various articles in which "Lo" delights were so displayed that the Indians returning to their "tepees" with their money could hardly fail to be tempted to dispose of a good part of it.

Temporary dancing booths—a dime for a dance—were constantly thronged, and the wheezy sounds of an old violin, the broken English of the half-breed floor manager, and the thump, thump of moccasined feet tirelessly treading out the Red River jig, went on without cessation.

A little farther away the sound of the tom-tom told to the initiated that the great gambling game, "Moccasin-ah-tat-e-wine," was in progress. The players sat around a blanket spread upon the ground. Two musicians, one on either side, beat upon the "tom-tom" or native drum, with sticks to which were appended birds' beaks, bears' claws, in fact the "lizard's leg and owlet's wing" and as many other uncanny things as ever Macbeth's witches used to furnish their "charm of powerful trouble." The players kept time to the sound of the drum with a droning sing-song "How-ah-ah-oh-how-how-ah," which they accompanied with wild oscillations of the body, rolling up their eyes and finally becoming oblivious to all about them.

In playing the game an Indian who was very expert distributes bullets—which they used to take the place of dice—hiding them under or inside moccasins provided for the purpose. The gambler watches these swift manipulations and the "boodle" is apportioned to him according to his success in pointing out the whereabouts of a certain marked bullet. The "heathen Indians" I was told, are passionately addicted to this game, and the medley of hats, pipes, sashes, etc. for which they gamble often absorbs about all their possessions that can be removed. Sometimes, before the game is finished, one victor triumphantly walks off with the whole.

We found the ceremony of paying the treaty money was well under way, when, after going the rounds, we arrived at the school house. While the Indian Agent and his assistant attended to the payments, the chief in scarlet uniform with gold braid trimmings and the grave councillors in black frock coats with red facings went to and fro among the Indians, witnessing each payment . . . [and] . . . settling disputes. . . .

The chief, a man of fine presence, appeared quite impressed by the introduction of a lady into the governmental sanctum. When I was presented by the agent, he greeted me with a dignified handshake and the universal "How," and directed the interpreter to provide seats at once. Accordingly we were escorted to a row of boxes and invited to make use of them. We were told, these boxes held the two-ounce biscuits (we should call them crackers!) which, at the rate of two a day, are served out, a sort of "reward of merit" for regular attendance, as a noon-day lunch to each child. If he fails to appear in the afternoon, no lunch for him the next day.

The last interesting feature of the occasion was an Indian wedding solemnized on the green by a very grave-looking person. At the conclusion of the ceremony his keen eyes, looking out through immense green goggles searched the assembly for witnesses to sign the marriage certificate. After securing the Indian agent and his clerk, his eye fell upon me, with the result that the "Boston paleface squaw" was invited to affix her signature to the document.

## A Saskatchewan River Trip

On her second visit to Winnipeg a few years later, Colcleugh was invited by officials of the Hudson's Bay Company to be their guest on a journey of a thousand miles up the Saskatchewan River.

A drive to Selkirk, which at that time was the port from which all supplies were shipped, a short sail on Red River, and several days on Lake Winnipeg brought us to Grand Rapids, the post at the mouth of the Saskatchewan.

Well named is that post for with Grand Rapids indeed does that wild river enter Lake Winnipeg. Several days were spent at the post, above the rapids, while the supplies our steamer had brought were transferred by a primitive tram-way. As I waited for the arrival of the river steamer I was interested in watching the Indian women (whose embroidery on caribou skin I have rarely seen equalled) and looking out at the mad whirl of waters before us. Suddenly the chief, as one of the young braves flashed by in a birch canoe, said, "You shoot 'em?" I had heard that he used to be famed for his dexterity in shooting those rapids but did not do it any more. So I replied, "Yes, if you take me." Neither of us could back out after that and!! "Nine mile," he said, and I only know it was the swiftest nine miles I ever went in fifteen minutes. If he said "ninety" I should have been in no mood to contradict him. Wonderful!! it was, but I never wished to repeat it, and when, years later, I visited Grand Rapids I saw the old chief and learned that it was the last time he ever made the mad trip.

To the long journey up the Saskatchewan river space cannot be given, replete as it was with interest. The little settlement at "The Pas," memorable as the place where Sir John Franklin wintered before his last ill-fated expedition, was of interest for various reasons, but I remember it as the scene of my first ride on a dog-sled. "How in the summer?" was what I said, when, in talking to the factor in charge of the Hudson Bay post there I had expressed a desire to try that special conveyance, and he assured me he could arrange it. Surely enough he did. A few brief orders and, in a short time, the dog-team resplendent in gorgeous embroidered blankets (see cats. 68, 136) and the Cree driver equally decked out appeared and I soon learned that on the short, dry grass the sled was swung along with ease—to the great satisfaction, evidently, of the crowd of Indians that speedily appeared from no one knew where. It was a "show" for them evidently, and an experience for me (ESC VI).

*The Mackenzie River
Journey: Into the North*

In 1894 Emma took an extensive journey "into the North" as a guest of the Hudson's Bay Company. The following excerpt is from the *Evening Bulletin* of September 10, 1932.

To Mr. C. C. Chipman (at that time the chief officer of the company) and his associates in Winnipeg, I was indebted for one of the most interesting trips I ever had. At that time, a yearly expedition was sent to take supplies to the "posts" north of the Arctic Circle, and to bring back the year's catch of furs. As a personal favor I was allowed to go.

From Winnipeg to Calgary, over the Canadian Pacific Railway, thence north to Edmonton on the Saskatchewan River, was familiar ground to me. Captain Robertson, an official sent out by the Government to inspect the steamboats in the north, awaited us.

We lost little time, and late that afternoon a decidedly nondescript outfit bore us away from the Alberta Hotel. Upon a long wagon were piled three trunks, an array of bags, my tent, bundles of bedding, sacks of oats, and the indispensable receptacle for provisions, "grubbox," in local parlance. In the rear, high above all, towered—at the start—a miniature haystack, while baskets swinging beneath, and frying-pan and tea-kettle fastened on in some way, the mysteries of which were known only to the driver, supplied all needed variety.

Early evening found us at camp on the Sturgeon River. Supper had been eaten, my tent put up and the men had taken the horses down to the river. As I was left alone on that wilderness hill-side, I never felt so remote from civilization, so much as if I had cut loose from all my former world. Behind me lay friends and news of friends; before me, far to the northward, lay long leagues of untrodden lands, and months of separation from all I had known in life. "Into the North" had, in those few lonely moments, a power of meaning I had never dreamed (fig. 11-7).

Fig. 11-7. Pad saddle, Plains Cree/Ojibwa/Métis, collected by Colcleugh at Athabasca Landing, 90 miles north of Edmonton, where travellers gathered to await the Athabasca River steamer. 1894. HMA 75–151.

Fig. II-8. "Traders leaving
Athabasca Landing for the
North, 1903." The steamer
*Athabasca* is in the background.
Colcleugh travelled for 13 days
on these small sturgeon head
boats, as well as on the steamer
in 1894. E. Brown coll. Courtesy
Alberta Provincial Archives.

A breakfast at 4:30, a noonday nap under an umbrella, while the men
prepared lunch, another sunset-camp and sunrise start, and we had climbed
the height of land between the Arctic and Atlantic rivers. For seven miles we
followed the bare, bald crest, then, all brakes on, we dropped down into the
valley of the Athabasca, where at the Hudson Bay Post, "Athabasca Landing," our steamer awaited us.

We found on board two sportsmen en route for the "Barren Grounds" to
shoot musk ox, a young woman, bound for the mission school at Fort Chipewyan, and the police inspector with one of his men. . . .

Starting at once, after a run of 40 miles, we picked up 30 men who had
been engaged for the boats which carry all freight down the hundred miles
of rapids between "Grand Rapids" and Fort McMurray (figs. II-8–11). At
five the second afternoon we reached the end of the steamer's run, a mile
above the island which is in the middle of the channel at the Grand Rapid.
Miss Thompson and I remained on the steamer for a week while the goods
for all the posts in the far North were taken from the steamer to the head of
the island, across which they were carried on a rude tramway. We then
walked through the lovely woods, two-thirds of a mile, to the landing at the
lower end of the island. Our tent was soon put up, a camp-fire blazed and a
tea-kettle sang.

Fig. 11-9. Many Subarctic métis were employed in the river traffic, portering supplies to isolated northern Hudson's Bay Company posts. At Grand Rapids, on the Athabasca River, goods had to be carried around the falls. Mathers coll. Courtesy Northwest Territories Archives, PWNHC.

I made it my first business to gather spruce boughs for our beds. Through all the North each traveller carries his own bedding. I had started so ignorant of this that all the time I was on the "Athabasca" my couch had consisted of my rubber sheet spread over the slats. I got on all right, of course, but had no intention of losing the chance of having a better bed when it could so easily be obtained.

To me, each hour of the strange wild life teemed with interest, but details must be omitted.

When, finally the brigade of five boats was ready our boat led the way. Our steersman was the guide to whom all looked for directions. It was late when we started, so we only ran a few miles before camping for the night. At four the next morning the sharp blows of a willow wand on the side of our tent aroused us and we were off.

With the exception of occasional stops to "boil the kettle," all that day (and several others) we rushed, whirled, shot and drifted, while about us curled and twisted the smooth green hollowing curves of great whirlpools,

Fig. II-10. "Running a Scow through Grand Rapids, Athabasca." When emptied of goods, the scows were taken through by a few men. Courtesy Alberta Provincial Archives.

dashing chutes, foaming cascades, dangerous eddies—every kind of angry vagary in which water could possibly indulge.

One felt a little sympathy with one of the native boatmen, who, starting the morning after a most uncomfortable night and a terrible time the previous day, looked back at the surging torrent with "Sacre Cascade" several times repeated, meanwhile wrathfully shaking his fist.

Fort McMurray was reached, passed, and, after 200 miles of perfect solitude, we rounded a little promontory from which a flag with "H.B.C." on it waved us a welcome.

Irreverent persons have been known to translate these initials, "Here before Christ." Fort Chipeweyan can hardly claim to be prehistoric but the fact that Mackenzie started from there when he explored the great river bearing his name, that Sir George Simpson, Franklin, Rae and other explorers rested there before penetrating the trackless wilderness beyond, all these and many incidents connected with the olden days of the fur trade cast a halo of romance about this old post.

Of interest to me was the mission school, where sweet-faced sisters cared for little Indian waifs, but, although far from all they had previously known, they were anxious to hear news "from outside."

Fig. II-11. "The Hudson's Bay Company steamer *S.S. Grahame* on the Athabasca River, 1896." The women on board are probably wives of Hudson's Bay Company men or teachers in the missions. E. Brown coll. Courtesy Alberta Provincial Archives.

Only the barest outline of the wonder-journey across Lake Athabasca, down the Slave River, a detour taking ten days to reach the post on the Peace River, thence back to Smith Landing, where the goods were landed, and a portage of 16 miles was made to Fort Smith, while our steamer turned back (fig. II-12).

It must be remembered that all steamers had to be carried in pieces and put together where they were to be used. One at Athabasca Landing, another at Fort McMurray, and the little "Wrigley" at Fort Smith. . . . (fig. II-13).

In the early morning the little steamer—83 feet long—started out on her long voyage. She was a staunch little craft, riding the mountain waves of Great Slave Lake, and stemming bravely the swift rapids on the Mackenzie.

She had to visit two posts on Great Slave Lake, five on the Mackenzie, and the Arctic post on Peel River, 40 miles up from the Mackenzie delta.

As I noted the miscellaneous cargo that crowded every available bit of space, I thought how much depended upon the safety of that boat and its cargo, including, as it did the year's supplies for all those far-away outposts.

Fig. II-12. "Freight wagons leaving Fort Smith, 1898." At Smith's Landing the *Grahame* returned south, while its freight and passengers continued north by way of a 16 mile portage around the rapids. Riding in one of these ox-drawn "Red River" carts squeezed amidst packing bags and boxes, Colcleugh travelled from Smith's Landing to Fort Smith in relative comfort, arriving at 3 A.M. Here she awaited a third steamer, the *S.S. Wrigley*, which each summer carried supplies from Fort Smith to the mouth of the Mackenzie River, stopping briefly at all of the Hudson's Bay posts en route. At each post, residents lined the banks to watch the steamer arrive with its anxiously awaited supplies, and shook hands with each crew member and passenger who climbed the banks to the settlement. C. C. Sinclair coll. Courtesy Manitoba Archives.

Fig. II-13. "The *S.S. Wrigley* on Great Slave Lake." This steamer was built at Fort Smith in 1886. Photo by Henry Jones. Courtesy Sophie Rusler.

Although we frequently dodged great ice-cakes on Great Slave Lake, the sun shone nearly 24 hours in the day.

The first port visited after entering the Mackenzie July 4, was strangely enough, Fort Providence. I could only celebrate by taking a few snapshots of the little Indian girls drawn up to meet Bishop Grouard, adding by request the Mother Superior and some of the sisters. This school, established somewhere in the sixties, affords a home for 40 dusky converts. It is in charge of sisters from the Grey Nunnery at Montreal.

Special interest naturally centered at Fort Simpson, as the residence of the Anglican Bishop—Bishop Reeve—and the headquarters of all the Mackenzie district. There was so much business to be transacted there that we spent some days and I had an opportunity to learn much of the life in the North.

Although many would call existence at the outposts dreary and uninteresting, and although hardship is the rule, still from father to son descends the love for the strange, wild life.

Although accustomed to solitude, these men never lose interest in outside affairs and the word "Welcome," frequently inscribed over the entrance to the fort enclosure, is no misnomer.

In the Journal of St. David's Mission, Fort Simpson, for July 1894 are two entries recording Colcleugh's visit: "July 5th: Steamer arrived from Fort Smith this morning bringing a large packet, for which we are thankful. The B[isho]p returned, and all those who left with her. Mrs. Colcleugh, (a tourist) is with the steamer. July 6th: Steamer left for Peel River this morning, the Bishop has gone to Norman and will await her return. July 18th: Steamer arrived from Peel River at 4 A.M. . . . Mrs. Colcleugh with the S.S. on her return. Indian Prayers as usual. Good Congregation Service conducted by the Bishop. July 19th: Steamer left again for Fort Smith at 4:30 P.M. Quite a crowd of passengers. The B[isho]p has gone to Smith in hopes of meeting Mrs. Reeve. Mr Camsell and Mr. Christie to Athabasca. . . . . Mrs. Christie, the wife of the accountant has left for a visit to civilization."[9] In the language of the day, "a visit to civilization" or to "go outside" meant returning to the southern part of the western provinces, while "going inside" or "going in" meant descending the Athabasca River and entering the vast sparsely inhabited northern territories (Russell 1898: iii).

Mr. Camsell, the officer in charge, was to join us (figs. 11-14–17). Mrs. Camsell finally decided to take the trip, thus adding greatly to my pleasure. At Fort Good Hope there was much to interest me but I remember it as the place—on the Arctic Circle—where I gathered dozens of the most beautiful wild roses I had ever seen. Beyond Fort Good Hope we began to meet the Eskimo, but, interesting as we found them, my attention really centered in the variety and luxuriance of the flowers along the banks. I had never been able to grasp the fact that hot sun and almost continuous daylight forces vegetation into almost tropical luxuriance. Replete with interest was every

Fig. II-14. Fort Simpson officers' house, the headquarters of the HBC and the dwelling house of Mr. and Mrs. Julian Camsell and their nine children. Chief Factor Camsell was in charge of the Mackenzie River District of the HBC from 1882 to 1900, and he frequently travelled on the steamers. When his wife decided to accompany him from Fort Simpson to the mouth of the Mackenzie River and back, she provided a most compatible companion for Colcleugh. Augusta E. Morris coll. 1881–83. Courtesy Hudson's Bay Company Archives, MPA.

Fig. II-15. "Indians landing at Great Slave Lake with birch bark canoes, coming to trade at Resolution." C. W. Mathers, Edmonton. Courtesy Northwest Territories Archives, PWNHC.

Fig. II-16. "Skin Lodges of the Dog Rib Indians in front of HBC's Fort on Great Slave Lake." C. W. Mathers, Edmonton. Courtesy Northwest Territories Archives, PWNHC.

Fig. II-17. "Peel's River Post. Priest and men looking over supplies." Augusta E. Morris coll. 1881. Courtesy Hudson's Bay Company Archives, MPA.

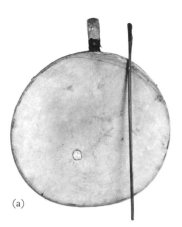

(a)

(b)

(c)

Figs. II-18 a–c. Objects in the Haffenreffer Museum collected by Colcleugh in the Eskimo community of Fort McPherson, Peel's River, Mackenzie Delta, 1894: (a) drum and drumstick, (b) quiver and arrows, (c) ivory needle case and thimble holder.

minute of the stay at Peel River, where we visited the Eskimos, and from their strange comments on the unusual "two white women," had an unusual opportunity to see ourselves as others see us (fig. II-18 a–c).

On the journey south up the Mackenzie River, a log entry made by the captain of the *S. S. Wrigley* notes that the steamer reached "Mrs. Colcleugh's Island," which lay between Forts Norman and Wrigley, on July 16, 1894 (HBC Archives B.200/a/39). The island is referred to again by this name in the *Wrigley's* log for 1895. No explanation of the naming of the island appears in Colcleugh's writings. But its existence seems to indicate a significant local awareness of this lady from "outside," so much so that she, like Mackenzie, Rae, Simpson and others, left her name as a permanent imprint on the North.

On our return trip the unforgetable memory is our journey up the Athabasca. With what I now consider inexcusable stupidity I had taken it for granted that we had finished the excitement connected with the rapids on our way down stream. How I fancied we were to pursue the even tenure of our way like a placid old canal boat in the rush, tumble and whirl of the waters, I know not. I soon found my mistake. Only the bowsman and steersman remained in the boats, and the crew of eight men, with leather bands about their chests, attached to a long line from the boat, walked along the shore dragging our unwieldy boats. This was our sole motive power for over one hundred miles.

To tell of the strange wild life, the excitement of the moose hunt—always followed by a night of feasting—the bears encountered and the strange scenes as Bishop Grouard gathered the dusky sons of the wilderness about him for prayers—all this is now impossible, but they loom large in the memory of a never-to-be-forgotten summer (ESC X).

Having proved herself as an able travel journalist who was willing to undergo physical duress and who had the determination to get to the right people to make a good story, Colcleugh was given assignments, in later years, of increasing social and political significance. At the close of the Spanish-American War in 1898, she was sent to Cuba by her newspaper to investigate and bring to public notice that country's poor health and living conditions, especially among women and children. A few years later she was in Puerto Rico describing for the newspaper's readers the aftermath of a disastrous hurricane which had struck the island.

In 1902, at the age of fifty-six, she was asked by her editor if she would be willing to be a passenger on the first train over the Uganda Railway, journeying from Mombasa, British East Africa, to Wyanda, Uganda. Although she contracted a fever during her three month stay in Africa, which recurred in succeeding years and kept her from further rigorous adventures, Colcleugh never complained about the adversities of travel,

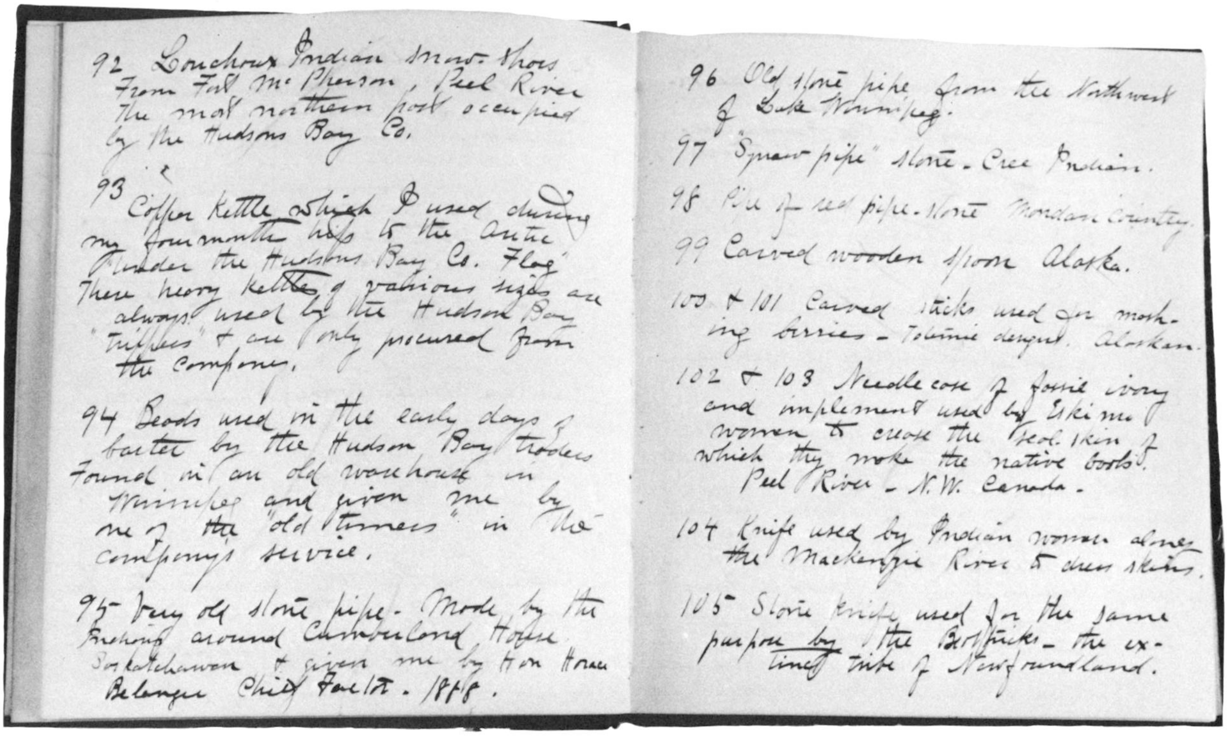
92 Loucheux Indian snow-shoes
From Fort McPherson, Peel River
the most northern post occupied
by the Hudsons Bay Co.

93 Copper Kettle which I used during
my four months trip to the Arctic
under the Hudsons Bay Co. Flag.
These heavy kettles of various sizes are
always used by the Hudson Bay
"tripmen" & are only procured from
the company.

94 Beads used in the early days of
barter by the Hudson Bay traders
Found in an old warehouse in
Winnipeg and given me by
one of the "old timers" in the
company's service.

95 Very old stone pipe. Made by the
Indians around Cumberland House
Saskatchewan & given me by Hon Horace
Belanger Chief Factor. 1888.

96 Old stone pipe from the Northwest
of Lake Winnipeg.

97 "Spear pipe" stone. Cree Indian.

98 Pipe of red pipe-stone Mandan country.

99 Carved wooden spoon Alaska.

100 & 101 Carved sticks used for mash-
ing berries. Totemic design. Alaskan.

102 & 103 Needle case of fossil ivory
and implement used by Eskimo
women to crease the seal skin of
which they make the native boots.
Peel River. N.W. Canada.

104 Knife used by Indian women along
the Mackenzie River to dress skins.

105 Stone knife used for the same
purpose by the Beothucks - the extinct tribe of Newfoundland.

Fig. II-19. Collection notebook of Emma Shaw Colcleugh.

taking as her motto "If you don't have what you like, make yourself like what you have!" (ESC XI). Her final long trips were taken in comfort on the "floating hotel" of the cruise ship *S. S. Bluecher*, stopping at major ports in Brazil, Argentina, and Chile. She went as a passenger in 1910 and as lecturer the following year. She continued her work with the *Journal*, as Club Editor and Reviews Editor for travel books, until her retirement in 1928.

In 1932 she wrote the final series of nineteen articles (excerpted above) for the *Evening Bulletin* entitled "I Saw These Things." They are based on earlier field notebooks and letters, and are illustrated with her own photographs (all, unfortunately, lost). These articles provide additional documentation to the collection notebook which accompanied the 218 artifacts she sold to Rudolf F. Haffenreffer Sr. in 1930 (fig. II-19). The Colcleugh objects became part of his private collection of American Indian materials, and were housed in the King Philip Museum, later to become the Haffenreffer Museum of Anthropology, Brown University. Until 1940 Emma Shaw Colcleugh lived in retirement in her childhood home of Thompson, Connecticut. At the age of ninety-four, having taken the train alone to Florida for a vacation, she died. Her career as teacher, traveller, adventuress, collector, poet and journalist had spanned more than half a century.

Collections of native Subarctic arts gathered by Victorian travellers contained objects that were integrated to varying degrees within a native community. Some objects were functional within the traditional community; that is, they had long been made by the society for its own use before being noticed and desired for purchase by outsiders. In the Subarctic this group included bows, arrows, quivers, drums, pipes, firebags, tobacco pouches, snowshoes, moccasins, mitts, leggings, shirts, moss bags, hoods, bark containers, stone and wood utensils, and tools.

A second group of objects functioned well in the historic era to bridge the gap between insider and outsider in the community. A highly ornamented firebag or jacket might be commissioned by the local Hudson's Bay Company factor for his own use, or a beaded altar cloth might be made as a gift for the resident missionary. These objects often stayed within the community, reinforcing the maker's pride and pleasure in creativity.

A third level of objects functioned as a means for the native artist to participate in a cash economy. Made by native people in quantity for sale to tourists along the more travelled routes, this group included elaborately beaded pouches, silk-thread-embroidered picture frames and greeting cards, glasses cases, card cases, place mats, and embroidered, slipper-type moccasins. Favorite excursion points, such as Grand Rapids, on the western shore of Lake Winnipeg, to which lake steamers brought visitors from Winnipeg, became centers at which such goods were offered for sale. In Colcleugh's words (ESC VI): "As I waited for the arrival of the river steamer I was interested in watching the Indian women whose embroidery on caribou skin I have rarely seen equalled." In the late nineteenth century there were more such centers of trade in the Lake Winnipeg area than farther north. In the more isolated areas of the North, along the Slave-Athabasca-Mackenzie river chain, tourists were so few that their purchases had little effect on the types of objects made, which continued to be those that were useful within the community. However, the activity of the river transport system encouraged movement of goods and native-made items by way of the men — most of them of mixed native and European ancestry — who worked on the river as porters, trackers, helmsmen and as general crew for the little steamships. Hence, beaded and quilled objects from Great Slave Lake and even farther north might well be found in southern centers of commerce such as Winnipeg and Edmonton.

Many objects were made with native and natural materials: bark, wood, bone, hide, porcupine and bird quills, dentalia shells traded from Puget Sound, swan's feet, stone, babiche and sinew. Others were made with trade items which had become an important part of the artist's repertoire—glass seed-beads, polished iron beads, silk thread, wool and cotton cloth. Some objects were made with techniques long existent in the community: porcupine-quill weaving, the tailoring of skin clothing, the cutting, folding and incising of birch bark, and the looping of babiche to form netted containers and snowshoes. Other objects were created using new skills learned outside the native community: silk-thread embroidery, glass-bead embroidery, and the tailoring of Western-style wool and cotton clothing.

Many objects made by native women were used by both men and women: for instance, beaded, quilled and silk-thread-embroidered moccasins, and other items of clothing, and pouches and wall pockets for storing household items. Some objects were made by women for use by women, such as sewing bags; other objects were made by women for use by men, such as firebags, gauntlets and dog blanket sets. Drums, bows, quivers, arrows and stone pipes were made by native men for their own use. A complete nineteenth-century collection from the Subarctic includes a combination of these various art expressions.

FACTORS IN SELECTION

It has often been said that objects, to be collectible, must be "suitcase-sized." They must also be durable, and not given to organic disintegration or destruction through packing and storing, since most nineteenth-century travellers were on extended tours of many months, and carried their purchases with them in steamer trunks, valises and boxes. Bead embroidery on hide or cloth was particularly suited to withstand such rugged storage conditions and became a popular take-home item. The Colcleugh collection contains one exception to this pattern of collecting non-bulky objects: a chair made of wood with a netted babiche seat, which was purchased at Fort Good Hope on the lower Mackenzie River (see cat. 93). Although certainly not of suitcase size, the chair had the positive attribute of providing a place for Emma to sit while on shipboard!

Collections of native artifacts made by nineteenth-century men and women generally reflected the personal interests of the collector and his or her ideas about what objects had inherent interest, beauty, or value and were worthy of being saved. In surveying the Colcleugh collection from the Subarctic, it seems clear that small, decorative objects, useful in the household or as ornament for dress occasions, were her favorites. Most of the collection consists of bead- and silk-thread embroideries and porcupine-quill weavings, made and used by women. However, there are two gun cases, two babiche bags, two octopus bags, a firebag, a pair of mitts, and a dog blanket set—all men's belongings—although made by women and highly decorated. There is a pair of snowshoes, made and used by both men and women. Two of the stone pipes, carved by men, are small and of the type that she noted were also used by women.[10]

In comparison, a collection made by the aristocrat-sportsman Lord Lonsdale in the Mackenzie River area in 1888 (Krech 1989), and now in the Museum of Mankind, British Museum, contains almost no bead or quill embroidery and is heavily oriented toward men's hunting and other utilitarian equipment. Another collection from the Mackenzie River area is that made by Frank Russell in 1893 for the University Museum of the University of Iowa. It contains examples similar to those in the Colcleugh collection, but with a wider range of types of objects, and more balanced representation of those made and used by both men and women. Unlike Colcleugh and Lonsdale, whose collections reflected their personal interests, Russell was consciously attempting to collect in a scientific manner for a university museum, in order to present a fairly complete inventory of late nineteenth-century Mackenzie River material culture.

Native expectations were another factor that determined a collector's selections. Certain objects might have been offered to a man, and others to a woman, according to native perceptions of the collector's interests. Emma may have been offered especially fine bead and silk embroideries because, like other women, she was assumed to be an embroiderer herself, or because she expressed particular delight in their beauty, or perhaps only because the native women expected her to like what most other women liked. A man, on the other hand, might only have been offered an embroidery if he mentioned that he wanted it for a female relative. Lord Lonsdale, for instance, collected some decorated clothing from the Arctic mainly as a gift for his wife.

Still another factor in determining the make-up of a collection was the visitor's access to the native craftsperson. Introductions may have been made through the captain of a river steamer, a teaching nun at a mission, a Hudson's Bay Company official, or the guide of a hunting expedition. Each would have had access to different kinds of artifacts. Emma Shaw Colcleugh often identified the source of particular objects in a notebook of her collection (see fig. II-19: ESC NB 93, 94, 95).

In summary, the aesthetic tastes, particular interests, and gender of collectors, their relations to and within the community, the purpose of their visit, the degree of acculturation of the community, and the size and durability of objects are all factors determining the composition of the Victorian museum collection. The exhibition of these different kinds of collections in museums gives us, then, our view of what objects were available within a culture at a particular time.                    BAH

1 "ESC 1" refers to the first in a series of nineteen articles written by Emma Shaw Colcleugh for the *Evening Bulletin*, published by the Providence Journal Company, entitled "I Saw These Things," in which she recalls highlights of her trips. Excerpts from these articles have been included here. Providence Public Library, *Evening Bulletin*: B: 8:30:32–9:21:32.

2 Christian Feest has defined four levels of native art: tribal, representing art indigenous to a culture; ethnic, or art collected by Westerners during the period of their early exposure to a native culture, thought by them to be typical of it, and eventually produced primarily for outsiders; pan-Indian, or art produced for the art market of the dominant white society because it is considered native, and which has been adopted by many different native groups for whom it had not been a functional part of their culture; and Indian mainstream art, produced by artists who happen to be Indians, which is competitive with all other art because of general artistic principles, rather than representative of a particular culture (Feest 1980: 14–16). The Colcleugh collection falls into the first two categories: tribal art, such as babiche bags and snowshoes, and ethnic art, such as floss embroidered slippers and picture frames.

3 See Middleton, Dorothy, *Victorian Lady Travellers*, New York, Dutton, 1965; Russell, Mary, *The Blessings of a Good Thick Skirt*, London, Collins, 1986; Halliburton, Richard, *The Royal Road to Romance*, Garden City, N.Y., 1925.

4 In the same month that the Manitoba Free Press ran an article on Colcleugh's return from her three-month journey down the Mackenzie River, it featured the return of Mrs. Graham, a prominent worker in the Women's Christian Temperance Union, and Lady Aberdeen, wife of the Governor General of Canada, from participation in this conference (*Manitoba Free Press* 10:9:94). Lady Aberdeen subsequently addressed the ladies in Prince Albert, Northwest Territories, on the aims of the National Council of Women (U.S.), whose meeting she had attended in Washington, D.C. It is interesting to observe, in this same month, that almost no mention was made of native affairs, while a great deal of attention was given to economic concerns— fisheries, non-native land settlement, mineral rights—and to politics.

5 October 1894. Other literary works by Colcleugh include "Nahanni," a poem celebrating the beauty of a mountain range visible from the lower Mackenzie River; *Worldwide Wisdom Words*, a book of philosophical and humorous quotations from many parts of the world; and *Alaskan Gleanings*.

6 See the Elizabeth Taylor Papers, private collection of James Taylor Dunn, St. Paul; also "Paris to Peel's River in 1892," Grace Lee Nute, *The Beaver*, March 1949.

7 As a result of this concentration of interest in hunting two nearly extinct species, the Unorganized Territories Game Preservation Act of 1894 was passed, which established closed seasons and a permit system.

8 For late nineteenth-century Mackenzie River visitors see "Grandees, Tourists and Sportsmen: Travellers in the Mackenzie Basin," in *Ribbon of Water and Steamboats North, A History of Fort McMurray, Alberta*, D. J. Comfort, Fort Smith, 1974. See also Pike, Warburton, *The Barren Ground of Northern Canada*, London & New York, Macmillan & Co., 1892; Tyrrell, J. W., *Across the Sub-Arctics of Canada, A Journey of 3,200 Miles By Canoe and Snow-Shoe Through the Barren Lands*, London, T. Fisher Unwin, 1893; see also Russell 1898, and Krech 1989.

9 Journal of St. David's Mission, Fort Simpson, July 1894. Diocese of the Arctic Collection. M71–4. Series II–5a, vol. 1, Box 7.

10 The objects she obtained in the Arctic from Mackenzie Eskimo and Alaskan coastal peoples represented a greater proportion of men's equipment than of women's— quiver, arrows, drum, ivory story knife, pipes, harpoon, and feast bowls—perhaps indicating that her collecting was determined as much by availability as by preferences relating to gender.

# III Styles and Style Change

## Central Subarctic Regional Styles

Fig. III-1. Ribbon appliqué on Cree-Métis, Chipewyan-Métis mitten cuff, mid-nineteenth century, cat. 21.

Fig. III-2. Horizontal, triangle, diamond, and zigzag patterning on Ojibwa twined bag, Wisconsin, 1885, DAM 1931.45.

THE INITIAL GEOMETRIC DESIGN COMPLEX

When European floral designs were introduced into the central Subarctic in the mid-nineteenth century, they joined a long-established, broadly based geometric design complex that seems to have originated north of the Upper Great Lakes area extending north and south, and to have existed since pre-contact times. In a variety of media, including paint, quills and natural fibers, there was a preference for treating design areas with repeated horizontal bands of zigzags, triangles and diamonds enhanced by subtle color alteration.

Some of the eighteenth-century Algonquian panel bags from the Upper Great Lakes area (see Feest 1987; Glenbow 1988: figs. w 88, w 91) were painted with bands of contiguous same-size triangles. Late in the century, designs of repeated rows of zigzags, triangles and diamonds had become fully developed on Cree ribbon appliqué on fabric hoods, leggings and other clothing (Conn 1980: 12). Such patterning in ribbon work continued in the nineteenth century (fig. III-1). Similar designs were woven into nineteenth-century Great Lakes fiber bags (fig. III-2), particularly those incorporating wool yarn (Whiteford 1977). A variation used on such bags that was also especially common in ribbon-work designs breaks the series of diamonds or triangles at intervals with a linear extension of the horizontal axis. The beaded "otter tail" edging that dates at least to the eighteenth century on finger-woven sashes and also appears on nineteenth-century Great Lakes bandolier bags (fig. III-3) is a variation of this pattern. Here a row of repeated diamonds is varied not by extending the space in between, but by expanding a diamond into a lozenge shape at intervals. In each of these nineteenth-century variations, the equilateral triangle provides the basic design element, and repeated elements are the same size and adjacent, be they triangles, diamonds or V's forming the zigzag.

On both ribbonwork and fiber bags, color was often manipulated to create a subtle optical interplay defying a defined figure-ground relationship. For instance, when color was changed along a horizontal axis bisecting a row of diamonds, the rows of triangles thus created related to the adjacent rows on both sides, simultaneously completing both a

Fig. III-3. Beaded "otter tail" design, on bandolier bag, HMA 77–16, Great Lakes, 1860–80, collected from the Cree in Alberta.

row of diamonds and a band formed from interlocked triangles. This fascination with the spatial ambiguity created by splitting color along a band continued as a hallmark of later Great Lakes ribbonwork after curvilinear, foliate-like profiles dominated.

Farther north in the central Subarctic, among the Athapaskans, the old basic geometric design complex was the same. An equilateral triangle, repeated in horizontal bands of adjacent same-sized diamonds, triangles and zigzags, formed the foundation and appeared primarily on woven quillwork bands used on clothing. In a common variation found on both quillwork bands and bead-edged fabric appliqué from the eastern Athapaskans, a check is inserted between the zigzag points. Although the foundation forms are the same, the Athapaskan dynamic is different from the Algonquian one. Repeated zigzags on either side of a central diamond band, expanding it outward, are the most common configuration on Athapaskan quill belts (fig. III-4).[1] Color is symmetrical along the horizontal axis and pulsates outward. If diamonds are interlocked, they remain diamonds, solidly or concentrically colored within each diamond and are seldom color-split, as are the Algonquian examples just discussed. (See also discussion of Athapaskan quill design with belts, cat. 3 A–H.)

When appliqué borders appeared on eastern Athapaskan garments about the mid-nineteenth century, they continued this basic patterning.

Fig. III-4. Athapaskan woven quill designs, 1890s, detail of belts (cat. 3).

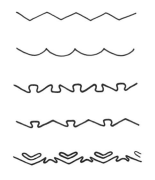

Fig. III-5. Athapaskan appliqué edge patterns on garments and bags ca. 1860–1900.

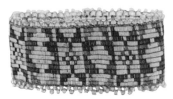

Fig. III-6. Algonquian quill weaving, napkin ring, 1890s, cat. 1.

Appliqué edges (fig. III-5) were most often cut in a simple zigzag or with checks inserted between the triangles (Duncan 1980). Appliqué fragments in the Haffenreffer Museum collections (cat. 76 and 77) illustrate slightly more complicated variations.

This widespread central Subarctic approach to patterning continued in Athapaskan quill-weaving and Cree/Cree-Métis ribbonwork even as floral styles became more popular in the nineteenth century. These geometric designs survive today primarily in the woven quill bands that a few Athapaskan Slavey women continue to make, and in the ribbonwork of the Osage, a Great Lakes tribe now living in Oklahoma.

Another geometric style practiced by Lake Winnipeg area Algonquian groups during the early nineteenth century appears to have been influenced, if not inspired, by Euro-Canadian designs. Best known on woven quillwork such as the napkin ring (cat. 1; fig. III-6) and needle case (cat. 2), this style has been called Algonquian (Duncan 1989), Red River Métis (Brasser 1976, 1988) or Red River Ojibwa (Brasser 1988, Phillips 1988). These designs differed fundamentally from the type discussed above. They were formed of separate, multi-element motifs composed primarily of tall obtuse or right triangles and rectangles of different sizes, joined to create forms such as eight-pointed stars and lozenges. Motifs were usually alternated in an ABAB (occasionally an AAAA) pattern along bands.[2] The motifs, the thin connecting lines, and the proportion of positive to negative space, suggest the influence of Caucasian rug designs similar to those that seem to have affected the development of the beadwork patterns of the Western Sioux.

## SOME MAJOR CREE FLORAL STYLES

The earliest references to beads in the central Subarctic report their use in a woven technique. In the 1740s James Isham (1949: 107–8) observed Cree women in the Fort Churchill-York Factory area weaving beaded bands on a simple sapling loom. Hudson's Bay Company records for 1768 speak of women at Churchill "making bead belts for the trade" (HBC B42a 70). These were probably also loom-woven and, because of the technique, geometric in patterning. But the "deer, birds, straight and curved lines, etc." that Factor Andrew Graham saw beaded on rectangular hoods during the 1770s and '80s when he was assigned to posts on Hudson's Bay, indicate that by that time, beads were sometimes sewn directly onto a hide or fabric ground (1969: 145). Floral designs followed in the nineteenth century.

Establishing exactly when floral embroidery was first produced in the central Subarctic is difficult, but it seems to have been well established in the Lake Winnipeg area in the 1840s. At present some specific nineteenth-century styles can be identified and dated, and the evolution and relationships of floral styles and particular types of items, such as the woven-panel firebag, can be traced. More work remains to be done.

The Haffenreffer Museum collection includes examples of major nineteenth-century floral styles of the Lake Winnipeg area. Although commonly called Cree or Métis, some of these styles were shared by Saulteaux people living east of the lake.

*The James Bay Cree Style* — A beaded hood from the Haffenreffer Museum (fig. III-7), one of a group of elaborate floral beaded hoods usually attributed to the James Bay Cree, illustrates the earliest datable floral style found on Cree work. This same style appears in silk-floss embroidery on two octopus bags collected about 1860 (RSM L.304.128 and NMNH 2022), and in bead embroidery on both octopus and panel bags. Two James Bay-style octopus bags were "presented to Sir George Simpson by Cree Indians at the time of the Franklin Expedition" (LFG 2257 and 2260; fig. III-8), and thus date to the 1840s. These bags and hoods include many of the same motifs, particularly outlined rosettes with suggested rather than delineated petals, serpentine stems edged with small almond-shaped petals, thistles or related variations, and several distinctive profile blossom

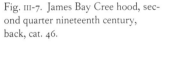

Fig. III-7. James Bay Cree hood, second quarter nineteenth century, back, cat. 46.

Fig. III-8. Octopus bag, given to George Simpson at Red River in the 1840s, LFG HBC 2260, also in the James Bay Cree style.

forms. The motifs on beaded examples tend to be slightly less detailed than those in floss; for example, what is clearly a thistle when embroidered in floss becomes stylized into a range of bud and flat-topped bell forms on beaded pieces. Floss examples are too faded to determine original colors, but beaded work shows preferences for white, pink, blue, green and crystal. British whitework embroidery with "leaf stems" is likely the European prototype for this style which may have developed in the Red River area under the influence of British women, particularly those associated with the Anglican missions there.

*The Lake Winnipeg Small Flower Style*

A later floral style, the delicate "Lake Winnipeg small flower style," is represented on several floss-embroidered pieces from the Haffenreffer Museum collection (figs. III-9 a & b). The style combines groups of tiny sinuous motifs of similar scale to form fluid, asymmetric sprig arrangements. Characteristic motifs include rosettes in shades of red and rose, alone or with teardrop-shaped lobes wrapping part way around them; composite serpentine leaves constructed by the attachment of individual green S-shaped leaves along a curving central core of lighter or darker green; and tendrils with a single loop, often embroidered in blue. Pink teardrop-shaped lobes are sometimes wrapped along the tops of leaves. Berries are also occasionally included, often in blue.

The Lake Winnipeg small flower style was usually embroidered in buttonhole stitch using a fine, tightly twisted silk floss. Available examples show original bright colors now often faded to shades of rust, avocado green and gold. The style appears mostly on Victoriana, such as picture frames, wall pockets, and lamp pads from the last decade or so of the nineteenth century, but also on moccasins. Some of the Haffenreffer Museum items appear to have been purchased at Cree-speaking Grand Rapids on Lake Winnipeg, but work in this style was probably also produced in other communities in the area. At least two variations on this style developed farther north around the lake.

Fig. III-9. Lake Winnipeg small flower style: (a) silk-embroidered center of New Year's card, cat. 15 (b) silk-embroidered insert in picture frame, cat. 12.

(a)

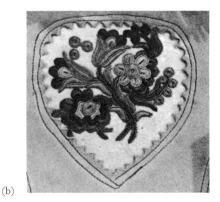

(b)

*The Norway House Style*

The flamboyant floss-embroidered style that centered around Norway House, Manitoba, in the 1890s and through the first two decades of the twentieth century, was related to the Lake Winnipeg small flower style. This "Norway House style" (fig. III-10 a & b) utilizes the basic motifs of the earlier style, but settles on several preferred motifs and dramatically enlarges the rosettes and serpentine leaves. Rosettes are formed of one or more layers of elongated petals wrapped with one or more outer layers of scalloped (unarticulated) petals. The color dominance in designs leans to the reds and pinks of the rosettes. See page 168 for discussion.

The Norway House style was produced not only at Norway House but also in related communities such as Cross Lake. Although documentation of examples is not yet sufficient to define community variations, at least two community styles seem to be represented in the treatment of the rosettes.

Fig. III-10. Norway House style. (a) Jacket back yoke, cat. 32. (b) Characteristic motifs: (1) expanded rosette (2) tendril (3) bud with three-part top (4) serpentine composite leaf.

(a)

(b1)

(b2)

(b3)

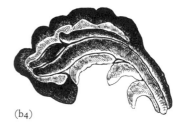

(b4)

*The Lake Winnipeg*
*Cascading Lobe Style*

A less flamboyant style, using beads rather than floss and related to the Lake Winnipeg small flower and the Norway House floss styles, was also produced at the turn of the century by women of northern and eastern Lake Winnipeg. The use of beads no doubt determined some of its characteristics, but there are also clear preferences for a certain repertoire of motifs, each configured in particular proportions. Firebag (cat. 50) is typical of the "Lake Winnipeg cascading lobe style."

Designs are asymmetric sprays primarily composed of: a motif formed from stacked tear-shaped lobes with petals attached along one side; small rosettes with tear-shaped lobes or petals wrapped part way around them; four-petal rosettes placed against broad pointed leaves; flat-topped bells with an interior line of a second color; and berries. White stems with hairs on each side connect the motifs.

In all cases the design is beaded directly through paper that was later pulled away where not covered by beads. Multiple examples with the same design indicate that the paper served as a pattern (fig. III-11).

The Haffenreffer collection also includes examples of several other floral styles from the Cree- and Saulteaux-speaking areas. Slippers (cats. 22 and 23) with their combination of thin, sinuous leaves and profile blossoms constructed of broad petals stacked behind each other, represent a style that also appears on a few jackets, probably from the same

Fig. III-11. Ramona Sinclair, Edmonton, 1916. Ramona was the daughter of Charles Cuthbert Sinclair, who in the 1890s served as clerk and factor at various posts, including Norway House. Ramona is wearing a "Norway House style" costume embroidered with silk floss, and leggings and a panel bag beaded in the "Lake Winnipeg cascading-lobe style." Ramona's uncle was related to Emma Shaw Colcleugh's husband. Ramona's panel bag, now in the Lower Fort Garry Museum, is one of several similar to cat. 50 on right. Courtesy Garbutt Collection, Hudson's Bay Archives, MPA.

Fig. III-12. Motifs prominent in Cree floral work: (a) rosettes with undelineated petals, cats. 52, 55 (b) variations on the moss rose with its groups of tiny pointed petals at the upper points of the calyx, cats. 17, 31 (c) broad, pointed leaves backing rosette petals, particularly on four-petal rosettes, cats. 16, 50 (d) tiny pointed petals placed in a row or in pairs along the edge of a blossom, or, occasionally, the edges of a leaf, cats. 29, 37 (e) a sinuous leaf with S-shaped leaves and sometimes lobed petals attached along either side of a prominent central stem, cats.33, 10 (f) almond or tear-shaped petals stacked behind each other or wrapped along the edge of another motif, cats. 50, 54.

community and perhaps the same maker. Other styles, represented by single examples, are discussed in individual catalogue entries.

In general, nineteenth-century Cree floral designs included certain motifs, as well as preferences for relating those motifs that continue today. Awareness of these trends is useful in the attribution process (fig. III-12 a–f).

## ATHAPASKAN REGIONAL STYLES

During the second half of the nineteenth century, regional floral styles also developed among Subarctic Athapaskan groups. The Athapaskan region is far larger than the Cree, Saulteaux and Northern Ojibwa areas, and several regional beadwork styles developed, shared by groups socially connected because of the trading posts they frequented. Duncan (1989) identifies and discusses five Northern Athapaskan style regions, calling them the Great Slave Lake–Mackenzie River Region, the Liard-Fraser Region, the Yukon-Tanana Region, the Tahltan Region and the Interior Coastal Region. These names refer to the waterways which were instrumental in determining contact affiliation in each region.

More of the Athapaskan material in the Haffenreffer Museum comes from the Great Slave Lake–Mackenzie River Region than from any other Athapaskan region. The early establishment of fur trade posts on the Slave and Mackenzie rivers meant that boats servicing them could allow travel for an occasional adventurer, such as Emma Shaw Colcleugh. Farther west, travel was more difficult. In the 1940s, some Athapaskan people in remote areas of the Yukon could remember the first white man they had seen.

*The Great Slave Lake–Mackenzie River Region Style*

The Great Slave Lake–Mackenzie River Region floral style was remarkably homogeneous in the late nineteenth century, so much so that without specific documenting information, it is usually impossible to attribute an example to a single language or tribal group. Women from across the region had been trained together in mission schools and later traveled between communities, thus reinforcing a unity of style.

Great Slave Lake–Mackenzie River Region designs were formal, ornate and internally complex. Occasionally an object was floss-embroidered, but most were beaded on black velvet with dense bouquets of frontal and profile blossoms, leaves, berries and tendrils. Most motifs

Fig. III-13. Detail of dog blanket showing ornate, complex foliate style of Great Slave Lake–Mackenzie River Region beadwork, 1890s, cat. 68.

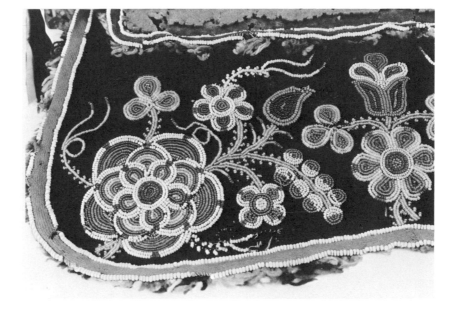

Fig. III-14. Motifs prominent in the Great Slave Lake–Mackenzie River Region floral beaded style: (a) rosette with metal beads in the center of the outer layer of petals (b) petals and wisps with metal beads at points (c) wisps and tendrils (d) bud-like motif, sometimes called "beaver castor" or "spider bump" (e) split-color berries.

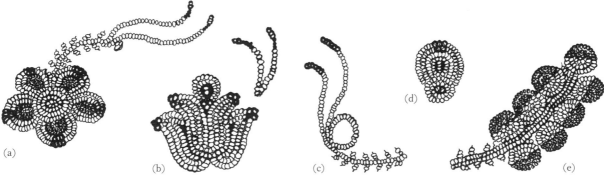

were constructed by elaboration—the attachment of petals and leaves onto a central core element. Color followed the contour and typically changed with each two bead rows, in shaded layers of pinks, greens, aquas and golds. Round, berry motifs were sometimes color-split through their centers. Accents of silver- and gold-colored metal beads usually high-lighted the points of leaves, petals and tendrils, as well as the center of the outer color layer on petals. Rosette and leaf centers were sometimes constructed of metal beads. The beading was precise and formal, the overall effect cheerful and ornamental (see figs. III-13, III-14 a–e, and cats. 60–73).

*Western Athapaskan Styles*

West of the Great Slave Lake–Mackenzie River corridor, floral designs were more open and less ornate, with fewer, simpler, more stylized motifs. Those from the Liard-Fraser Region (fig. III-15) tended toward a free exuberance of unpredictable motif and color combinations. Parts of designs were often abstracted fillers generated during the beading process. Liard-Fraser Region designs were never alike, but shared the tendency toward background elaboration.

In the Yukon-Tanana Region, motifs were often open rather than solid, with color often changing across or along the axis of the form rather than along its contour. Many motifs were single-element and simply outlined or solid; more complex ones consisted of two or three outlined parts, each very simple and usually tangent rather than overlapping. The Haffenreffer Museum's gold poke from the Klondike (fig. III-16) and wall pocket, cat. 83, are examples of this style. The Tahltan and the Interior Coastal Region are not represented in the Haffenreffer collections.

KCD

Fig. III-15. Sekani bag, Liard-Fraser Region, cat. 78, with simpler, stylized motifs and abstract fillers.

Fig. III-16. Gold poke, Klondike, Yukon-Tanana Region, cat. 82.

## Visual Perception, a Factor in Design Change

> ... when by some circumstance the mind is freed from its usual allegiance to the complexities of nature, it will organize shapes in accordance with the tendencies that govern its own functioning . . . . the principal tendency at work here is that toward simplest structure, i.e., toward the most regular, symmetrical, geometrical shape attainable under the circumstance.
>
> ARNHEIM (1974: 145)

Much of the floral beadwork of North American native groups is undocumented—the maker, place and time of origin have not been recorded. But the objects themselves can reveal a great deal, and attribution is often possible via comparative analysis of style, whereby undocumented objects are grouped with like objects of known history on the basis of similarities in the class of artifact, methods of construction, and applied designs.

As we analyze floral bead and silk work from the northern Plains and the Subarctic comparatively, confusion is sometimes caused by similarities in designs that other evidence indicates have been produced at a distance from each other. However, since we know that floral design was introduced into the central Subarctic from an outside source, and then adapted and modified by native people, an examination of the way in which two-dimensional designs are perceived—and are likely to change when they are reproduced—may be helpful in the search for factors to explain these similarities. If there are universals at work in the perception-reproduction process, an understanding of them may help to explain why designs produced by different groups about the same spatial or temporal distance from an initial point of design introduction can be similar to one another. It may also suggest the placement of particular objects along spatial and temporal continua of design evolution, thus assisting in the attribution process, and helping to produce an overview of the patterns of design change across time and distance. The conclusions of psychologists studying the mechanisms of visual perception are helpful in addressing these concerns.

### VISUAL PERCEPTION THEORY

Students of visual perception group their observations under a broad principle they believe to be universal, the "law of the good gestalt."

"Gestalt" refers to perceptual totality, and "good gestalt" to the most easily perceived mental order or structure of that totality. The "good gestalt," then, is the simplest one, because "any stimulus pattern tends to be seen in such a way that the resulting structure is as simple as the given conditions permit" (Arnheim 1974: 53). When ambiguous stimuli are presented, the brain chooses the least complex alternative by simplifying and regularizing the visual pattern, particularly by making it symmetrical, by leveling (dropping out information), and by sharpening (enhancing or exaggerating information).

Experiments in visual perception show that when participants are asked to recall or reproduce a visual pattern, the number of structural features and details that are remembered, decreases. Individual shapes and overall configurations become regularized in memory, and both symmetry and repetition of parts increase. Forms within a pattern that share proximity, size, shape, slope, color or brilliance, tend to be thought of and recalled together, a phenomenon termed "common fate association." The elimination of some details and recall of others perceived as a unit simplify the pattern. Such perceptual mechanisms are thought to have developed as a necessity for survival in a complex visual world where the mind must be able to discard "visual noise," and to focus on essential information and retain it for future recognition. Thus in perceiving an object visually, the brain simplifies the complex of stimuli, organizes it, regularizes it, and forces structure and order onto it. The regularization of information in a pattern presents a more coherent perceptual totality, one in which the number of different kinds of visual information for the brain to decode has decreased.

Because perception operates in this way, such simplifications and structural modifications are likely to be reflected in the changes that occur when a design is reproduced, particularly when the original design was detailed or unfamiliar. Conversely, when such changes have occurred in the evolution or reproduction of a design over time, we may suspect its ancestry to be found in a more complex original that was geographically or temporally distant. This would particularly be the case if the original were borrowed from another culture.

A scholarly debate about visual perception theory has continued over the last fifty years, with published studies supporting or refuting aspects of Gestalt school theories.[3] It is not the intention here to join the debate but to point out the correlation between the observations of visual perception specialists of the Gestalt school and the changes that occur in two-dimensional floral designs across the Subarctic. We suggest that an awareness of the nature of such changes is helpful as we seek to attribute examples and understand the history of the art.

## VISUAL PERCEPTION AND
## CENTRAL SUBARCTIC FLORAL DESIGNS

In the mid-nineteenth century, elaborate floral designs based on European embroidery patterns were introduced into the Lake Winnipeg and Great Slave Lake areas. The new two-dimensional designs spread rapidly, away from the sites of introduction, and changed as people saw and adapted them. The principles isolated in visual-perception studies suggest that certain predictable changes will have occurred during this process. A comparison of the initial and derived designs tests this prediction.

*Early Floral Designs from Central Subarctic*

The mid-to-late nineteenth-century floral styles of the native peoples of the Lake Winnipeg and Great Slave Lake–Mackenzie River regions, where European floral patterns were directly introduced, are usually complex and full of detail. Designs are often asymmetrical, and normally include many different foliate motifs connected by short stem segments. The foliate motifs are usually composed of several parts, constructed by the elaboration of a central core element with additional underlapped elements. The application of color within each element is normally intricate, especially in beadwork from the eastern Athapaskans of the Great Slave Lake–Mackenzie River Region, where color changes in subtle gradation every two bead rows. Most eastern Athapaskan designs also include metal bead accents, particularly at the center of the outer color layer of petals and at the points of leaves, petals and tendrils, adding further visual complexity.

On floral designs of the same period from the Lake Winnipeg area, small motifs with intricate details are the rule. When larger motifs occur, they are composed of numerous parts. Designs usually incorporate many colors, normally contrasted within each motif.

*Related Designs Geographically or Temporally Distant*

According to the predictions of visual-perception research, we would anticipate that, in designs from more remote areas and later times, individual motifs would be less complex and more regular, and that they would have fewer parts and internal details, less underlapping of parts, and fewer color changes. There would likely be increased symmetry both in individual motifs and in entire designs, and more repetition than variety in structural relationships. Prominent deviations on the original would probably be retained.

These predictions are confirmed by nineteenth century Subarctic embroidery produced away from the communities where European floral designs were first introduced, and also by Subarctic work from the twentieth century. On each, in comparison to the originals just described, both the entire designs and the individual motifs are almost

(a)

always composed of fewer parts, and are more regular and symmetrical and less detailed. Within designs there are fewer motifs and fewer different motifs—a limited number of motifs are apt to be repeated. Many motifs consist of a single element, often the outline of a total form (a blossom, bud or leaf), or, if more complex, are composed of only a few elements, which are more often tangent than underlapping. Frequently stems are actually connected networks, and function as a single motif rather than as multiple ones. The limiting of the number of elements and elimination of underlapping within individual motifs simplifies and regularizes motif contours. There are also fewer colors on these examples, both in each individual motif and in entire designs.

One important characteristic from eastern Athapaskan designs is remarkably tenacious, however. In eastern Athapaskan designs, metal beads, (particularly polished iron ones, now often rusted or tarnished) were once very bright. As accents at certain prescribed locations (the centers of petal edges and the points of pointed motifs), they contrasted sharply with the surrounding colored beads, and were united visually by color, brightness and predictable location. Such accents continue in western Athapaskan designs, but become smaller (leveled), or conversely, become so enlarged (enhanced) that they split the design element horizontally into two blocks of color. The point accents are often limited to one or two metal beads or a bead of contrasting color placed at the points of leaves, petals and tendrils. In many cases this occurs in addition to a horizontal (transverse) color split, providing a double

(b)  (c)

Fig. III-17. (a) Octopus bag (LFG 2260), given to George Simpson about 1840 at Red River by Cree or Cree-Métis, and another (San Diego 28370) are two of several octopus and panel bags with similar basic designs on the body. Central and up- or down-turned stems issue from a central rosette. Small leaves line the stems, which themselves terminate in buds or rosettes. The latter are detailed, often elaborate. (b) Cree-Métis panel bag (cat. 49) and (c) Naskapi round-bottomed bag (cat. 43) both retain this basic configuration, but demonstrate the simplification and regularization that visual perceptionists predict will occur in visual memory. The panel bag seems to date closer to mid-century, and also to have been made at a distance from the original design source, probably to the west, the direction in which the panel bag form was dispersed (see Chapter III Bag Forms). The Naskapi bag was made late in the nineteenth century, east of James Bay and Lake Winnipeg, far from the point of introduction of European designs.

emphasis of this very prominent visual characteristic of eastern Athapaskan designs (see cat. 82). Whether such accents have been leveled or sharpened, the number of color changes and individual intersections where colors meet are fewer, and the visual complexity in regard to color has decreased.

The dominant stems on many western Athapaskan pieces are also a result of "common fate" recall and enhancement. Although eastern Athapaskan beadwork in the collections of the Haffenreffer Museum tends to have gold stems, white is equally common for stem segments from that region. Originally, these white stem segments, like the metal accents, stood out against a busy, multicolored composition and stark black background, and were easily remembered. In western designs, stems are both regularized and enhanced. Stem segments are joined and placed symmetrically to form a dominant central stem network, or are regularized into a pattern of identical repeated stem segments. In both cases, the number of different kinds of perceptual information has been reduced.

Cree / Cree-Métis designs dispersed both east and west from the Lake Winnipeg and James Bay Cree areas, and in both cases underwent similar transformations. One composite that appears on many early Cree bags, a central rosette with upswept stems emerging from either side, is a clear example. On these early examples, both the stems and the primary components of the rosette are white. United in memory by common fate association of brightness, color, and proximity, they are maintained in a simplified form on many western Cree bag designs and on the Naskapi round-bottomed pouch (fig. III-17 a–c). "Leaf stems," the stems with small almond-shaped leaves projecting from either side that appear on early Cree work such as the hood, cat. 46, and on related early bags (fig. III-17a), are also retained in a simplified form on distant examples. Their descendent, the "hair stem," with its angled two-bead projections, appeared occasionally on later Cree work, but became especially popular with the Athapaskans, and remains so today.

The motif most frequently present in the initial designs, the frontal rosette, maintained its importance as designs became simpler. In nineteenth-century designs from both the Great Slave Lake–Mackenzie River Region and Lake Winnipeg, the frontal rosette was the most common motif, always regular and sometimes larger than other motifs. Although the embroidery version was adopted from European designs, the rosette form was also very common in the natural environment (wild rose, ground dogwood, etc.), so it is not surprising that it maintained its importance. The other most common early eastern Athapaskan motifs, the split bell and the rosebud, were also retained, but in simplified forms in western and more recent Athapaskan designs.

### EXAMPLES IN THE HAFFENREFFER MUSEUM COLLECTION

Certain older examples in the Haffenreffer Museum collection reflect the changes that visual-perception principles predict in designs developed at a geographic distance from the European introduction of floral design. The simple small motifs, dominant central stem network, and limited colors on the upper part of Cree / Cree-Métis panel bag (cat. 49) suggest such an origin.[4] Panel bag (cat. 48) is less far removed. Naskapi bag (cat. 43) demonstrates regularizations and simplifications in comparison to the somewhat earlier Cree / Cree-Métis bags to which it is related (fig. III-17 a–c). Style characteristics of the three-tabbed octopus bag (cat. 80), when compared with octopus bags such as cat. 54 clearly argue for a more distant origin (fig. III-18 a & b).

The floral sections on early twentieth-century panel bag (cat. 50) seem almost as busy as earlier floral designs, but there is actually considerable regularization through repetition. The geometric woven panel below demonstrates even more clearly the bag's distance from mid-nineteenth-century panel bags (fig. III-19 a & b). Comparison with earlier bag (cat. 48), which shares similarities in the geometric designs, demonstrates that the triangles, once functioning as part of a coherent overall pattern in the earlier bag, now float, small and alone, against a dominant white ground on the later one. On the earlier bag, the corner rectangles are composed of triangles, and the large triangles at either

Fig. III-18. The design on (a) Cree/Cree-Métis octopus bag (cat. 54) is a spray of multi-part flowers with levels of individual underlapped petals and connected by small stem segments. The color changes in layers within each petal. (b) Cree/Cree-Métis octopus bag (cat. 80) retains the basic idea of a central rosette with stems and additional motifs, but the overall design has become symmetrical, and the individual motifs are far simpler in both shape and color application. Both bags seem to date near the end of the nineteenth century.

Fig. III-19. Comparison of the woven panel portions from two Cree/Cree-Métis panel bags, (a) (cat. 48), from the mid-nineteenth century, and (b) (cat. 50) dated about 1900, demonstrates the "leveling" of visual information that occurs in the perception/reproduction process. Both the internal complexities of motifs and the connectors between motifs have dropped out in the later design.

side are formed from a triad of smaller ones. On the later bag, they are no longer composite motifs—the connectors have dropped out and the internal design integrity has been lost.

Although there are no late-nineteenth-century Great Slave Lake–Mackenzie River Region Athapaskan wall pockets in the Haffenreffer Museum collection, the floral work on firebag (cat. 60), tobacco pouch (cat. 61), leggings (cat. 65), and watch pockets (cats. 62, 63 and 64) is typical also for wall pockets. Comparison of the floral designs on Yukon-Tanana Region wall pocket (cat. 83) with these eastern designs from the same period clearly demonstrates visual-perception principles at work (fig. III-20 a & b). In contrast to the complexity of the examples from Great Slave Lake, the design on the Yukon-Tanana pocket is simpler, with a limited number of basic symmetrical motifs in a limited color range, repeated in a sparse symmetrical composition against a broad, open background. The embroidery on Sekani moccasins (cat. 42) shows simplification and regularization when compared with eastern Athapaskan counterparts such as moccasins (cat. 39 and cat. 41) from the same period. Other early examples are the Yukon-Tanana Region belt (cat. 84), gold poke (cat. 82) (fig. III-16), and knife sheath (cat. 81), with their dominant central stems and simple outlined foliate motifs. (Note the transverse color splitting on the gold poke). Sekani firebag (cat. 78, fig. III-15) demonstrates many expected simplifications and regularizations, but also reveals a new impetus for background elaboration that begins to transform it toward greater design complexity.

Comparison of old and recent material in the Haffenreffer Museum demonstrates that many of today's motifs are simplified, regularized descendents of motifs important to beadworkers and embroiderers in the late nineteenth century, and that they reflect the changes from the

(a) (b)

Fig. III-20. (a) Firebag (cat. 60) is typical of late-nineteenth-century work from the Great Slave Lake-Mackenzie River Region Athapaskans. Multipart motifs constructed by the elaboration of a core element with underlapped elements, and complex color changes within motifs, are typical. Athapaskan examples from farther west are far less complex and more regular. On both (b) wall pocket (cat. 83) (bottom pocket section) from the Yukon-Tanana Region and Sekani firebag (cat. 78), motifs are single-element or constructed of only two or three elements that touch but do not underlap. The number of colors in individual motifs and in designs as a whole is limited. On the Yukon-Tanana Region bag, the stems dominate the beads and hide ground. As is typical on work from the Liard-Fraser Region, the maker of the Sekani bag has used her basic design to launch a purely visual exploration where she fills in sections of the background whimsically, using already established contours to suggest new shapes.

Fig. III-21. The repeated diamonds and zigzags typical of nineteenth-century Athapaskan woven-porcupine-quill belts are also the basic motifs on later twentieth-century belts, but normally in less intricate versions. Compare (a) earlier belts (cat. 3 c, d [detail]) with (b) recent wristlets (cats. 122, 123, and 124).

(a)

(b)

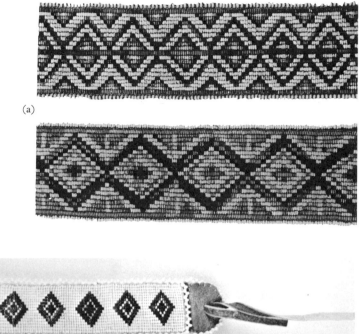

earlier, more complex sources that visual perception principles suggest will occur. Contemporary designs are, as a whole, far less complicated than earlier ones. Motifs are usually simpler and composed of fewer elements. There is less color complexity. Many motifs tend toward symmetry and strict regularity, and are apt to be repeated in a design.

Among Athapaskan examples, one may compare the late-nineteenth-century Athapaskan dog blanket (cat. 68) with cat. 136, made in 1984; older moccasins (cat. 67 and cat. 41) with the range of contemporary examples; and older moss bag (cat. 74) with recent bag (cat. 141). Contemporary Athapaskan woven quill designs are also similar but usually far less intricate than older ones. Compare cat. 3 c, d and cats. 122, 123, 124 in fig. III-21.

Among Algonquian examples, compare older gloves (cat. 37) with new ones (cat. 142); the range of older bags with the recent bag (cat. 151); and old and new moccasins and slippers.

Contemporary Algonquian work retains certain favored motifs and preferences for relating parts within a motif, but in simplified versions (fig. III-22 a-d). For example, the motif of stacked teardrop shapes on the mid-twentieth century moccasins from Saskatchewan (cat. 147) is a modern version of the curve of stacked lobes on the turn-of-the-century Island Lake-type panel bag (cat. 50, fig. III-22a). The upright teardrop positioned symmetrically within a motif and backed with petals on contemporary Island Lake barrette (cat. 150) and purse (cat. 151), and vamp patterns from Cross Lake (fig. IV-7), is a relative of the more complex groupings of teardrops on nineteenth-century Cree examples, such as octopus bag (cat. 54, fig. III-22b). The modern version has fewer parts and no color changes within the petals.

Fig. III-22. Certain favorite motifs and ways of constructing motifs that are apparent in late-nineteenth-century Cree/Cree-Métis (a-d) and Athapaskan/Athapaskan-Métis (e, f) floral designs, are retained in simplified versions today. Cree/Cree-Métis: (a) The wrapped teardrop lobes on early twentieth-century panel bag (cat. 50) are echoed on recent moccasins (cat. 147). (b) Motifs composed of symmetrically stacked teardrop shapes, which occur on late-nineteenth-century examples such as cat. 54, remain important although diminished on cat. 150 and fig. IV-7, both beaded in 1985. (c) A particularly simple bud and also blossoms formed of non-articulated, lobed layers rather than individual delineated petal layers are both characteristic of late-nineteenth-century Norway House-type designs, such as that of the pillow cover (cat. 35) and leggings (cat. 57). Both ideas are retained on recent moccasins (cat. 144). (d) The moss roses on late-nineteenth-century examples, such as the slipper tops (cat. 17), leggings (cat. 56) and tobacco pouch (cat. 61), are far more complex than their simple, regular descendants on contemporary examples, such as the mukluks (cat. 138) and dog blanket (cat. 136). Athapaskan: (e) The more complex dip-petaled rosette on late-nineteenth-century leggings (cat. 65) is recalled in its simpler recent cousin on the moss bag (cat. 141). (f) Earlier band designs, such as that of the garter (cat. 70), are more complex than recent ones like that on the moss bag (cat. 141).

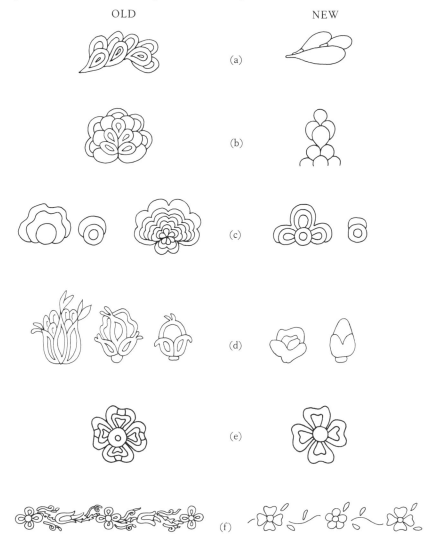

OLD                    NEW

(a)

(b)

(c)

(d)

(e)

(f)

Round petals, wrapping part way around a blossom, and exactly echoing the set of petals underneath rather than alternating with them, were particularly popular both frontally and in profile on turn-of-the-century floss-embroidered Norway-House-style examples (cats. 35, 57, 34, 37, and 33). They still appear on contemporary Cree material (cat. 144), but are less complex compared with the older Norway House examples, which include more layers of attached petals and more internal color changes (fig. III-22c). Late-nineteenth-century embroidery includes elaborate three-calyx moss rosebuds with characteristic tiny leaves attached at the points, and more commonly, two-calyx buds such as those on examples of Cree floss-embroidered slipper tops (cat. 17), leggings (cat. 56), and the Athapaskan tobacco pouch (cat. 61) and firebag (cat. 60). The rosebuds on contemporary examples (cats. 138, 139, and 136) are descendent but far less complex (fig. III-22d). Clearly, a strong tradition continues in the Subarctic. Contemporary embroidery is directly linked with the past along a continuum of design evolution.

In the case of contemporary beadwork, differences in the available materials and the realities of day-to-day life have also contributed to the simplification and regularization of forms. Larger beads and less delicate embroidery threads are common today, other activities compete with time once spent in handwork, and the consumer is often unwilling to pay for more complex work.

Certainly visual perception factors have not been the only influences in the evolution of floral design across the Subarctic. However, the mechanisms that operate in the processes of perception and reproduction have clearly been important. An awareness of those helps to clarify the history of floral design across this large geographic region, and can be usefully applied elsewhere in studies of design evolution, particularly where complex designs are adopted from an outside source.     KCD

III-40  III-30

III-36  III-24  III-35  III-23

III-39  III-29  III-38  III-28  III-31  III-34  III-33a

Map: The panel and octopus bag forms are dispersed across the North American continent.

## The Evolution of Two Algonquian Bag Forms

Ornamented bags have been important to Woodland and Subarctic Indians for centuries. Bags associated with personal medicine powers or with sacred smoking were observed by the first Europeans to visit the North American continent, although few examples dating to the eighteenth century have been preserved in museum collections. In the nineteenth century, a man generally owned one or more bags to carry tobacco, flint and steel for firemaking and, after the introduction of the muzzle loader, shot and shooting accessories. A successful hunter might have owned several ornamented bags and worn more than one on dress occasions. In the literature, the terms "firebag," and "shot pouch," have been used somewhat interchangeably, with preference for one term or the other when talking about different regions. Larger bags with wide straps have been usually termed "bandolier bags" in reference to the strap.

There are enough nineteenth-century bags known to permit discrimination of tribal and regional styles in both bag forms and applied decoration, and in some cases to trace their evolution. The most dramatic change, compared with earlier bags, came in the replacement of the geometric patterning in paint and quills found on eighteenth-century bags, with elaborate floral designs in beads on nineteenth-century bags. By the end of the nineteenth century, firebags were used primarily for dress occasions, and some were probably also made for sale to non-natives.

By early in the nineteenth century, central Subarctic Algonquians preferred two distinct types of firebags: the panel bag, a pouch from which hung a rectangular woven panel, and a tabbed bag now called an octopus bag, in reference to the four pairs of tabs hanging at the bottom. Both forms have long histories, still only partly understood.[5] DeBry recorded a tabbed bag in the late sixteenth century. Both bag types were collected in the 1760s somewhere in the upper Great Lakes area from Algonquian speakers. Panel bags are known from about 1800, yet by the end of that century the octopus bag was clearly preferred. Examples of both types of bags in museum collections are remarkable for their lack of documentation, but many—particularly the panel bags—are regionally attributable and generally datable due to the style of the floral embroidery on the pouch section. Octopus bags reveal a broader range of floral bead styles than panel bags, and also display regional preferences in their proportions.[6]

These two especially popular bag types were introduced across Canada in the nineteenth century, especially by Cree and Cree-Métis hunters working in the fur trade, by Cree wives of Hudson's Bay employees traveling with their husbands, and by Cree bands moving west and settling with other tribes. Regional variations of both bag types developed in the Plains, on the southern and northern Plateau, and among the Tlingit on the Northwest Coast. Although Ottawa and Ojibwa fur-trade employees moved west as well, it was the Cree and Cree-Métis with their strongly established styles who exerted the greatest influence on bag design.

The following discussion traces the panel and octopus bag forms across the continent. The bags illustrated have been chosen as representative of regional variations.

*The Panel Bag*

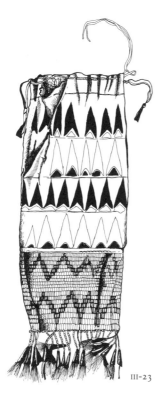

III-23

Precursors to the mid-eighteenth century Algonquian panel bags from the upper Great Lakes area (fig. III-23) have yet to be identified. These bags had two ornamented components: a smooth pouch of tanned hide painted on both sides with geometric designs, and a textured rectangular panel below, formed of hide thongs wrapped alternately in pairs with porcupine quills. The bottom and occasionally the sides were finished with tassels formed from quill-wrapped thongs tipped with dyed animal hair and metal cones.[7]

In the early nineteenth century, variations of the panel bag developed in the central Subarctic, the southern Great Lakes, and on the Plains incorporating new materials and designs. Woven bead panels and fabric pouches with designs in couched beads replaced the wrapped quill panels and painted hide pouches. The central Subarctic bag of the Cree in turn spawned variations on the Plateau and the Northwest Coast.

The Subarctic Cree/Cree-Métis panel bag of the nineteenth century was a descendant of the early hide panel bag just described. On it the pouch was made of wool fabric (black or red) and the panel below was of woven beads. The bead panel was usually fringed on three sides. Sacred images, such as the sun and thunderbird outlined on the pouches of some of the earliest examples (fig. III-24), suggest that they were used as medicine bags. A century later, some individuals such as the old uncle of Harry Sanderson, Cree-Métis of The Pas, still kept his herbs and medicines in a beaded panel bag hung from his house rafter (Sanderson, pers. comm. 1985). A mid-century variation is fig. III-25, given to Dr.

III-24  III-25  III-26  III-27  III-28

John Rae. This drawstring pouch has an embroidered rather than a woven panel and a decorative band around the top.

By the latter half of the nineteenth century Cree/Cree-Métis panel bags incorporated elaborate floral motifs beaded on both sides of a pouch of black wool above the single geometric panel of woven beads (figs. III-26 and III-27). The pristine condition of many collected about 1900 suggests that by then such bags were used primarily for dress occasions. The Haffenreffer collection includes beaded panel bags in several floral styles.

The widespread Sioux-Assiniboine-type pipe bag form (fig. III-28) was also kin to the eighteenth-century Algonquian panel bag. The proportions were altered so that the pouch section was tall and narrow,

III-29

III-30

III-31

III-32

in order to allow the bag to be tied to the pipestem or held in the hand, but the earlier combination of pouch, hanging panel and fringe was maintained. As on the early Algonquian bags, the hanging panel of the pipe bag was formed from quill-wrapped hide strips, but they were wrapped in pairs vertically rather than in the alternated segments common on the thong wrapping of the early prototype.

The similarities between eighteenth-century painted Algonquian panel bags, their nineteenth-century beaded Cree and Cree-Métis counterparts, and panel bags produced on the western edge of the continent demonstrate that it was Cree speakers who carried the type west. Many were involved in the fur trade and some entire bands migrated as far west as British Columbia. A few panel bags were produced on the Plateau during the 1840s, and by the 1890s they were being made in Southeast Alaska by the Tlingit.

The panel bag (fig. III-29) was made briefly on the Plateau in the mid-nineteenth century. It was almost identical in proportion to its Cree prototype. The pouch was made of wool and embroidered with a few schematic foliate-like motifs. The primary design area was the hanging panel, which was woven of large seed beads and incorporated angular figures of quadrupeds and stylized eagles like those on Wasco-Wishxam twined bags.

The Tlingit also made the panel bag (fig. III-30) for only a short period, but later in the century. Both black and red wool were used for pouches, and the woven panel was geometrically patterned and normally quite short, sometimes ending in bead-strung tassels. Beadwork was concentrated on the pouch portion (usually on both sides), in a loose quasi-floral style precursor to the fully developed Tlingit foliate scroll style of the turn of the nineteenth century.

During the nineteenth century, as the Cree version of the panel bag evolved and was carried westward, another bag type that seems at least in part to have been influenced by the eighteenth-century Algonquian panel bag developed in the Great Lakes. The later nineteenth-century Great Lakes bandolier bag (fig. III-31), with its large woven panel and row of short woven tabs hanging along the bottom retained the idea of a woven panel below a more simply ornamented upper area, but, on it, the woven panel dominated and formed the front body of the pouch. When a contrasting decorated section existed, it was a narrow, beaded floral band formed by the extension of the back of the pouch above the opening. Whiteford (1986) has also pointed to the firebag with two horizontal geometric bands of woven porcupine quills alternated with bands of simple quilled foliate forms as a precursor to the Great Lakes bandolier bag (fig. III-32).

*The Octopus Bag*    The other prominent nineteenth-century Cree/Cree-Métis bag type, the octopus bag, can be traced to prototypes produced in the mid-eighteenth century alongside the panel bags. But the form was recorded even earlier. Two Carolina Algonquian bags, one an animal pouch with two legs and tail making three tabs (fig. III-33a), the other with four freehanging tabs (fig. III-33b) are pictured in DeBry's engraving of John White's drawings of 1590. The record then lapses until the eighteenth century, when bags with two rounded, closed tabs or three pairs of pointed free-hanging tabs were collected in the upper Great Lakes area. By the mid-nineteenth century, a florally embroidered fabric octopus bag with four pairs of tabs had emerged as the most popular bag among the Cree and Cree-Métis.

The early nineteenth-century Great Lakes two-tabbed medicine pouch (fig. III-34), made of dark-dyed hide, was tall, rectangular and constructed with two broad round or square-ended tabs closed along the edges so that the pouch extended into them. Long fringes, sometimes with bells attached to the ends, hung between the tabs. Such bags were embroidered in quills with abstract geometric symbols or representations of manitous or spirits, and were clearly sacred (see Phillips 1984).

The three-tabbed painted hide bag (fig. III-35), dating from the mid-eighteenth century, consisted of a pouch and three pairs of free-hanging

III-33a

III-33b

III-34

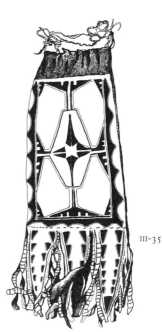

III-35

pointed tabs, each pair separated by long fringes like those on the medicine pouches just discussed. The geometric patterning painted on both the pouch and the tabs is not so clearly symbolic as that of the two-lobed medicine bag, but both bags seem to be related to medicine bags made from the bodies of animals such as otters, weasels and skunks, such as those sketched in the 1830s by Karl Bodmer on the Upper Missouri. On these bags, the legs and tail of the animal created three tapered extensions, perhaps the precursors of the later triple tabs. The sixteenth century bag pictured by DeBry (fig. III-33a) clarifies this connection centuries earlier.

By the early nineteenth century the octopus bag form had become conventionalized (figs. III-36 and III-37). Now made of fabric, most such bags had four pairs of tabs, each tab rounded or indented at the end. They were decorated florally, almost always on both sides. Most were beaded; a few were floss-embroidered. Tab and bag edges were carefully bound with ribbon, calico or wool twill braid, and the tab pairs were usually connected at the bottom where short tassels were attached. A few of the earliest beaded four-tab examples maintained the long inter-tab fringes of the earlier two and three-tab hide version, stringing the fringes with beads. The octopus bags in the Haffenreffer Museum collection, like those elsewhere, exhibit a range of floral styles.

Although uncommon, a pipe bag version of the tabbed bag was occasionally made in the Plains in the nineteenth century (fig. III-38).

III-36

III-37

III-38

Such bags retained the pointed tabs of the eighteenth-century Musée de L'Homme bag, sometimes using two, sometimes three single stiff tabs rather than pairs of tabs. The pouch was tall and rectangular, and the solid beading on the lower end of the pouch sometimes extended to cover the tabs.

In the nineteenth century the tabbed bag was introduced into the southern Plateau, where two versions developed, and into the northern Plateau in British Columbia where it was picked up by the Shuswap and Thompson River peoples. In the southern Plateau, tabbed bags completely woven of beads were made briefly at mid-century on the Columbia River, probably in the Wasco-Wishxam area (fig. III-39). Each bag had four pairs of woven tabs, and both pouch and tabs were patterned with the animal and bird motifs found also on panel bags from the area. Tabbed bags also incorporated geometric motifs, particularly diamonds and triangles. A few more conventional four-tabbed octopus bags are also known from this area, usually made of red wool and embroidered with schematic, outlined semifoliate motifs. Near the end of the nineteenth century, farther north on the Plateau in British Columbia, the Salish-speaking neighbors of Cree bands who had moved into the area began making heavily beaded octopus bags. These were similar to central Subarctic ones in being floral and sewn with the couching stitch, but had more flamboyant individuated designs.

By the late 1870s, the octopus bag had made its way to the Tlingit of the Northwest Coast, and by the 1890s had become a favored form there (fig. III-40). Most Tlingit octopus bags in collections are beaded on only one side, with characteristic split-color, foliate-scroll motifs.

The Subarctic Athapaskans also came to prefer certain forms for firebags during the nineteenth century. In some communities, such as Fort Chipewyan, Crees and Athapaskans lived together, and Cree-speaking wives of Hudson's Bay personnel were in most of the Great Slave Lake and Mackenzie River posts in the nineteenth century. Yet neither of the two common Cree bag forms, the panel bag and the octopus bag, were ever popular among the Athapaskans. However, at least one (fig. III-41) was collected from the lower Mackenzie River area.

Brasser (1975, 1976, 1988) has pointed out the métis preference for the octopus bag, suggesting it to be a métis invention, but it is clear that links with bags as early as the sixteenth century identify a more complex history and development. Such early prototypes have not yet been identified for the panel bag, but there were no doubt versions predating the eighteenth century examples known. KCD

1 Some twentieth-century woven belts such as those in the large Slavey collection at the GAI have designs that alternate blocks of motifs, but they are typically Athabaskan motifs like the adjacent diamonds.

2 This ABAB alternation of motifs also appears on the painted bands on late eighteenth- and early nineteenth-century European-style coats, usually called Upper Missouri River, on which this style of woven quillwork often appears.

3 The literature on visual perception is scattered, made up of older texts by psychologists of the Gestalt school (Koffka 1935, Ellis 1939, Kohler 1947), more recent surveys with a surprising range in focus and projected audience (Bloomer 1967, Cornsweet 1970, Kaufman 1974), and a variety of articles, primarily in psychology journals, usually reporting on experiments with humans or animals. Zusne (1970) comprehensively surveys the studies on visual perception of form dating through the 1960s. Gibson and Hochberg are prominent names. Gombrich (1961, 1979) and particularly Arnheim (1954, 1969, 1974, 1981) are the art historians who have been most interested in visual perception.

4 Unless otherwise noted, all examples are from the Haffenreffer Museum of Anthropology, Brown University.

5 Existing documentation on museum specimens indicates that during the nineteenth century the panel bag and the octopus bag were used primarily and dispersed together across the continent by Cree speakers. Therefore, they will be called Cree/Cree-Métis here. However, further research may clarify a greater Ojibwa role, particularly earlier than the nineteenth century in regard to the panel bag. Jasper Grant was stationed in Ojibwa country when he collected several panel bags between 1800–1809 (Phillips 1984). During some periods in the nineteenth century at Red River and in the southern Lake Winnipeg area and possibly elsewhere, Ojibwa often called themselves Cree.

6 One of the earliest dated floral beadwork styles, found also on James Bay Cree hoods (cat. 46), appears on both panel and octopus bags from the mid-nineteenth century, demonstrating the close relationship of the two bag types at that point in time. Compare octopus bags fig. III-36 and fig. III-8 and several similar ones with panel bag APM H67.269.5 and related examples. The beaded designs of the later panel and octopus bags of the Tlingit are stylized versions of this earlier style, demonstrating the simplifications and regularizations predicted by visual perception studies (see Chapter III Visual Perception).

7 See Glenbow 1988 and Feest 1987 for other painted panel bags from this period.

FIGURE CAPTIONS

Fig. III-23. Panel bag, painted hide and wrapped quills, Great Lakes, United States or Canada, 1760 or earlier, MH 78.32.136.

Fig. III-24. Panel bag, thread-embroidered fabric and woven beads, Cree or Cree-Métis, collected 1800–09, NMI 1902.323.

Fig. III-25. Panel bag, thread-embroidered hide, Cree or Cree-Métis, collected 1850s, RSM L.304.129.

Fig. III-26. Panel bag, beaded fabric and woven beads, Cree or Cree-Métis, mid-nineteenth century, cat. 48.

Fig. III-27. Panel bag, beaded fabric and woven beads, northern Lake Winnipeg Cree or Cree-Métis, ca. 1900, cat. 50.

Fig. III-28. Pipe bag with panel, beaded hide and wrapped quills, Plains, Teton Dakota type, early twentieth century, HMA 57–502.

Fig. III-29. Panel bag, beaded fabric and woven beads, Plateau, Wasco-Wishxam type, collected 1849–50 in Oregon or Washington by Dr. William F. Edgar, LACM A5627-69.

Fig. III-30. Panel bag, beaded fabric and woven beads, Tlingit, Klawak, Alaska, last quarter nineteenth century, BrM 1-1480.

Fig. III-31. Bandolier bag, beaded fabric and woven beads, Great Lakes, last quarter nineteenth century, HMA 57–495.

Fig. III-32. Bag, hide with woven quill panels, Ojibwa, ca. 1900, UMP 45.15.812.

Fig. III-33. a & b. Two tabbed bags, hide, Carolina, sixteenth century, adapted from DeBry's 1590 engravings of John White's drawings (Harriot 1972, p. 64, 61).

Fig. III-34. Medicine pouch, quill embroidered hide, Great Lakes (Ottawa-Eastern Ojibwa?), collected 1800–1809, NMI 1902.325.

Fig. III-35. Octopus bag, painted hide, Great Lakes, United States or Canada, 1760 or earlier, MH 78.32.126.

Fig. III-36. Octopus bag, beaded fabric, James Bay Cree type, ca. 1850, SD 28370.

Fig. III-37. Octopus bag, beaded fabric, Cree or Cree-Métis, fourth quarter nineteenth century, cat. 54.

Fig. III-38. Plains pipe bag with tabs, beaded hide, Cheyenne, Oglala and Assiniboine type, ca. 1900, HMA 57–493.

Fig. III-39. Octopus bag, woven beads, Plateau, Wasco-Wishxam type, owned by Tam-a-has, the Indian who killed Marcus Whitman in the massacre of 1847, OHS 2007.

Fig. III-40. Octopus bag, beaded fabric, Tlingit, Klukwan, Alaska, ca. 1900, MAI 5-410.

Fig. III-41. Octopus bag, beaded fabric, lower Mackenzie, collected 1894 by Emma Shaw Colcleugh, cat. 71.

Fig. IV-1. The route between Norway House and York Factory, Manitoba, a river journey of several weeks involving about a dozen canoes, was travelled again in 1985. Journalists and dignitaries accompanied native and métis people on the journey, dressed in sturdy clothing made of home-tanned hides and trade materials typical of that worn by past voyageurs and traders. Myrtle Muskego, (standing, third from left) was one of several Cree and Cree-Métis women from Norway House who made clothing for use on the journey. All looked forward to several weeks of wilderness canoeing and camping, living in the bush as their predecessors had done (Hail-Duncan photo 1985).

Fig. IV-2. York boat races between crews of Cree residents of the Norway House area are an annual event on northern Lake Winnipeg, recalling the past importance of this wooden craft in the old water transportation routes from Hudson Bay inland and back, through which food supplies and trade goods were carried in, and fur pelts out. In the nineteenth century these boats were manned by native and métis employees of the Hudson's Bay Company (Hail-Duncan photo 1985).

# IV Subarctic Arts Today

## Maintaining Traditions

The nineteenth-century collections of native Subarctic material culture made by Emma Shaw Colcleugh and others are linked to the arts of the present, as many native and métis women actively continue to produce traditional arts while also exploring new techniques and media. In many central Subarctic communities, particularly the more northern ones of the Great Slave Lake–Mackenzie River region, there are those well known for their abilities in bead or floss embroidery, babiche looping, caribou and moose-hair twisting and tufting, or porcupine quillwork. Some men are also still active in the production of traditional tools and hunting equipment, although these objects, because they no longer figure in daily life, are usually made only when commissioned by an individual or a museum, or funded through a heritage-preservation project.

The importance of traditional native heritage is emphasized in many activities that enjoy wide support from the Canadian government and from the non-native community. This resurgence of interest in native identity should be viewed in the political context of the 1970s, when attention was focussed on the native population through issues created by mineral resource activities, native land claims and settlements, and new governmental educational policies for native students. Added to this, a new sense of Pan-Indianism—recognition of a set of common problems and a common cultural world-view—created greater unity of purpose and sharing of ideas among native people of both Canada and the United States.

As a part of this cultural revitalization came the desire to establish a strong native identity with clear distinctions between Indians and non-Indians, through an emphasis on native history and native material culture. Among the events centering on native history have been well-publicized re-enactments of old trading company canoe journeys. Such communal projects become focal points of group solidarity and reinforce cultural and ethnic identity (fig. IV-1).

Other events that develop pride and awareness of heritage, such as the annual York boat races at Norway House on Lake Winnipeg (fig. IV-2), traditional competitions in weight packing and jig dancing, community feasts and arts and crafts exhibitions, are encouraged on a regular basis by the Canadian government. In the 1980s a major government-sponsored project, "Operation Heritage," provided materials and wages to members of the Dogrib band at Rae, Northwest Territories, to re-create traditional moose-hide clothing, caribou-hide tents, snowshoes with babiche netting, and sinew and rawhide utilitarian objects. The nearby Mountain Indians built and navigated down river a large old-style moose skin boat. The boat and many other objects were later installed as permanent exhibits in the Prince of Wales Northern Heritage Centre at Yellowknife, serving to remind the large native population that frequents the museum of their recent past and their legitimate place in the nation's history.

Revitalization has created a renaissance both in aboriginal arts, such as porcupine-quill weaving, and in post-contact arts, such as bead embroidery, and these arts have become a means of stating the existence of a separate culture. But as Nicks (1982:51) has pointed out, it was its use as a distinguisher—not the particular form of the material culture—that was important to revitalization. For some of the younger native people especially, their separate cultural identity could as well be expressed in "message" T-shirts and lapel buttons as in moose-hair tufting. For the older craftspeople, however, the renewed emphasis on and interest in skills they had learned when young has brought pleasure in itself. In almost every home, a middle-aged or elderly woman can retrieve from some private corner a bundle of embroidery materials—perhaps old silk thread saved from before World War II, tiny seed beads in colors no longer made, or even faceted, polished-iron beads, dyed horsehair, bits of home-tanned hide, and paper patterns. Handling them brings back pleasant memories of earlier times, of working with mothers and other female relatives on delicate embroidery. Pride in the skills of the past is apparent; as Maria Houle, a bead embroiderer from Fort Chipewyan said, looking with admiration at an old, intricately beaded garter: "They made *everything* long ago, the old people, everything!"[1] Many women feel that it is important to pass on these skills, part of the native heritage, to children and grandchildren. Even younger women, now able to pursue careers outside the home, often retain traditional artistic skills and want to use them to create something for their children (fig. IV-3).

Community recognition of the work of particularly skilled women encourages novices to learn. Another incentive is greater economic independence for a woman—for there are people "from outside" who will pay well for fine quality bead and floss embroidery, quill weaving and moose-hair tufting.

Fig. IV-3. Margaret Leishman, Kakisa Lake, Northwest Territories. Traditional values are strong, even among educated young Athapaskans who work in non-traditional areas. Margaret works as interpreter for the territorial government at Yellowknife among Slavey and Chipewyan people. She is making mukluks for each of her four sons to remind them of their native heritage. "I started beading these mukluks when they were babies, and they may be grown-up before I finish, but I intend to keep working on them because I want my boys to have something that I made for them" (Leishman, pers. comm. 1985).

Still, most older women, many of whom attended mission schools where they received regular instruction in embroidery, recognize that young girls today are not as interested in learning fancy handwork, perhaps because of a wider variety of activities and opportunities open to them. As Kathleen de la Ronde, a Métis of Cree and Scots ancestry from The Pas, Manitoba, said of the art of birch-bark biting: "We children all used to do biting; we bit the designs on leaves. . . . because we had nothing else to do" (pers. comm. 1985). Also, in the last generation, children learned bead and floss embroidery as an economic necessity in order to help their mothers complete objects made for sale. Kathleen remembers making wool pompons for mukluks from two pieces of paper, "wrapping the yarn around them like a doughnut." Her brothers were also expected to help, in order to get the pieces finished in time. Especially during the 1930s and '40s financial imperatives forced young people to practice the traditional arts.

Older women realize that many of the elaborately embroidered objects of the past are no longer being made. In 1985, when asked whether anyone was still making beaded panel bags (such as cat. 50), Maria Houle said: "No. Nobody. Long ago they make this kind. They die, everybody, you know. We can't keep alive!" (pers. comm. 1985).

Yet in the North many are searching for a way to keep traditional culture alive. Recently the Department of Culture and Communications and the Department of Education of the Northwest Territories sponsored an oral history project among the older residents of Fort Providence through which they recalled the days of their childhood and youth. In the resulting book, *Our Elders* (Slavey Research Project, 1987), the words of these Dene people evidence deep regret that with changing times and the loss of a common language their arts and their knowledge of survival in the North seem no longer valued by their grandchildren.

*Traditional Objects and Techniques*

Subarctic arts that have survived from pre-contact times include the tanning of animal hides for clothing and other uses, twining of bird quills, moose and caribou-hair twisting, porcupine-quill weaving and embroidery, the production of bitten patterns on birch bark and of folded birch-bark containers, and looping in babiche and hareskin. Techniques surviving from historic times to the present are bead and silk embroidery. In the 1920s and recently, hair tufting has been popular.

Because they are still functional, certain objects—hide jackets, hide footwear, mittens, gauntlets, snowshoes, drums, and in some areas, moss bags and cradles (fig. IV-4 a & b),—have continued to be made over the past hundred years for use within the community and sale outside it. Other objects continue to be made but usually as revivals for

(a)

Fig. IV-4 (a) Mothers proudly present their babies laced in board cradles. Maria Portage, Manitoba, 1926. Rev. R. T. Chapin collection, Western Canada Pictorial Index; (b) St. Theresa Point, Island Lake, Manitoba, 1985 (courtesy Alex Bignell, Cree, The Pas, Manitoba). In the more recent photo, the cradles are highly decorated with beads, a revival of late-nineteenth-century styles.

(b)

outside buyers. These include looped babiche game bags, bark containers, and decorated dog blankets. Many objects that played an important functional and aesthetic role in earlier years, such as women's long ribbon-appliquéd or bead-embroidered cloth hoods (cat. 46), popular among the Cree and Cree-Métis during the first half of the nineteenth century, are made no more.

At the turn of the century, medicine bags and other decorated bags used for tobacco, strike-a-light equipment and cartridges were designed primarily for native use, but occasionally were sold to outsiders, as were carved stone pipes. In areas where there was a market, silk-thread-embroidered picture frames, lamp pads and wall pockets were intended primarily for sale, but occasionally were also enjoyed within the community. These arts are no longer practiced.

Both today and in the past, community aspirations, new ideas and new materials affect form and function. For instance, the use of decorative wall ornaments was a sign of upward mobility in Colcleugh's time ninety years ago. In the 1890s a silk-embroidered caribou-hide wall pocket or picture frame might be proudly displayed in the home of its maker. In the 1980s a tufted moose-hair picture or picture frame is equally admired.

Some art forms popular now did not exist in Colcleugh's time, including moose-hair tufted pictures, round-toed moccasins, fish-scale pictures, and probably decorated mukluks. Western-style clothing made from traditional materials of smoked moose hide and bleached caribou hide, with floral embroidery in floss or beads, was popular then and now, with changes in form responding to current high fashion.

*Teaching and Learning*

Before the days of formal school instruction, young girls learned skills of all kinds by watching and imitating their mothers and female relatives, boys by observing their fathers and male relatives. Even after mission schools were established in the North in the second half of the nineteenth century, much learning took place informally within the extended family. In the minds of older craftswomen, this informal learning was the most important. Maria Houle learned to sew "from my mum and auntie, since I was 12 years old; I'm 60 years old now, and still sewing." Where did your mother learn? "I don't know; her mum, I guess." Was she passing it on to her children? "Yes. . . . to my grandchild, who is 14 years old, I teach her beadwork; and to another, 16 years old; and to my sister's daughter that is married." Her grandchildren and others come to her home, "sometimes two hours. . . . twice a week." She draws beadwork patterns for them, teaches them how to start, and to finish.

Fig. IV-5. Teacher Margaret Van Dell, Slavey, holds sampler of embroidery stitches made by a student in her 1985 home economics class at the Fort Providence school. The class provided formal instruction in basic sewing, including thread-embroidery stitches, making hide clothing, and bead embroidery. Each girl made a sampler notebook of floss stitches. Learning projects progressed from the basic "Traditional Needle Kit" and "Making a Bead Loom" to the more difficult pattern-cutting and stitching of an Alaskan Dene parka (Hail-Duncan photo 1985).

About some other young teenage girls in the community who did not bead, she lamented: "They can't put thread to needle and catch it, most girls now, nothing." Why not? "Their mum never taught them things like that, you know" (Houle, pers. comm. 1985).

For more structured learning, in the past decade provincial governments have established classes, sometimes within local "friendship centers," that provide instruction and sponsor exhibitions with competitions that are judged and awarded prizes. In Manitoba there are seventy friendship centers, whose aims are to foster fellowship and promote progress in the educational, social, economic, athletic and cultural life of both native and non-native Canadians. Programs offered include home economics classes and beadwork instruction; the centers include display and sales areas for handcrafts. Manitoba also sponsors a program entitled Native Effort for Talent, which supports native youth in art, dance, writing, sports and other areas of self-expression. In Alberta, in recent years, an annual fair has been held in Edmonton each November, sponsored by the provincial government through the Native Arts and Crafts Division of the Alberta Vocational Center. Entries are sought throughout the North. Sometimes seed money has been given to selected craftspeople in different communities to provide them with supplies and to encourage them to enter their work in the fair. Exhibiting artisans have been flown in to Edmonton from their northern communities. Creativity in arts production has been fostered by such competitions.

In some communities a regular curriculum in the traditional arts has been developed within the provincial and territorial school systems. For instance, in Fort Providence, Northwest Territories, children learn sewing skills from second grade through high school. In 1985 the class members exhibited their work at the end of the school year, and the pieces were raffled to help raise funds for more materials (fig. IV-5).

Such formal instruction follows a tradition established in the nineteenth century in mission schools from Red River to the mouth of the Mackenzie River, where embroidery skills were taught as a part of the school curriculum. In this century at Fort Providence, two Sisters of the Order of Grey Nuns have given special impetus to the work. In the 1930s and 1940s, Sister Beatrice Leduc organized silk-thread embroidery classes. Usually she drew the patterns and the students, both native Slavey and Slavey-Métis, executed the work.[2] Fancy work was introduced to fill the extra hours profitably, but the nuns did not consider it as important as the academic curriculum. Many of the finest pieces were sent out of the North as gifts to church dignitaries or other visitors.

In the 1950s and 1960s Sister Ann Cooper, herself of mixed native-white ancestry, encouraged bead, quill and silk-floss embroidery at Fort Providence. She organized a craft shop as part of the mission nursing station where women's pieces could be sold to visitors from the outside. When she left the community in the early 1970s, the inventory of the mission shop was transferred to the Slavey people and provided the base for their cooperative, the Red Willows Craft Shop, which operates successfully today.

*Marketing*    Revitalization and commercialism have been mutually reinforcing, as heightened awareness of Indian identity has enhanced the market potential for crafts in both native and non-native communities (see Nicks 1982). Various agencies have been established at the provincial and federal levels to aid native art production and distribution. Among the most influential of these are the Canadian Handicrafts Guild, established in 1935, and the National Indian Arts and Crafts Cooperative, established in 1975.

One artist in bead and thread embroidery from a northern community seemed puzzled in 1985 by the number of people from "out" who found their way to her door. "All the time they come; all over, from Calgary, Yellowknife, all over: there are enough women sewing here, you know; I don't know why they come to me; everybody comes; somebody sends them in here to me." Actually, the Alberta Indian Arts and Crafts Society had been publicizing this artist's work in Edmonton, as a part of a program to support native handiwork. They had printed flyers with her picture and a brief biography, along with order forms with prices for various types of bead and yarn embroidery.

Commonly, a more informal marketing strategy is used. Potential buyers hear of skilled artists and seek them out. One member of an extended family may serve as a collection agent for the products of many, and sell directly from her home (fig. IV-6). Only when pressed does she provide the identity of the maker, as this is not considered particularly important.[3]

In Cross Lake, Manitoba, the Cree/Cree-Métis community markets much of its handwork through a small shop operated from the home of Frances M. Ross. She assures an inventory by drawing patterns for moccasin vamp designs and jobbing them out to specialists in beadwork (fig. IV-7). Others complete the moccasins, some cutting the skins and some sewing them together. Her energetic marketing methods cause many people to bring their finished products to her shop for sale.

Often non-natives, such as bush-plane pilots who bring visitors to remote fishing camps, motel owners or restaurant managers, serve as

Fig. IV-6. Families and extended families often market each other's crafts; Georgine Albert, Jack River, Norway House, creates and sells her own work and that of her family from her home (see cats. 142, 143; Hail-Duncan photo 1985).

intermediaries in marketing. There are a few seriously interested intermediaries such as Memoree Philipp of Fort Providence, who began buying local porcupine-quill weavings some twenty years ago, both for her private collection and to sell at her inn's shop. Her interest has insured a steady market that has encouraged Slavey women to practice this old and difficult art. Philipp also takes commissions from museums wishing to acquire examples of contemporary yet traditional Slavey art. This encourages the women to attempt more time-consuming—and therefore more costly—projects than those earmarked for casual tourist sales (see cats. 117,118), and also to re-create other articles, such as the hareskin jacket (cat. 169) no longer used. Through such projects, the knowledge of almost-lost art forms has been kept alive, providing a limited source of income for some of the elders of Fort Providence. Perhaps as important, practicing the old skills is a source of pleasure and pride for the craftswomen.

Non-native shops, some in business for almost half a century, provide another important market for native arts as well as employment through jobbing out piecework to native people. Some stores send out moccasin vamps to be bead-embroidered by women skilled in this art; other women cut the hides to form moccasins, mukluks, mitts and jackets, and still others sew them together (see cats. 148,149).

Because the northern communities are isolated, the Hudson's Bay Company and other traders have determined to a large degree what materials are available. Hudson's Bay Company stores have provided a regular marketing outlet for native products for many years, but this

Fig. IV-7. Moccasin vamp patterns (HMA 85–673), beaded with thread through lined notebook-paper and two pieces of hide, separated by a wrapping-paper stiffener. Beaded by Adelaide Blacksmith over a pattern drawn by Frances M. Ross. Swampy Cree, Cree-Métis, Cross Lake, Manitoba.

Fig. IV-8. (a) beading needles and (b) beads currently available in northern trading company stores.

(a)

(b)

was more important in earlier times than it has been in the last quarter century. Fifty years ago the mothers of some of the current artists interviewed could state what sizes and colors of beads they wished to use, and the company would order them (figs. IV-8a & b). Some objects, when completed, were sold either in the local post store or in one of the larger outlets. None of the consultants recalled that the Hudson's Bay Company commissioned goods, rather, they said, it bought whatever finished pieces the women chose to bring in. World politics also affected availability of materials. For instance, silk floss for embroidery was available and popular from the second half of the nineteenth century until World War II, and excellent examples of floss embroidery exist from that period (see cats. 19, 20, 24). When current examples were sought, women complained that they no longer could get the fine-strand silk thread necessary for small-flower designs; it had been replaced on

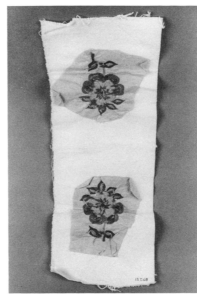

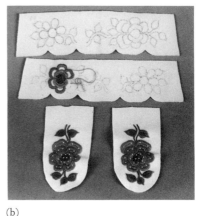

Fig. IV-9. Some women have achieved excellent results with the thicker floss; see (a) HMA 87–231, tuppies (front and reverse), and (b) HMA 87–232, parts for moccasins, made by Dora Migui, Dogrib, Fort Rae.

(a-front)          (a-reverse)          (b)

the shelves by rayon, cotton and wool or synthetic-blend yarns fig. IV-9(a-1, 2; b). Because silk is now once more available from the Chinese market, a few women have begun using "real" or "thin" silk floss again (see cat. 140).

Marketing of native arts is also carried out through advertising, by privately owned shops, native cooperatives, and by the Canadian government as they promote tourism in such magazines as *Up Here* and *The Beaver*, and in travel literature. In the major cities of Winnipeg, Edmonton, Calgary, Saskatoon and Yellowknife, government-sponsored arts and crafts associations provide project-consultation service, serve as raw materials depots, and aid native craftspeople in developing marketing and retailing techniques. Occasionally native arts are enhanced through the television media: from Churchill a channel that reaches most communities in Manitoba features in-depth stories on native artists. Recent major Canadian museum exhibitions in conjunction with world expositions and with the Olympics have substantially increased appreciation of Subarctic native arts and culture among an international audience.

The successful continuance of native Subarctic traditional arts rests ultimately on the meaning of these arts to the people. To many residents of growing northern communities there is a nostalgia for the old days of simpler living. Many older people withdraw to their "fish camps" in the bush during the summers, in order to practise time-honored skills of fishing, drying fish on racks, smoke-tanning hides, berry-picking, and executing porcupine-quill weavings (figs. IV-10, 11). Fearful that their

(a)

(b)

Fig. IV-10. (a) Ben and Mary Marcel, their daughter Alice Marten, and Alice's children, at Jackfish camp, Chipewyan Reserve, Alberta.
(b) Like many older Athapaskans, the Marcels love to spend time in their summer fish camp, away from the community of Fort Chipewyan where they live in the winter. They practise the time-honored skills of smoke-tanning hides, fishing, and sun-drying fish on racks. Their lives are quiet and family centered. The boys attend an outdoor skills camp run by the Fort Chipewyan band council where they are taught the ancient skills of wood and animal lore (Hail-Duncan photos 1985).

Fig. IV-11. Victoria Mercredi, Chipewyan, cleaning fish in preparation for sun-drying them on racks; Jackfish River camp, Chipewyan Reserve, Alberta (Hail-Duncan photo 1985).

Fig. IV-12. A member of the Fort Chipewyan band council holds sphagnum moss, gathered from deep within a moss clump and used traditionally as a kind of diaper lining in moss-bags. He is serving as instructor for teen-age Chipewyan boys in traditional wood lore and survival skills at the Old Fort Chip outdoor camp (Hail-Duncan photo 1985).

young people are growing up without knowledge of traditional native skills of survival, in Fort Chipewyan the band council runs an outward-bound type of camp for teen-age boys on the rocky shores of Old Fort Chip, the previous site of the settlement. Accessible only by boat, the isolated camp provides a chance for instruction in wood lore, tracking, and methods of living off the land (fig. IV-12). As long as this interest in the old ways continues, and with it pride in the skills that were developed for coping with and beautifying life, and as long as there is a desire to pass this knowledge and accompanying world view on to the next generation, the traditional arts will survive in the North.    BAH

## Native Craft Production in Brochet, Manitoba 1978–1980

Craft production in the North can best be understood as a series of networks—resource, production and market—that contain important social components with strong economic overtones. In Brochet, Manitoba, a community of 650 people of mixed Cree, Chipewyan and Métis ancestry, craft production expresses ethnic and artistic identity, and functions as a cottage industry.

Brochet lies 850 kilometers (530 miles) northwest of Winnipeg, Manitoba, on the northeast shore of Reindeer Lake,[4] accessible only by air or boat. The nearest settlement with a road, Lynn Lake, lies 120 km (74 miles) to the south. In 1978 there was no television or telephone service in Brochet, although a single radio phone was available. Commercial radio reception was remarkably poor, and mail came twice a week. Thus Brochet was more isolated than settlements much farther north that enjoyed those amenities. The economy of the community included trapping, commercial fishing and intermittent wage labor (fig. IV-13).[5]

### Resource Networking

The few raw materials required to produce Brochet's craft items—native and commercially tanned leather, cloth, beads, needle and thread, and fur—were often difficult to procure, particularly leather. Native-tanned leather was considered to be vastly superior to commercially tanned leather, which lacks the water repellency of native-tanned products and is more difficult to use for beadwork. The commercial leather available in the community, usually split moose hide or deer hide, was purchased in Winnipeg (in person or by mail-order) or provided by the consignor of a special order. The most commonly used mail-order source for leather was the Winnipeg Raw Fur Exchange. Colored suede was available in wine, blue and green as well, but non-native purchasers did not care for this medium and discouraged its use.

Several factors combined to make smoked leather increasingly difficult to obtain in recent years. Moose hides provided the majority of smoked leather for utilitarian items, but increased hunting near the settlement had depleted the local moose population, forcing hunters to go farther afield. A fresh moose hide adds considerable weight to a sled heavily laden with fresh meat, so it is often abandoned in the bush. In

Fig. IV-13. Mr. Cook and son preparing to go on the trap line, Winter
1980 (Michelle Tracy photo).

addition, tanning moose hide, a labor-intensive process, is no longer
practiced by many younger women. To keep pace with the demand for
crafts, some women imported hides from other communities where
home tanning was more prevalent, paying between $135 and $150 for
a tanned moose hide (fig. IV-14).

Caribou hide was reserved for fancier items made for sale to non-
natives, such as women's mittens and slippers and, when plentiful,
mukluks and jacket yokes. The presence of a caribou herd is more
unpredictable than that of moose, a solitary animal; in some years, there
were virtually no caribou near the settlement, while in other years the
herd was very close. In previous years the Kaminuriak Herd, which
ranges into the Keewatin District, was the primary source of caribou
for Brochet. Recently, however, the Beverly Herd has migrated closer.
Like moose hides, caribou hides were frequently left in the bush due to
their weight, particularly when the herds were so distant that planes had
to be chartered to reach them. Most caribou hides purchased in Brochet

Fig. IV-14. Scraping a moose hide. Mrs. Angelique Merasty, Cree, and Michelle Tracy, Spring 1980 (William Tracy photo).

were from settlements farther north and closer to the caribou range; in 1980 a smoked caribou hide cost between $30 and $35. Since caribou are particularly susceptible to warble flies, whose bite leaves scars in the hide that open into holes during the tanning process, it is quite unusual to find hides free of such holes. Smaller items, such as moccasin vamps and cuffs, are often made from such hides that are unusable for larger garments. Caribou hides may be used either smoked or unsmoked, but the milky-white unsmoked hides are highly desirable. Hides are sometimes smoked to cover an uneven coloration of the white hide, which may result from uneven scraping.

Cloth was occasionally used as a backing for beadwork. Black duffel, velvet, and heavy woolen stroud were reintroduced as beading backgrounds in the late 1970s, and were readily accepted, perhaps because they were easier to bead on than hide. However, the craftswomen had no ready source for these materials, which usually had to be provided by the consignor. The lining of items such as jackets, vests and moccasins, varied from high-quality rayons and satins, sometimes provided by the consignor, to simple lightweight cottons purchased at the Hudson's Bay Company store or salvaged from other garments.

Fur was readily available in Brochet. Furs that could not fetch premium prices on the raw fur market were used for trimming parka hoods, mukluks and gauntlets. Pelts were acquired from one's own family through purchase, or as gifts from non-relatives. The availability of any given type of fur was unpredictable, and only rarely did a consignor provide a special pelt for the trimming of an order.

Although beading needles, thread and beads were available at the Hudson's Bay Company store, the selection was very limited. Serious beadmakers tended to purchase those items outside the community in Lynn Lake, Thompson, The Pas and Winnipeg. It was also possible to purchase supplies by mail. Sometimes craft work could not be done because there were no beading needles in the store. Most beadworkers felt that obtaining materials was a major problem and wished they were more available in Brochet.

*Production and Design*

The techniques for beading were relatively simple. Belts, headbands and sometimes wristbands were loom-woven. Looms were simply constructed from a bowed tree-branch. Nearly all other beaded items were made by sewing beads directly onto leather with a couched stitch. Plastic kitchen wrap was placed over the leather by some women and beaded through, in order to keep the leather clean while it was being worked, particularly important when the background was white caribou hide. The protective covering was left on the item by the beadworker and removed by the purchaser. Chalk was sometimes applied to the hide to enhance its whiteness just before an article was sold.

A common method of transferring a pattern onto leather was to draw half the design on a piece of tissue paper, then fold the paper with the design to the inside and rub with a spoon. Unfolded, the paper pattern would be perfectly symmetrical. The tissue could then be stitched loosely onto the leather, and beads could be applied with the tissue sandwiched in between. After the piece was finished any tissue showing was carefully pulled away. When white caribou hide was used, the design was drawn on a piece of paper with a pencil, and the paper was laid face down on the hide and rubbed vigorously with the back of a spoon to transfer it onto the hide. Some of the older women drew the design directly onto the leather with a ball-point pen or felt marker. (Occasionally red ink rather than blue was used because it was less visible on the hide.) Designs could be repeated by folding the leather so that the inked pattern could be rubbed onto the next desired location.

(a)

(b)

(c)

Fig. IV-15. Beading patterns for moccasin vamps (a–d) and mukluk (e). Continued next page.

A thin cardboard layer (often from a cereal box) was normally used to back a piece in order to maintain a desired level of stiffness. A piece of white cloth might serve as a final layer of backing.

The production of craft items was an intensely personal experience and a manifestation of the craftworker's ethnicity. Although craftswomen operated within definable boundaries, sufficient latitude for self-expression existed.

The majority of beadwork appeared to be based on designs created by the beadworker. Responses to one questionnaire indicated that seventy-five percent of the respondents had patterns they followed. Some designs appeared to be "owned" by some of the older women. The women kept their patterns on pieces of paper and stored them together with their beading supplies; an older woman might have more than a hundred patterns and combinations. It was considered improper for one woman to use a design belonging to another; permission had to be obtained before the design could be used or, at the very least, it was expected that verbal acknowledgement be made to the "owner." This is not to suggest that the designs were in any way totemic or family property (fig. IV-15a–e).

Inspiration for designs came from any number of sources. One particularly adept beadworker modified a floral element from a pillowcase purchased at the Hudson's Bay store. Another beadworker copied the decal of the head of a Plains Indian chief found on the prow of an aluminum canoe sold by the Bay.

Books were a major source of inspiration.[6] Perhaps the most commonly available craft book in the North is *American Indian Beadwork* by Hunt and Burshears. The patterns for loom-woven pieces in it are charted so a weaver can actually count the beads and create exact copies of the designs. Designs from several traditions are often combined. Inspired by the book, one Chipewyan woman made a belt that contained geometric Sioux and floral Ute elements.

Floral designs were by far the most common, although a few women used anthropomorphic and zoomorphic designs on specially ordered pieces. The latter were usually regarded as male designs and were used on male items, such as knife sheaths, rifle cases, and men's mukluk and gauntlet sets. The sheaths and cases occasionally contained references to sky, land and water such as birds, caribou and fish. The woman who most frequently used these designs did not draw them herself—her husband did. Some older craftswomen felt certain patterns were appropriate for male garments, others for female garments. Men's designs were likely to be larger and of stronger color than women's. In some cases a beadworker would use flowers with rounded elements on

(d)　　　　　　　　　　　　　　　　　　　　　　　　　　　　　　　　　(e)

women's clothing, and angular or pointed flowers on men's clothing. Specialization existed to a limited degree among the beadworkers. One woman might primarily make mukluks, mittens, gauntlets and moccasins, while another would concentrate on beaded crests (coasters).

Twenty-five craftswomen, when surveyed by the author, identified the following items as most commonly made: mukluks (48%); gauntlets (28%); belts (20%); slippers (16%); jackets (16%); necklaces (8%); moccasins (8%); vests (4%); crests (4%); watchbands (4%); earrings (4%); and wallets (4%). The results of this sample perhaps say more about the perception of the craftswomen than actual production. Small items such as watchbands, earrings and wristbands were in fact fairly common but rarely identified as items frequently made. Conversely, although mukluks and gauntlets were said to be frequently produced, they were not particularly common. What this survey seems to record is the women's perceptions of items they felt were important. When one beadworker began making beaded drop earrings and selling them for $3 to $4, younger women realized that these small items could be produced quickly and inexpensively and began making them. They were able to make more money in a shorter period of time on these items than on larger pieces, because earrings were popular with the non-native community. However, not all small items realized this same profit ratio. One of the older women made miniature beaded gauntlets and mukluks for pulls on parka zippers, but said she could not price them according to the actual amount of time invested.

*Marketing Networks*

The principal market for crafts production in Brochet was the local non-native community, consisting of school teachers, the nursing staff, and the staff of the Hudson's Bay Company trading post. The clergy in the community, by virtue of their long tenure there, tended not to purchase craft items. Department of Public Works employees, the agent for the local airline, and a free trader offered other outlets. During the 1960s and 1970s, the local free trader (not associated with the Hudson's Bay Company) was the principal buyer, and offered cash or groceries for crafts.

The real viability of the market lay not so much with a given category of non-natives, but with individuals. Each individual entering the community automatically became a potential customer. However, each buyer had to be approached and explored separately to determine if the potential source was indeed a reality.

The local native community also offered a market, although largely not a cash market. Items of clothing were made for extended family members, either for practical use (mukluks, mitts, moccasins) or for dress wear, primarily for children who were traveling out of the community (vests, headbands, purses). Most utilitarian items were not heavily beaded. A son of one prominent craftswoman persuaded his mother to make him a pair of wrap-around moccasins with fully beaded vamps; when he wore his new moccasins hunting with his father, his feet got so cold that he was forced to exchange moccasins with his father. The beads held the cold against his feet "like a block of ice." On reaching home, he cut off all the beadwork.

Although silk-thread embroidery was nearly a lost craft in Brochet at the time of the survey, older members of the community viewed thread embroidery as a superior decorative technique because it did not hold the cold in, and because of its lighter weight. This concern with weight is understandable for articles such as mukluks and gauntlets, but also extended to other articles. Members of the Royal Canadian Mounted Police in Lynn Lake ordered two beaded plaques from a noted craftswoman, who commented that she had no idea what anyone would do with something like that: "They are so heavy." Heavily decorated items were usually for show rather than utility and were normally worn only on trips outside the community.

Beyond the community the market was confined to special orders from individuals or institutions that offered a stable, if limited, market. The Manitoba Museum of Man, as well as the Canadian Museum of Civilization, has been known to purchase crafts from Brochet. However, outside buyers were difficult for the craftswomen to reach and, in the past, although the prices received might be considerably higher than in town, one often had to wait an extended period of time for payment, creating economic hardship. Craft items are frequently made for the express purpose of meeting a cash shortfall in the household.

Prices for beaded objects in Brochet generally doubled from 1970 to 1980. The higher-priced objects, commanding up to $100 or higher, were: jackets (ranging from $100 to $300, averaging $175 in 1980, up from the 1970 average of $60); mukluks ($30 to $100 with $60 average, from $32 in 1970); and vests ($35 to $100, averaging $62, fifty percent higher than the 1970 average).

The rather wide fluctuation in price relates to the ages of participants in the survey: older women tended to undervalue their work, while the younger women set higher market values. One fifty-three-year-old respondent indicated that a jacket ought to sell for $100 while several craftswomen in their mid-twenties felt $250 was a proper price.

Door-to-door sales rose as Christmas approached and the need for cash increased. Articles previously unsold reappeared at reduced rates. Conversely, special orders were more difficult to acquire in the week before Christmas as the women were busy making items for their own families. However, even those items might be sold if there was no money for groceries. Many of the men were on the trapline just before Christmas, so the family depended on the mother.

In 1979 the Arctic Trading Company, which had enjoyed great financial success by developing a mail-order business for native crafts from its head office in Churchill, Manitoba, purchased the independent trading post in Brochet. The company encouraged the local post manager to recruit women in Brochet to bead moccasin vamps to be shipped to Churchill, where sheepskin-lined bottoms would be attached. The finished moccasins would then be sold through the mail. In Brochet this attempt met with failure. The post manager approached the most prominent craftswoman in town and placed an order for one hundred vamps. The order was not treated seriously by the woman; she felt that, because he placed such a large order, the manager did not understand the work involved. He further belittled her creativity by not ordering a complete item. Finally — the greatest transgression — he intended to make a profit from *her* work. Because of this, very few women participated in the project. It is worth noting that eighty-nine percent of the women surveyed indicated they would make more items for sale if the market were larger, yet clearly the approach taken by the trader so offended them as to override economic considerations.

*Training in Traditional Skills, Perception of Self, and Ethnic Identification*

Beadwork techniques were not necessarily taught by mother to daughter, partly because children are sometimes reluctant to learn traditional skills from their parents. As a case in point, one ninth-grade student completed her first beadwork as part of a work experience program. She had been taught by her mother, but was interested only when encouraged by an outside authority, the school.

Women most frequently began beading in their early to mid-twenties in an effort to earn extra money for their families. They were as likely to learn the skills from older friends or contemporaries as from their mothers. Beading was often a social activity where groups of two or three women, usually of similar age, would congregate in someone's home to bead, chat, drink tea and eat cookies. In Brochet, a Catholic community, there was a general prohibition against beading on Sunday.

Craftswomen were modest in appraisals of their own work, and the finest beadworker in town vehemently denied the accolade, suggesting several others in her place. Yet fierce competition sometimes existed among craftswomen. The response to the 1979 crafts competition was enthusiastic. Many became secretive about what they were making for the contest. One woman confessed that she would hide her work when someone knocked on her door; another who produced a moss bag, unusual for the community at that time, refused to divulge even to the judges what she was making until it was time to turn in her entry. Ironically, craftswomen tended to judge the beaded items carried by the trading post on technical merits rather than on being handcrafted, hence commercially beaded belts were very popular, since they were ranked high on tightness of beading, composition and color selection.

Native crafts, particularly beadwork, did not function as an ethnic identity marker at Brochet because most there were natives, and highly decorated clothing was not regarded as particularly functional in cold climates. Outside the community, however, there was a greater need to reinforce ethnicity, and special items were created for children going on a school trip or adults participating in a winter carnival at Lynn Lake. However, the beadwork appeared to reinforce *individual* identity rather than mark *ethnic* identification.[7]

Within the ethnic groups (Cree, Chipewyan and Métis) in Brochet there seemed to be little to distinguish Métis beadwork from Cree or Chipewyan work. Chipewyan beaders tended to use fewer and larger floral motifs for decoration, while the Cree used more and smaller motifs. One Métis beadworker appeared willing, for occasional special orders, to use anthropomorphic designs as well as floral designs.

There seemed to be a slight tendency for Chipewyan women to use more caribou skin than Cree women, particularly in small items such as knife sheaths, rarely in larger items such as vests. This may correlate with a somewhat heavier Chipewyan reliance on caribou as a subsistence source during the historic period, and a greater familiarity with the resource and applications derived from it. A piece of beadwork introduced into Brochet from outside was usually identified by its point of origin rather than by its maker, for instance, from Lac Brochet rather than Chipewyan.

Craft production in Brochet, as in so many northern communities, is problematic. Scarcity of resources, particularly, is one of myriad problems facing the beadworker. There is little doubt that adaptation to new materials can be accomplished, but of greater concern is the fragility of the market. Since the majority of the work produced in Brochet is for sale, production will rise and fall to match demand. A protracted period of little or no market demand locally may lead to an abandonment of craft production as a means of supplementing the family income. Income from crafts cannot compete with income gained from wage labor. Furthermore, it is questionable whether local consumption is sufficient to ensure continued production. So far, attempts to mechanize the crafts in this community have not met with success. Craft production in small communities such as Brochet is subject to the vagaries of other aspects of the northern economy, which are as intimately interwoven as they have been for centuries.                                                            WAT

NOTES TO SUBARCTIC ARTS TODAY

1 The information in this chapter provides a general impression of the forces affecting continuation of the traditional arts, kinds of objects available, teaching and learning opportunities, competitions and marketing arrangements in the North in the 1980s. It is based on field interviews among native and métis artisans during August 1985 and August 1987, at Winnipeg, Norway House, The Pas, Edmonton, Fort Chipewyan, Hay River, Fort Providence, Yellowknife and Rae. Only a limited number of consultants could be interviewed, but the opinions of those quoted reflect more widely voiced sentiments.

2 Although much of this work, now in the collection of *Les Soeurs Grises, Maison de la Mère Musée*, Montreal, is attributed as "half-breed," both native and métis girls attended the school and were probably working on embroidery. When native families were away in the bush tending their trap lines their children were often taken out of school to go with them, while métis families were more likely to stay in the Fort Providence community. Since their children spent more time in the schools they would likely have produced more of the work (Lemire, pers. comm. 1986). On the other hand, Sister Neumier, a resident Grey Nun in Fort Providence in 1985, noted that native children often boarded at the school while their families were in the bush, and that hand work was taught them as a way of filling evening and weekend hours (Neumier, pers. comm. 1985).

3 Native-owned craft cooperatives, on the other hand, which have had guidance from trained government marketing personnel, usually attach a card to each object, with the name and band affiliation or community of the maker, as well as the materials used. Usually the artist establishes the price, and the cooperative takes a percentage, resulting in a wide variation in price for similar workmanship.

4 William Tracy and his wife, Michelle, lived in the small, isolated native community of Brochet from 1978 to 1980, while he worked on a doctoral dissertation in anthropology and she taught in the public school. During their stay they gathered data on the production and marketing of native crafts through standard ethnographic techniques. The "ethnographic present" is 1978–80.

5 See James G. E. Smith 1978.

6 The Tracys kept a modest library of museum catalogues and monographs illustrating beadwork. The series *Central Cree and Ojibway Crafts*, published by the Department of Indian and Northern Affairs, was quite popular, perhaps because one of the illustrated pieces was from Brochet. It was a common pastime for women to stop by the Tracy house for tea and peruse these books. Occasionally a piece would produce the comment, "My mother used to make something like that" or "I bet I could make that." Often a woman would reappear several weeks later with a similar piece for sale.

7 Since a great many non-native individuals living in the North wore gauntlets, jackets, mukluks and other beadwork as a means of identifying themselves as Northerners, a case could be made for beaded native winter clothing as a Western Canadian symbol second only to Inuit carvings.

EPILOGUE  # Women's Work, Women's Art

In image and text, this volume documents the artistry of the native women of Subarctic America from the mid-nineteenth century to the present. It richly reveals the reworking of European-derived motifs in the evolving native aesthetic traditions. The collection displays as well the variety of trade materials that women incorporated into their decorative art: glass beads, silk floss, horsehair, wool yarn, stroud, velvet, braid and silk ribbon.

Except for a few scraps of evidence that may be recovered by archaeologists, a visible record of Subarctic Indian women's handiwork in prehistoric times is lost to us. But as the historic era dawned successively from east to northwest through the boreal north, accounts of the earliest European observers tell of the embellishment that Indian women, using only indigenous materials, lavished upon clothing, footgear, and accouterments. One hundred and five years before Emma Shaw Colcleugh descended the Mackenzie River on the steamer Wrigley in 1894, the first European ventured on those waters. On his downstream journey by canoe to the Arctic Ocean in 1789, Alexander Mackenzie encountered an encampment of Slavey and Dogrib Indians clad in decorated leggings and fringed garments of "well dressed" caribou and moose skin. Some tunics were "embroider[ed] very neatly with Porcupines Quills & the Hair of the Moos Deer painted [colored] Red, Black, Yellow & White." Belts and garters of porcupine quills woven with sinew were, Mackenzie recorded in his journal, "the neatest thing of the kind that ever I saw" (Lamb 1970: 184).

By the last quarter of the nineteenth century in the Mackenzie region, cloth apparel (cat. 72) was well on its way to replacing the Indians' basic clothing of dressed skins. Whatever this shift to manufactured materials may have lacked in the way of exoticism to the eye of the Euroamerican traveller, it brought a substantial reduction in women's labor on hide preparation. When a family was clad entirely in dressed skins, furred or sueded, the demand on women's time and energy must have been great indeed.

In the Mackenzie region, hides of moose and caribou continued in constant use for mittens and moccasins through the mid-twentieth century. Until government inducements began to pull people into the expanding trading-post settlements in the 1960s, almost all Indian families lived in the land and off of the land—hunting, fishing, and trapping for furs. For "bush" activities through the long winters, nothing could equal native hand- and footgear. It was a woman's responsibility to keep her family shod year-round in moccasins.

One moose hide is barely sufficient to meet the moccasin needs of two adults for a year. About ten pairs of moccasins can be made from one moose hide: a woman needs three or four pairs and her husband at least four pairs per year (Helm and Lurie 1961: 98). Before the introduction of moccasin rubbers to protect the moccasin from destructive dampness in the warmer months, many more pairs per year were needed.

Preparing a hide is an intermittent but extended and sometimes arduous process. This is especially true of moose hide, which, when soaking wet as it frequently must be, is a brutally heavy and cumbersome object. The moose hide must be first defleshed, the bulk of the hair cut off, and soaked; then lashed to a frame and scraped, removing the rest of the hair (fig. IV–14); removed from the frame and soaked in a fatty substance (once brains, more recently commercial soap); thoroughly wrung and repeatedly pulled, usually two women working together, to soften it; then scraped again. The soaking, wringing and scraping sequence is usually repeated three more times. Different tools for fleshing and scraping are used at each stage. Finally, the hide is smoked over a smoldering fire of rotten wood (Helm and Lurie 1961: 99–100). All this is women's work.

A woman's aesthetic standards and pride in her handiwork do not start with the decorative elements with which, past and present, she has embellished items of hide apparel. The hide itself is subject to aesthetic appraisal. To gain approval, the dressed hide must be supple, smoothly and evenly scraped, and smoked an even, rich golden brown. An elegant pair of moccasins must display not only attractive designs and colors executed in fine floss-work or well-stitched beading; the hide must also be handsome.

Aesthetic judgments attach to many aspects of native crafts, as illustrated by an incident in the Dogrib trading settlement of Rae some years ago. The anthropology division of the National Museums of Canada had arranged for the construction of a birch-bark canoe in the aboriginal form that had been supplanted by canvas canoes in the early 1920s. That successful "sale," followed by another the next year, stimulated an elderly widower to repair to an island near Rae, where he spent the summer alone, crafting yet another birch-bark canoe. When it was finished, the canoe was brought to Rae, where it evoked a lively interest among the Dogribs. But the older men and women arrived at a collective judgment: "He should have had a woman do the sewing." Although "seaworthy," the canoe's stitching of spruce root that pieced the sections of birch back together was uneven. Spruce-root stitching, on birch-bark baskets or birch-bark canoes, is woman's work and should be executed handsomely.

To the earlier Euroamerican collectors, only a woman's handiwork, not the woman was of consequence. Those past artisans are nameless and unknown to us. In the native world, however, the creator of every piece of woman's craft was known. For many of the finest creations of a "bush" Indian wife, her husband served as a kind of travelling art gallery. When men went by dog team to the trading fort, particularly at Christmastime and Eastertime, to trade their furs, their wives usually stayed behind. But the embroidered or beaded yoke of her husband's parka and his decorated moccasins, newly-made for him to wear at the fort, advertised a woman's handiwork afar.

From afar in space and time, we admire the skill and artistry of the anonymous women whose accomplishments are revealed in this volume. One would like to think that these women, and those many more whose work has been lost to us, received in their lifetime the appreciation of their handiwork that young Slavey women knew in the early years of the nineteenth century when, we are told, "[the trader] Mr. Wentzel has often known the young married men to bring specimens of their wives' needlework to the [trading] forts and exhibit them with much pride" (Franklin 1824: II:81).

*June Helm*
PROFESSOR OF ANTHROPOLOGY
UNIVERSITY OF IOWA

Color Plates

and

The Catalogue

Woman's Hood, East Cree, James Bay type, second half nineteenth century, cat. 46.

Moccasins, Dogrib, ESC collected Fort McPherson 1894, cat. 41.

Purse, probably Saulteaux, and Wall Pocket, Cree or Cree-Métis, ESC collected Lake Winnipeg, Manitoba 1888–1894, cats. 20, 24.

Jacket, Cree or Cree-Métis, Norway House style, 1890–1910, R. Colonna collected North Bay, Ontario 1930, cat. 32.

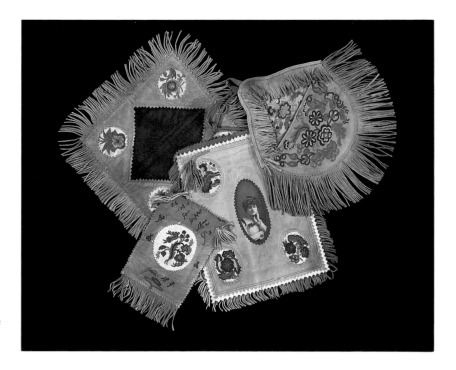

"Victoriana," Lake Winnipeg type, late 19th century, (clockwise from top left) cats. 13, 10, 11, 15.

Loom-woven Porcupine-Quill Bands, (top to bottom), Slavey, made in Fort Providence 1985–1986, cats. 123, 120, 117; Loucheux or Slavey, ESC collected on the Mackenzie River 1894, cat. 3 e,d,f,g,c,b,h.

Gun Case, Loucheux, ESC collected on the Mackenzie River 1894, cat. 4.

Octopus Bag, Great Slave Lake–Mackenzie River Region Athapaskan type, 1870; ESC collected 1894, cat. 71.

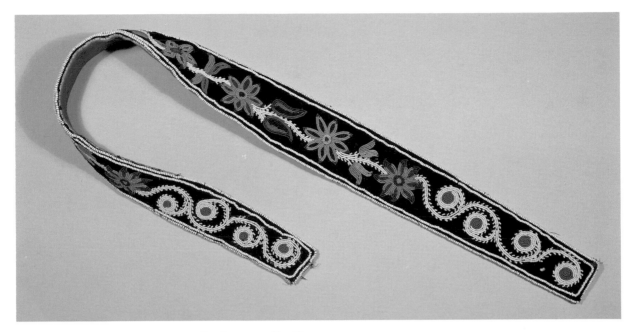

Baby Belt, probably Slavey, ESC collected Fort Simpson or Fort Norman 1894, cat. 73.

(clockwise from top left), Watch Pocket, ESC collected Fort Norman 1894, cat. 62; Firebag, ESC collected St. Peter's Reserve 1888–1894, cat. 60; Tobacco Pouch, ESC collected Fort McMurray 1894, cat. 61; all in Great Slave Lake–Mackenzie River Region style.

Octopus Bag, Cree or Cree-Métis type, second half nineteenth century, cat. 54.

Firebags with woven panels, Cree or Cree-Métis type, mid-nineteenth century, (l. to r.), cats. 49, 48.

Firebags with woven panels, (l.), Cree or Cree-Métis, northeast coast Lake Winnipeg, ca. 1900, cat. 50; (r.), Cree-influenced, second half nineteenth century, cat. 79.

Bark Storage Container, (l.) Montagnais-Naskapi, ESC collected Lake St. John, 1895, cat. 94; (r.) Bowl or Dish, Montagnais type, ESC collected Saskatchewan 1888–1894, cat. 95.

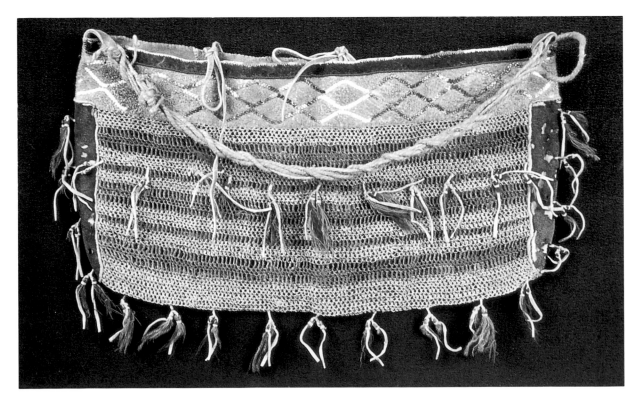

Game Bag, Dogrib, ESC collected Fort Rae 1894, cat. 90.

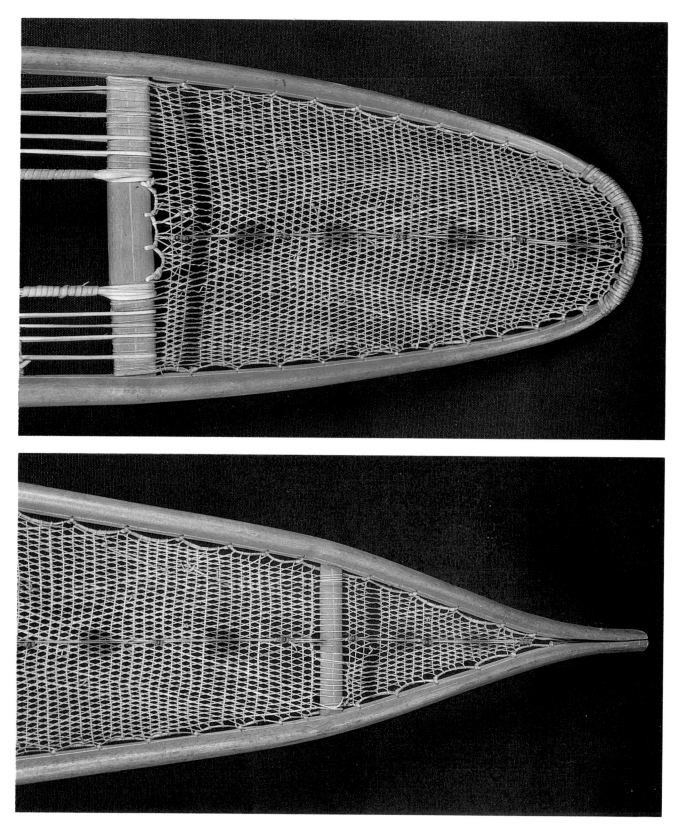

Snowshoe (details), Loucheux, ESC collected Fort McPherson 1894, cat. 92.

Pouch and Strap, Liard-Fraser Region Sekani type, early twentieth century, cat. 78.

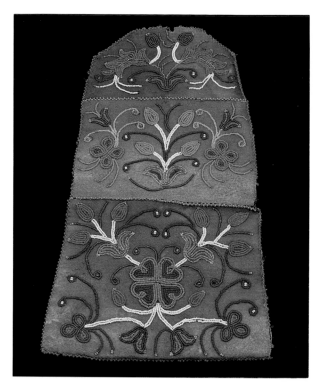

Wall Pocket, Yukon-Tanana Region Athapaskan type, early twentieth century, cat. 83.

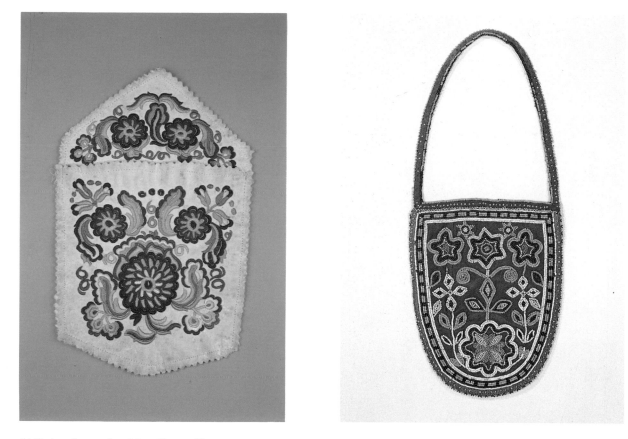

(l.) Pocket, Cree or Cree-Métis, Norway House style, 1890–1910, cat. 34. (r.) Cartridge Bag, Naskapi, early twentieth century, cat. 43.

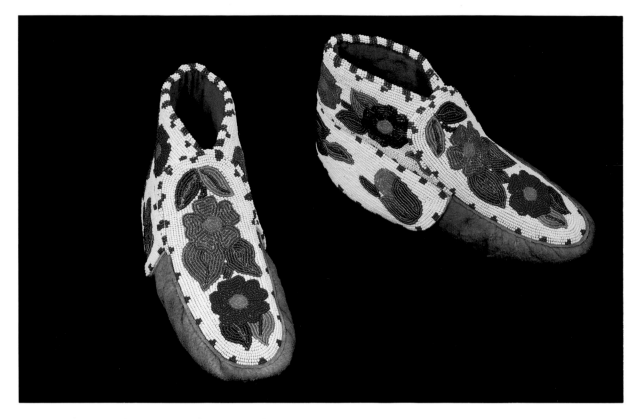

Moccasins, Chipewyan-Cree-Métis, Fort Chipewyan, Alberta 1972, cat. 161.

Dog Blanket, Chipewyan-Cree-Métis, Fort Chipewyan, Alberta 1985, cat. 136.

Moose-Hair Tufting (detail), Fort Providence, Northwest Territories, 1985, cat. 131.

Bark Containers, Fort Liard area, Northwest Territories 1985, cats. 175, 176.

Sled Dog Blanket, Great Slave Lake–Mackenzie River Region Slavey or Slavey-Métis type, ESC collected Fort Simpson 1894, cat. 68.

## PART I

The Old Collection:
Nineteenth and Early Twentieth Centuries

CATALOGUE DATA WILL FOLLOW THIS FORMAT:

oo  *Object*

>   Tribe or Region    Date of manufacture
>
>   Source (collector, collection date and location, and/
>   or museum acquisition date)
>
>   Dimensions
>
>   HMA catalogue number
>
>   *Collector's comments* (Emma Shaw Colcleugh)*

Description

Interpretation

Comparisons

When an object has been identified on the basis of research in the absence of collection information, and is typical of a known style, the word "type" follows the tribal or regional attribution.

* The Museum's largest single collection from the nineteenth century—sixty-eight objects—was collected by Emma Shaw Colcleugh, Rhode Island journalist and teacher, between 1888 and 1894 in Ontario, Quebec, Labrador, Manitoba and points north, in present-day northern Saskatchewan and Alberta, and Northwest Territories. Comments by the collector from two sources are written in italics, followed by "ESC" (Emma Shaw Colcleugh) and either "NB" (notebook) or "GL" (green list).

"NB" is a hand-written collections notebook in which she entered her comments about individual pieces.

"GL" refers to a typed collection list with a green cover which accompanied the collection when it came to the Museum. It lists 218 objects from her collection which she sold to Rudolf F. Haffenreffer Sr. in 1930. The list contains more objects than the notebook. It incorporates many comments from the hand-written notebook and was based on it and seemingly on her verbal information. The last page contains a handwritten agreement of sale and her signature. The numbering systems for NB and GL do not correspond.

# Porcupine Quills

## Algonquian Quill Weaving

Much Northern Algonquian quill-weaving seems to have been produced in the Red River area of Manitoba. It is best known on epaulets and other band ornamentation of hide frock coats, which were especially popular among the Cree- and Ojibwa-Métis of the area, and on a variety of pouches, particularly firebags. This work differs from Athapaskan woven quillwork in the motifs preferred, the ways in which they are related, and the colors most commonly used. Multi-element motifs are the most popular, particularly stars and braces but also lozenges and crosses, constructed chiefly from juxtaposed right triangles. Motifs are usually alternated in an ABAB fashion and may not necessarily touch. The proportion of positive to negative space is most often unequal, with the latter often dominating. A natural-quill background with red, blue-green, yellow and occasionally black is common; color layers within motifs tend to vary in width.

## 1 *Napkin Ring*

Northern Algonquian (Red River Métis?) type, late nineteenth century

Rudolf F. Haffenreffer Sr. collection

W: 3 cm   D: 5 cm

57–579

Natural, red, blue, and green aniline-dyed porcupine quills woven on light brown thread in a band pattern of repeated eight-pointed stars. Two-beaded edging in iridescent white seed-beads sewn with sinew. Backing of tanned hide.

Small items such as this napkin ring, pin cushion and needle case (cat. 2) were probably more commonly produced for sale to visitors than collections evidence.

## 2 *Pin Cushion and Needle Case*

Northern Algonquian (Red River Métis?) type, late nineteenth century

Rudolf F. Haffenreffer Sr. collection

60–4646 A & B

(A) Pin cushion: L: 4.5 cm D: 3.6 cm. Natural, red and blue-green porcupine quills woven on light-brown thread in a rose-trellis design. Two-beaded edging in translucent blue-green and iridescent white seed-beads sewn with sinew. Silk covered pad.

Compare with unattributed garters MMMN H4.3.41, with tulip design.

(B) Needle case: L: 7 cm open W: 4 cm. Natural, red, blue-green and yellow porcupine quills woven on light-brown thread in a pattern of eight-pointed stars. Two-beaded edging in translucent blue seed-beads sewn with sinew. Caribou hide lining.

1                    2 (A)                    2 (B)

## Athapaskan Quill Weaving

Eighteenth-century reports of Northern Athapaskan clothing comment on their fine porcupine-quill ornamentation but do not specify techniques. The earliest examples of Athapaskan garments were collected in the middle decades of the nineteenth century. Some include quill bands woven directly onto the garment, or loom-woven, then applied (Clark 1974a; VanStone 1981; Duncan 1989). The bands are placed at the breast, and sometimes at the cuffs and hem. The sophistication of design and skill of execution on these indicate that the art of porcupine-quill weaving had already been long established when they were made.

By the mid-nineteenth century, loom-woven belts were common. In 1862, Hudson's Bay Company factor B. R. Ross sent several single belts from the Dogrib and Slavey to the Industrial Museum of Scotland, now the Royal Scottish Museum (RSM 848.16, 849.2-4), along with a narrow belt attached to a man's tunic (RSM 558.39). He described quill weaving, in a report forwarded to the museum the same year:

The manufacture of Belts, bracelets and shot-pouch straps is precisely similar. A certain number of strands, according to the article to be made, of strongish sinew thread are stretched across a rod of willow, bent like a bow. A square piece of birch bark, through which a number of holes corresponding to these strands is pierced, runs on them keeping them at equal distances and firmly in their proper position. The first procedure then is to soak the quills in the mouth, where a supply is always lubricating during the manufacture. A strand of very fine sinew thread is then passed horizontally at right angles confining the blunt ends of the quills which are bent over it and then passed between the longitudinal strings. When the work is completed the pointed ends, which are all brought through on the reverse side, are cut off, and a lining of soft deerskin, ornamented around the edges with dyed goose quills or beads is sewn on. The most skilled work-women exhibit their adroitness by regularity of pattern and economy of materials—some using double the quantity of quills that others will. The patterns are innumerable and in most cases are designed during the process. When well done quill work is very pretty and the natives are proud and justly so of their skill in it. The quantity done in a day by a skillful operative is about 2½ inches of belt size—and one of these articles is completed in about a fortnight, when it would be bartered for about 8£-worth of goods (1862).

The making of belts remained popular through the nineteenth and into the twentieth century, and many are found in museum collections. A few women continue the art today (see Chapter IV). The process Ross describes is identical to that used today except that string has replaced sinew for the warp and weft and cardboard has replaced birch bark for the heddle.

## 3 Loom-Woven Porcupine-Quill Bands

Loucheux or Slavey, late nineteenth century

Collected by Emma Shaw Colcleugh on the Mackenzie River, 1894

57–278 A–H

*Belts made by Louchoux Indians. So far as I can learn this is the only tribe that does work anything like this. It is made on a small hand loom, the warp of sinew, each stitch represents one porcupine quill. When the weaving is finished, the quills protruding at the back are cut, the belt is then lined and the edges beaded* (ESC: GL 26).

(A) Belt. L: 77 cm   w: 4 cm. Natural, red, blue and purple quills woven on sinew in pattern of continuous expanded diamonds; white seed-bead edging, smoked-hide backing, metal hooks and eyes.

(B) Belt. L: 69 cm w: 3 cm. Natural, magenta and purple quills woven on sinew in pattern of alternated vertical bar and diamond with cross in middle; white seed-bead edging, smoked-hide backing.

(C) Belt. L: 65.5 cm w: 4 cm. Natural, rust, chartreuse and brown quills woven on sinew in pattern of contiguous diamonds formed of triangles placed along a center line; pink seed-bead edging, hide backing, red wool broadcloth section at one end and remains of black wool broadcloth section at other.

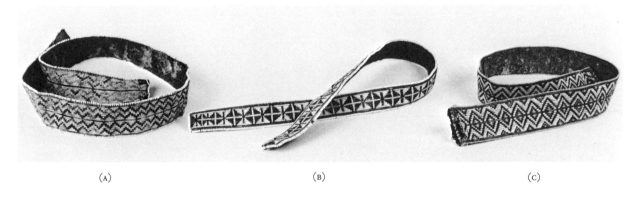

3

(A)          (B)          (C)

(D) Belt. L: 70.5 cm w: 4 cm. Natural, faded purples, magenta, red and yellow quills woven on sinew in pattern of contiguous diamonds; white seed-bead edging; unsmoked caribou-hide backing.

(E) Belt. L: 64 cm w: 4.75 cm. Natural, red, blue-green and chartreuse quills woven on sinew in central pattern of contiguous diamonds bordered with bands of checks and outer edge-borders of contiguous triangles; blue seed-bead edging,

unsmoked caribou-hide backing, black ribbon end-sections and ties.

(F) Belt. L: 72.5 cm  w: 5 cm. Natural, red, yellow, navy and purple quills woven on light-brown string in pattern of three parallel bands, one of contiguous diamonds and two of angled parallel lines facing out from the center; white seed-bead edging, smoked-hide backing, metal hooks and eyes, hide ends at one time covered with black fabric.

3

(D)          (E)          (F)

(G) Belt. L: 72 cm w: 4.2 cm. Natural, purple, gold, orange-red and bright blue (faded to aqua) quills woven on light-brown string in pattern of checked band bordered on each side with contiguous triangles; white seed-bead edging, smoked-hide backing.

(H) Garter. L: 34.25 cm w: 2.8 cm. Natural, lavender, purple and orange quills woven on light-brown string in herringbone pattern; white seed-bead edging, smoked caribou-hide backing, remnants of wool-yarn pompons at one end.

Athapaskan woven-quill designs are most often constructed of one or more horizontal bands in which a single motif is repeated contiguously in an AAAA fashion. Equilateral triangles, diamonds and V's joined to form a zigzag are by far the most common motifs. Color is normally applied in equal-width layers usually three stitches wide. The indigo blues and cochineal reds popular in B. R. Ross' time were joined later in the century with aniline reds, pinks, purples, oranges, yellows and greens.

The Colcleugh belts are typical late-nineteenth-century Athapaskan examples. The patterning of zig-zags, triangles and plain or expanded diamonds is that of earlier Athapaskan belts. Dyes are primarily aniline and have usually faded from their originally very bright tones. Golds and some reds are stable; purples, on the other hand, are not, and shades of purple and magenta have faded to a light lavender.

Porcupine quill weaving was practiced by women across the Great Slave Lake-Mackenzie River region and to a lesser extent by those farther west. It is also an Algonquian art. Although there is no reason to doubt Emma's statement that Loucheux (Eastern Kutchin) women made these belts, by far the greatest number of later Athapaskan quilled belts were made at Slavey posts such as Fort Simpson and Fort Providence. At the turn of the century, just as today, prices were determined by length. Today a few women at Fort Providence still weave quill bands.

Compare with woven bands: BrM 90.9.8.35, collected by Lonsdale in 1888–89 on his trip down the Mackenzie and Yukon Rivers; LFG C335 and BM 2-1141, both Loucheux; and collections of Slavey examples at RSM, GAI, NMM, AMNH, and MAI.

3

(G)                                    (H)

## 4 *Gun Case*

Loucheux (Eastern Kutchin), late nineteenth century
Collected by Emma Shaw Colcleugh on the Mackenzie
River, 1894

L: 123 cm including fringes  W: 19 cm

57–476

*Loucheux, Mackenzie River, 1894* (ESC: NB 127)

Two sections of smoked hide, ornamented with four bands
of woven porcupine quillwork with rows of diamonds and
triangles in natural, reds and teal blue. Straight-cut fringes
wrapped with quills of the same colors. Muzzle end is finished
with long, very thin twisted tassels wrapped at intervals with
lavender quills and tied into wool-yarn tassels of purple,
maroon, green and yellow. Thong and yarn tassels in same
colors at intervals along side seam. Quill-wrapped quill attached with sinew stitches to side seam. Hand-pinked upper
edge. Muzzle end padded.

The prestigious ornamented quiver of early contact
times was replaced, after guns became available, by an
ornamented guncase. Woven-quill bands trim many
Great Slave Lake-Mackenzie River gun cases. Fringes
are typical on the muzzle end of cases from this region.
Russell (1898: 178) emphasizes the importance of the
gun case. On hunts with the Dogrib in 1892–94, guns
were kept in their cases until the moment of firing.
According to Joe Laferte (pers. comm. 1982) of Fort
Simpson, it was common for the point to be of double
moose skin so that one could use it to test whether a
moose track was soft and fresh or older and frozen.

Compare UI 1090, Trout Lake Slavey, collected by Frank
Russell, 1892–94; HBC 373; RSM 1928.266; PH 93230, Athapaskan, probably Liard River, received 1927.*

* When no attribution is given to a piece from a comparative
  collection, there is no information available.

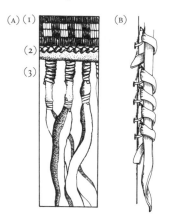

Detail:
A. (1) Quill weaving
   (2) One-thread, one-
       quill diagonal sewing
       (also called twisted, or
       simple line technique)
   (3) Quill wrapping
       around thong
B. Side view of quill-
   wrapped quill attached
   with sinew stitches
   along side seam

4

## 5 Quill-Woven Napkin Rings

Loucheux (Eastern Kutchin), late nineteenth century

Collected by Emma Shaw Colcleugh, 1894

57–279

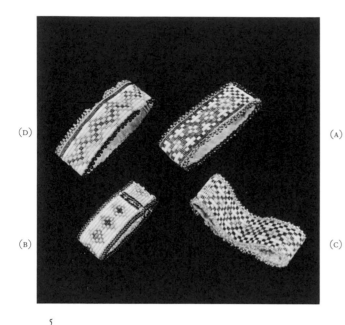

5

(A) L: 4 cm   w: 1.75 cm. Brown, red and chartreuse quills woven in pattern of connected diamonds on light-brown string; two-beaded edging of green seed-beads sewn with sinew, bias-cut ivory silk lining.

(B) l: 3 cm   w: 1.6 cm. Natural, red, green, and gold quills woven in pattern of separate diamonds on light-brown thread; single-beaded edging of red seed-beads sewn with thread, caribou-hide lining.

(C) L: 4 cm.  w: 2 cm. Natural, red, brown, green and yellow quills woven in pattern of checked diamonds on light-brown thread; two-beaded edging of crystal seed-beads sewn with thread, bias-cut ivory silk lining.

(D) L: 4 cm   w: 2 cm. Natural, aqua, gold, red and green quills woven in zigzag pattern on light-brown thread; two-beaded edging of crystal and black seed-beads sewn with thread, bias-cut ivory silk lining.

Simplified versions of the motifs common on larger woven bands are used on these smaller ones, probably napkin rings made to sell to visitors. Rings A, C and D were made as a set.

## 6 Gun Case

Slavey, late nineteenth century

Collected by Emma Shaw Colcleugh at Fort Simpson, 1894

L: 114 cm   w: 19 cm

57–486

*Gun case, Fort Simpson, Mackenzie River* (ESC: GL 32)

Two pieces of smoked moose hide ornamented with five bands of folded quills in lavender, purple, red, orange, green, yellow and yellow-orange in two-thread technique. Quill is wound around the sinew of the side-seam. Round piece inserted and sewn as cap at end, with fringe surrounding it; fringe pinked and wrapped tightly with quills in orange, natural, purple, pink and yellow.

Among the Athapaskans, folded-quill techniques are most common on Kutchin tunics from the mid-nineteenth century. They were also used to edge the vamps of late-nineteenth-century moccasins (see cat. 8).

(A)

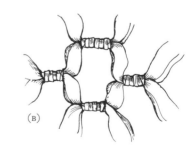

(B)

Detail:
A. Quill folded over two lines of sinew stitches to form zigzag
B. Quill-wrapped thongs in alternate pattern

(A)

(B)

6

## Moccasin Decoration

These are worn by all of the métis and Indians of the North; the whites in the country soon become accustomed to their use and are loath to return to the hard and cramping "English shoes." They are all made after the same general pattern: a single piece around the foot, a semi-elliptical more or less ornamented piece over the instep, and a top of light leather or canvas that folds around the ankle. Dressed moose leather is the best material obtainable by the Northern Indians for the manufacture of moccasins; caribou leather is also used, especially by the inhabitants of the caribou country, where few moose are to be found (Frank Russell 1898: 172).

Although many moccasins that have been preserved in museums are decorated—with silk, beads or quills—most nineteenth-century moccasins were utilitarian, sparsely decorated, sometimes pieced from hide scraps. One could go through several pair of moccasins a day on the trail, so keeping a man in moccasins was a continual job for many Subarctic women. Frank Russell (1898: 172), who walked with Dogrib to the Barren Grounds to hunt for musk-oxen, commented that "the moccasin is certainly the best form of foot wear for use in the fragile birch canoe or for walking upon snowshoes. But it is not a perfect protector of the foot, as the soft and flexible mooseskin will admit water as readily as blotting paper, and then wear away rapidly and stretch immoderately. Four or five pairs a day are sometimes required in tracking, and in spring traveling they are soon cut to pieces by the ice, though they are sometimes protected by a sole made from the skin of a caribou's leg with the hair on. They are sewed with sinew thread, which is strong and durable."

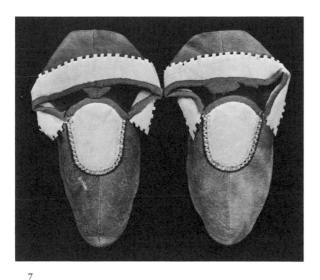

7

## 7 *Moccasins*

Eastern Athapaskan type, late nineteenth century

Collected by Emma Shaw Colcleugh at Athabasca Landing, Alberta, 1894

L: 25.8 cm   W: 14 cm

57–533

*Moose skin slippers, Athabasca Landing* (ESC: GL 40)

Soft sole, pointed toe of smoked moose hide, with T-shaped heel-seam and central toe-seam. Seams sewn with sinew. Vamp (tongue) of unsmoked caribou hide backed with smoked moose hide. Vamp edged with one row of horsehair wrapped with green horsehair, and two rows of four-quill plaiting in red-orange faded to salmon, purple and lavender, and light green faded to natural. Crenelated cuffs of unsmoked caribou hide; ankle edge bound with blue wool-worsted braid, now faded. Braid tab for hanging.

Colcleugh probably called these slippers rather than moccasins because they lacked high cuffs and wrap-around laces.

## 8 *Moccasins*

Eastern Athapaskan type, late nineteenth century

Collected by Emma Shaw Colcleugh, possibly at Fort Simpson, 1894

L: 26 cm

57–566

8

Soft sole of smoked moose hide, with T-shaped heel-seam and central toe-seam. Seams sewn with sinew. Double tongue (lower of white stroud, upper of unsmoked caribou hide), edged with two rows of two-quill plaiting, the first yellow and green, the second purple, followed by one row of horsehair wrapped with tan silk floss, a row of four-quill plaiting in purple, magenta and white, and two rows of horse-hair wrapped with red and green silk floss. Lower cuff of crenelated black wool, upper cuff of crenelated unsmoked caribou hide, wrap-around cuffs with pinked-front edge and tying thongs of smoked caribou hide; duffel lining. See cat. 40.

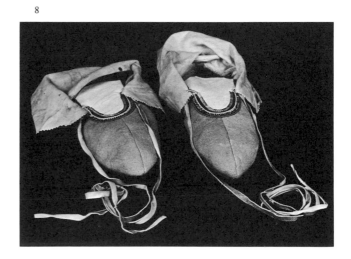

## 9 *Moccasins*

Eastern Athapaskan type, late nineteenth century

Collected by Emma Shaw Colcleugh, possibly at Fort Simpson, 1894

L: 24.3 cm

57–538

Soft sole of smoked moose hide with double tongue (lower of smoked moose hide, upper of smoked caribou hide), upper edged with row of purple porcupine quills folded to form a sawtooth (A), a row of paired four-quill plaiting in red-orange, natural, aqua and lavender (B), and three rows of natural, red and faded lavender horsehair wrapped around a horsehair core (C). Uppers of smoked hide show native mending, sinew-stitched. See cat. 40.

Compare with moccasins PWNHC 982.9.1.

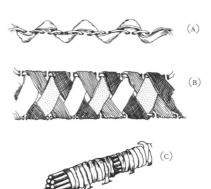

Detail, vamp edge
A. Sawtooth quill technique
B. Four-quill plaiting; pairs of quills laid together and plaited
c. Piping formed from bundle of horsehair wrapped around horse-hair around vamp insert

9

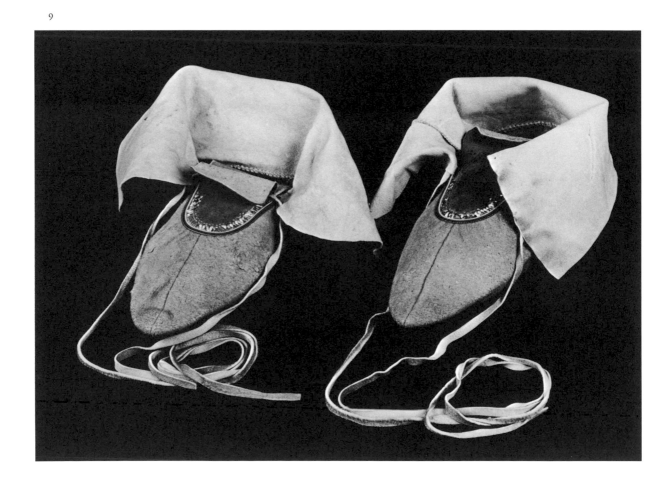

# Silk Thread

## Embroidery Materials

In the second half of the nineteenth century some native women of the Subarctic were embroidering hide moccasins, mitts, firebags and other personal equipment with silk thread using floral designs. Nineteenth-century inventories of Hudson's Bay posts show gradually increasing stocks of silk thread carried for sale to native communities and Company servants. At the Norway House Post in Manitoba, inventories from 1851 to 1857 distinguish bween silk thread (embroidery floss), stitching thread and linen thread, and indicate whether each was black, white or colored.[1]

Throughout Canada, at mission schools run by Ursuline Sisters, Grey Nuns and Anglicans, young Indian girls were taught embroidery skills as a part of their general education in homemaking and the domestic arts, just as their counterparts in European society were expected to master embroidery and needlework in their preparation for womanhood. Often designs were drawn by the teachers for the girls to copy and embroider. Some motifs were inspired by existing European fabrics.

Rectilinear and curvilinear designs were indigenous to the North, and had been executed in birch-bark incising and painted hide in the eastern Subarctic. The newly introduced floral and leaf design ideas from European embroidery sources were carried out in silk-thread and bead embroidery on hide and fabric. Variations in motifs were developed and expanded upon by Indian women as they made the designs their own. Native people in the twentieth century derive great pleasure from the floral designs they now use, and comment again and again on their beauty.

At the same time that silk embroidery was gaining popularity in the North, a less expensive look-alike thread became available to embroiderers. In England in 1853, John Mercer developed a technique of treating cotton fiber with a caustic alkali to strengthen it, making it more receptive to dye, and giving it a silky luster. The process was perfected in 1889 by H. A. Lowe (Joseph 1981: 267) and "mercerized" cotton embroidery floss began to be marketed. It is usually difficult to ascertain with the eye between silk and mercerized cotton thread in an embroidery.[2] Meanwhile, other substitutes were sought for silk. In the nineteenth century, sericulture, or the production of silk, was confined to China, Japan, Italy, and India, and changing economic and political situations meant that silk was expensive and often unavailable. By the first quarter of the twentieth century "artificial silk" was being manufactured by several means; one of its most popular forms was marketed as "rayon" in 1924 (Joseph 1981: 73). In the twentieth century wool and synthetic yarns have also been popular for embroidery, especially on mukluks and dog blankets (see cats. 136, 138).

While the fine strands of the early "thin" silk allowed delicate small-flower designs, the thicker yarns resulted in larger, more simplified floral forms. Mercerized cotton allowed finer work, although not as fine as the earlier silk. Many floss embroiderers of the 1980s refer to the early silk as "thin silk," and they treasure skeins of it among their work materials (Hail and Duncan 1985).

NOTES

1 Many Company servants were married to native or mixed-blood women, who embroidered with silk floss and beads. In July of 1857, at Norway House, Company servant James Flett purchased twenty skeins of colored silk thread for 10/1/8 pounds. At the same time he purchased flannel, Red River coating, duffel, fine white and gray cottons, tailor's scissors, green and yellow beads, nine yards of colored hair ribbons and two reels of white thread, all of these probably sewing materials for his wife (Norway House Records B 154/d/143: 34).

   In June and July of 1857 William Sinclair, C.F., purchased from the Norway House Post "two lists of colored thread, two lists of white stitching thread, and ten skeins of colored silk thread" (B 154/d/143: 279). Sinclair, a Chief Factor, was of mixed English and native descent. His descendant, Charles Cuthburt Sinclair, who served as clerk at Norway House at the end of the nineteenth century, married a cousin of Emma Shaw Colcleugh's husband, Frederick William Colcleugh. C. C. Sinclair's daughter, Ramona, is pictured in figure III-11 wearing a silk-thread-embroidered outfit.

2 Silk thread usually has a greater sheen than mercerized cotton, but even silk can lack luster when worked in a chain stitch rather than a satin or buttonhole stitch. The questions about why, when, and to what degree Subarctic embroiderers turned from silk to using mercerized cotton or artificial silks have been continuing ones for

museum researchers, so it was decided to test all of the "silk looking" examples dating from approximately 1888 to 1930 in the Haffenreffer Museum's central Subarctic collection. A chemical procedure was followed in order to make a gross fiber identification. A permanent slide was made of a part of a one-centimeter sample of shredded thread from the reverse side of each object in the collection. The remainder of the thread was placed in 10 milligrams of full-strength chlorine bleach. If the sample dissolved, it was identified as a protein, silk or wool. If it did not dissolve, it was identified as non-protein, a cellulose fiber such as cotton, flax or linen, or a synthetic. The procedure required twenty minutes, more or less, for each sample, varying with the tightness of the fiber twist. Each slide sample was then examined under a polarizing microscope at 150x to identify the specific fiber (Reid 1987).

All of the samples tested were identified as silk. They include the Colcleugh, Colonna and Haffenreffer collections. (The Bedford collection was not yet in the Museum.) The results indicate that, at the period when most of the Haffenreffer Museum material was collected, 1888–1930, silk was still very much the floss in use among native embroiderers in the central Subarctic, especially in the Lake Winnipeg area.

Detail cat. 35

## Lake Winnipeg Area

In the Lake Winnipeg area in the nineteenth century lived both Cree and Ojibwa-speaking people: particularly the Swampy Cree division of the Western Woods Cree, and the Lake Winnipeg Saulteaux, as well as the métis of both groups. In collections, if silk embroidered objects are attributed at all, they are usually called Cree. Colcleugh commented on the embroideries she collected as follows:

Cree embroidery, Lake Winnipeg Country. All Cree embroideries and most of that throughout the north are originally designed by the women. More than once I have sat on a river bank beside an Indian woman who drew her design from a flower using a porcupine quill for a pencil and her coloring matter the juice of some flower (ESC: GL 44; refers to cats. 19, 20, 24, 29, 30, 31).

On hide embroideries, remnants of the drawings are usually red, in a medium that looks like ink. Berry juice seems more likely to have been used than "the juice of some flower." Porcupine quills can be cut at an angle to create a reservoir and point, or can simply be dipped into a liquid. Contemporary Cree and Cree-Métis embroiderers remember their mothers and grandmothers drawing with porcupine quills. By Colcleugh's time some native women also had access to pens and red ink.

Designs were most often drawn free-hand by native women in the north; few women seem to have used the completely drawn-out patterns favored by non-native women, although some made paper templates of specific motifs that they might draw around. It is unlikely that templates were used for the type of delicate thread embroidery that Colcleugh collected.

## 10 *Wall Pocket*

Lake Winnipeg type, 1880–1915
Rudolf F. Haffenreffer Sr. collection

L: 31 CM   W: 33 cm

57–557

Smoked caribou hide with attached fringes; machine stitching; pinking; purple velvet backing. Front of pocket and back extension embroidered in floral design using buttonhole stitch. Silk floss in red, buff, greens, gold, aqua, lavender, and pink; faded. The craftsmanship of this embroidery is especially fine.

Compare with wall pockets: APM H67.269.6; and ROM HK 599, made for Mrs. Edmund Morris by a Cree-Métis. The leaves constructed of teardrop-shaped lobes are rare in thread, but common on beaded versions. Compare the elongated buds with those on the picture frames, cats. 11, 12.

## 10

11

## 11 *Picture Frame*

Lake Winnipeg type, circa 1890
Rudolf F. Haffenreffer Sr. collection
L: 29 cm    w: 24.6 cm
57–572

Smoked hide with under-edging of bleached caribou hide and smoked hide fringes; cardboard backing; all edges of cuts pinked; machine stitching. Center oval for photograph; at corners, inserts of bleached hide embroidered with silk-thread floral sprays in "Lake Winnipeg small flower style." Buttonhole-stitch embroidery, in faded greens, magenta, reds, aqua, blue-green, golds, yellow, blue, and purple. The cardboard backing probably came from a box that had been mailed; written on it is "Hudson's Bay Co, Michipicoten River, Algona District," a location on the northeast coast of Lake Superior. This frame may have been made by the same woman who made cat. 14.

## 12 *Double Picture Frame*

Lake Winnipeg type, circa 1890
Rudolf F. Haffenreffer Sr. collection
L: 36.6 cm    w: 22.9 cm
57–573

Smoked caribou hide; two oval cutouts for photographs and six teardrop-shaped inserts of bleached caribou hide embroidered in "Lake Winnipeg small flower style" with tiny floral sprays, some in buttonhole, some in chain stitch. All edges of cutouts pinked; cardboard-backed; machine stitched. Silk thread in red, green, magenta, brown, yellow, rose, and white.

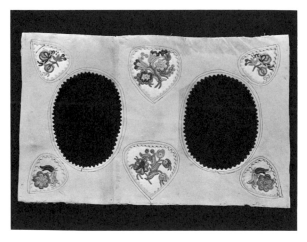

12

## 13 *Mat or Lamp Pad*

Lake Winnipeg type, circa 1890
Rudolf F. Haffenreffer Sr. collection
L: 31 cm    w: 31 cm
57–555

Square of smoked caribou hide with red velvet inset, edges pinked and trimmed; attached fringes; machine stitching; circular corner inserts of unsmoked hide embroidered in "Lake Winnipeg small flower style," using silk thread, buttonhole stitch, in buff, red, rose, greens, golds, and pinks. The original colors were probably those listed for cat. 14.

13

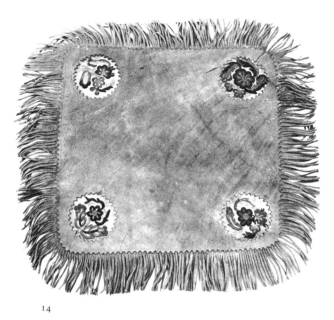

14

## 14 *Mat or Pillow Cover*

Lake Winnipeg type, circa 1890
Rudolf F. Haffenreffer Sr. collection
L: 33 cm   w: 31.6 cm
57–556

Smoked caribou hide, edges pinked; attached fringes; circular corner inserts of unsmoked hide embroidered with tiny floral cluster in Lake Winnipeg small flower style, using silk thread in buttonhole stitch. Thread colors: reds, aqua, purple, greens, golds; some greens faded to brown.

For cats. 11–15 compare valance MMMN H4.0.68, Inkster collection, 1819–1934, ornamented with similar small floral medallions, and chair cover ROM 958.65.1, made in 1897 by Mrs. Stout, half-breed wife of the Hudson's Bay trader at Nelson House, for the wife of J. B. Tyrrell. Nelson House was a Cree post.

## 15 *New Year's Greeting*

Lake Winnipeg type, 1889
Rudolf F. Haffenreffer Sr. collection
L: 20.8 cm   w: 12 cm
57–578

Wall-hanging of smoked caribou hide, cardboard-backed, edges hand-pinked; attached fringes; hanging thong. Insert of unsmoked caribou hide embroidered with floral spray in buttonhole stitch. An embroidered greeting, "With Best Wishes for a Happy New Year" and "Jan: 1889" in chain stitch. Silk-thread embroidery in brown, greens (some unfaded, others faded to olives) and golds, reds, rose, purples, maroon, and orange. Written in longhand on back: "With best love from Aunt Elga."

15

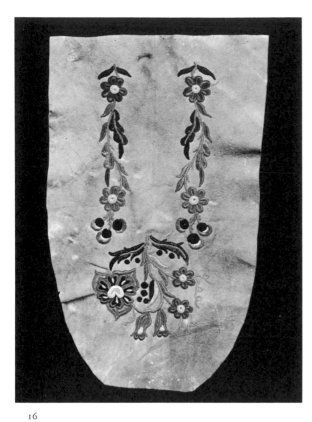

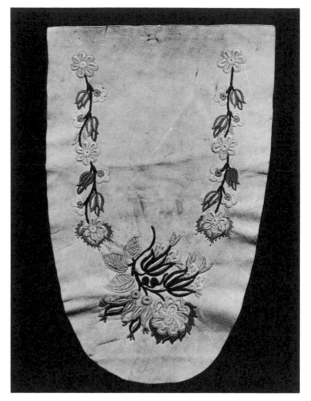

16

17

## 16 *Slipper Uppers*

Lake Winnipeg type, late nineteenth century

Collected by Emma Shaw Colcleugh at Old Fort
Garry, Manitoba, 1888–94

L: 28.9 cm    W: 17.5 cm

57–440 A & B

*Caribou skin slipper pattern. Red River Indians, Old Fort
Garry, Manitoba* (ESC: GL 86)

Smoked caribou hide; silk thread embroidered in buttonhole
stitch; central design a curved stem with rosettes, buds, tendrils and unattached berries; mirror-image side designs of
rosettes, buds, leaves and berries along a stem. Thread colors:
avocado, chartreuse and medium green, pink, red-orange,
magenta, gold, aqua, salmon, and salmon faded to buff.
Traces of paper support on back of hide.

Although the embroidery on these uppers is less
delicate and sure than that of cat. 17 (also collected at
Fort Garry), both share certain motifs: the fluid dip-
petaled rosette, fat calyx petals behind certain rosettes,
and bud centers that come to unusually sharp points.

The "Red River Indians" at Old Fort Garry were of
Cree, Saulteaux, and often French ancestry. Many attended the mission school at St. Boniface, and probably
learned silk embroidery there.

Compare with moccasins APM H.66.233.102, Darby Collection, 1890–1910.

## 17 *Slipper Uppers*

Lake Winnipeg type, late nineteenth century

Collected by Emma Shaw Colcleugh at Old Fort
Garry, Manitoba, 1888–94

L: 27 cm    W: 16.5 cm

57–439, 57–441

*Caribou skin slipper pattern. Red River Indians, Old Fort
Garry, Manitoba* (ESC: GL 37)

Lightly smoked caribou hide, thread embroidered in central
floral spray of a rosette, fat single leaves and single and
double moss-rosebuds with wisps; sides embroidered symmetrically with rosettes, buds and leaves along a serpentine

stem. Silk floss in dark, medium and light green, chartreuse, graduated pinks, salmon pinks, light blue, with touches of red, purple and gold; buttonhole stitch. Remains of paper support on reverse.

These slipper uppers picture the moss rose, a flower popular in nineteenth-century Britain. Its hairy calyx petals appear attached to small rosettes on the sides of the slippers; the extended attenuated points of the calyx contribute a sinuous elegance to the buds on the uppers. The tiny leaves attached in a row along the large central rosette may be an enlarged version of the calyx projections. Such leaves sometimes appear on Cree thread embroidery. When translated into beads, as sometimes happens, they lose their delicacy.

Tanned hide fades when exposed to light over a period of time. The fading of one of these uppers suggests that it was among mementos that Colcleugh displayed in her home. Elmer White, a neighbor of Mrs. Colcleugh in Thompson, Connecticut, recalled seeing the many beautiful objects in her collection on the walls and tables of her family home. He remembered that the neighborhood children were seldom allowed into the living room where the collection was displayed, and were never allowed to touch anything (White, pers. comm. 1985).

Silk embroidery thread is also very prone to fading. Certain colors, particularly blue shades, seem to fade more quickly than others. Some fade to a lighter version of the original; others may lose their original color almost entirely. On late nineteenth-century examples, orange-gold, red, orange and hunter green are very stable. Plum has often faded to rose, purple to lavender, and hot pink to light pink; salmon often fades to lighter shades or to buff; chartreuse to a brown-toned olive or avocado, then grey.

18

## 18 *Slippers*

Cree or Cree-Métis, late nineteenth century

Collected by Emma Shaw Colcleugh at Fort McMurray in 1894

L: 22.5 cm    W: 7.5 cm

71–5004

*Slippers from Fort McMurray, Athabasca River*
(ESC: GL 38)

Soft sole, bleached caribou hide, two-piece construction, with remnants of ermine fur at ankle; lined with white loose-weave cotton. Symmetrical floral design embroidered on front and sides in buttonhole and chain stitch in lavender, blue, maroon, green and chartreuse silk thread.

Compared with designs on slippers made in the Lake Winnipeg area (cats. 16, 17, 19), those on slippers made in Alberta show more symmetry and regularity. Compare with slippers: Northampton Museum D204/1975.15.

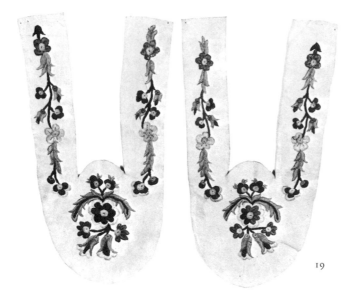

## 19 *Slipper Uppers*

Cree or Cree-Métis, late nineteenth century

Collected by Emma Shaw Colcleugh, Lake Winnipeg, Manitoba, 1888–1894

L: 23.5 cm    W: 13.5 cm

57–327, 57–328

*Cree embroidery, Lake Winnipeg country* (ESC: GL 44)

Bleached caribou hide, ankle opening cut out, silk-thread-embroidered in buttonhole stitch. Loosely symmetrical central spray of buds, rosette, small blossoms, long composite leaves with prominent central vein; sides embroidered with smaller versions of same motifs along stem. Thread colors: blue-green, red, light golds, chartreuse, faded salmon and maroon.

These are fine examples of the long multi-part leaves and tripartite buds of the Lake Winnipeg small flower style. They become more fully developed in the Norway House style.

Compare with moccasins: GAI 2278, Cree, Smith collection; and Northampton Museum D204/1975.15.

## 20 *Purse*

Probably Saulteaux, late nineteenth century

Collected by Emma Shaw Colcleugh, Lake Winnipeg, Manitoba, 1888–94

H: 12.5 cm    W: 16 cm

57–332

*Cree embroidery, Lake Winnipeg country* (ESC: GL 44)

Unsmoked caribou hide, lobed top and bottom, bordered with light green silk ribbon and netted openwork of clear seed-beads on thread; lined with purple silk brocade. Handle of plaited green and gold silk thread with tassels at ends; silver button closure. Embroidered with silk thread in chain stitch both sides, symmetrical floral designs in golds, dark blue-green, purple faded to rose, and magenta faded to brown.

These embroidered round fruit forms are similar to those on Ojibwa beadwork at the turn of the century. At the time Colcleugh visited, Ojibwa (called Saulteaux in the Lake Winnipeg area) were living south of Lake Winnipeg at St. Peter's Reserve, east of Lake Winnipeg at Island Lake, and on its southeastern shore at Berens River. Swampy Cree and Ojibwa (Saulteaux) of the Lake Winnipeg area frequently lived in the same communities and intermarried. It is likely that this purse reflects both artistic traditions.

21

## 21 *Mittens*

Cree-Métis or Chipewyan-Métis, circa 1860

Collected by Emma Shaw Colcleugh at Fort McMurray in 1894

L: 26.2 cm   W: 16 cm

57–542

*Half-breed mittens, Fort McMurray, Athabasca River, made extra large to permit wearing duffle underneath*
(ESC: GL 33)

Caribou hide, some smoked, some bleached, embroidered on the back of the hand and thumb with floral designs. Silk thread in chain stitch in pinks, greens, brown, red, blue, blue faded to gray, and yellow. Cuffs of brown velvet; band of silk-ribbon cutwork and attached silk ribbons in blue, red, pink, green and yellow. Fur edging (remnants).

Cutwork of rectilinear figures, formed by cutting and folding narrow superimposed silk ribbons, dates to the very late eighteenth century in the western Great Lakes region (Conn 1980). Silk ribbons became increasingly available to Native Americans when, as a result of new fashions introduced by the French Revolution, they went out of favor in European fashion (Marriott 1958: 54). Their use spread into the eastern Plains early in the nineteenth century and was introduced into the southern Plains by Prairie groups removed there in the 1830s and '40s. It continues there today. Ribbonwork was also produced in the Subarctic, and by the mid-nineteenth century was used by Cree and Cree-Métis women to ornament mitten cuffs and the front edges of the rectangular hood.

The motifs in this type of ribbonwork are variations on the zigzag, with straight extensions or elongation of sections of the zigzag occurring at regular intervals. In beadwork it is known as the "otter tail" motif. An "opposed half" color combination, where color changes along the horizontal axis of a motif, is the most common. On these mitts color is handled differently, with a central section (white in one case, yellow in the other) separating the two sides.

Mittens of this cut appear to have been particularly popular among the métis. Compare with mitts: RSM 848.7, Chipewyan half breed, collected 1857 by B.R. Ross; MMMN H4.31.76 and 77, Western Subarctic, 19th C, Inkster collection; MMMN H4.31.114, Cree, Isle a la Crosse, Saskatchewan, 1860s–70s.

22

23

## 22 *Slippers*

Cree or Cree-Métis type, late nineteenth century

Collected by Emma Shaw Colcleugh at Cumberland House, Saskatchewan or The Pas, Manitoba, 1888–94

L: 23 cm

60–924

*Slippers, Cumberland House, The Pas, Saskatchewan River* (ESC: GL 48)

Bleached caribou hide; separate soft sole; upper constructed of front plus two side pieces that join at heel and sides in vertical seams; silk-thread embroidered floral spray of fat rounded buds of stacked petals and multiple thin sinuous leaves, in shaded blues, salmon pinks, chartreuse, grey-greens, gold and maroon, using chain stitch; side tendril in running stitch; ermine fur at ankles; brown sateen lining.

Compare with motifs on shirt BM 2–4789, called Eastern Woodland, and coat McC ME 5153.

## 23 *Slippers*

Cree or Cree-Métis type, late nineteenth century

Collected by Emma Shaw Colcleugh at Cumberland House, Saskatchewan or the Pas, Manitoba, 1888–94

L: 21 cm

60–925

Bleached caribou hide; separate soft sole, vertical seams at heel and sides; silk-thread embroidered, in chain stitch, in

spray of rounded buds of stacked petals, a rosette, and thin leaves in salmon pinks, lavenders, grey-greens and light yellow; side tendril in running stitch. Ankle fur missing; aqua sateen lining. Probably by the same maker as cat. 22.

These slippers, with their thin sinuous leaves and fat bud forms of offset stacked petals, are characteristic of one of the several floral styles that appear in the western Lake Winnipeg area at the end of the nineteenth century. The soft white hide has been carefully tanned, then bleached, probably by hanging it outside in late winter when the sun reflected off the snow.

## 24 *Wall Pocket*

Cree or Cree-Métis, late nineteenth century

Collected by Emma Shaw Colcleugh, Lake Winnipeg, Manitoba, 1888–94

L: 19.1 cm   W: 14.8 cm

57–329

*Cree embroidery, Lake Winnipeg country* (ESC: GL 44)

Soft bleached caribou hide bound at edges with purple silk ribbon, unlined; silk thread embroidery in chain and buttonhole stitch in shades of blue, green, magenta, purple, gold and salmon; some fading.

Compare wall pocket, MMMN H40.798A, D. C. MacTavish Collection, 1860s–1910.

24

## Embroidered Fragments

Some of the unfinished and completed embroidery on hide in the Haffenreffer Museum's collection was probably the work of children in mission schools. The examples exhibit varied skill.

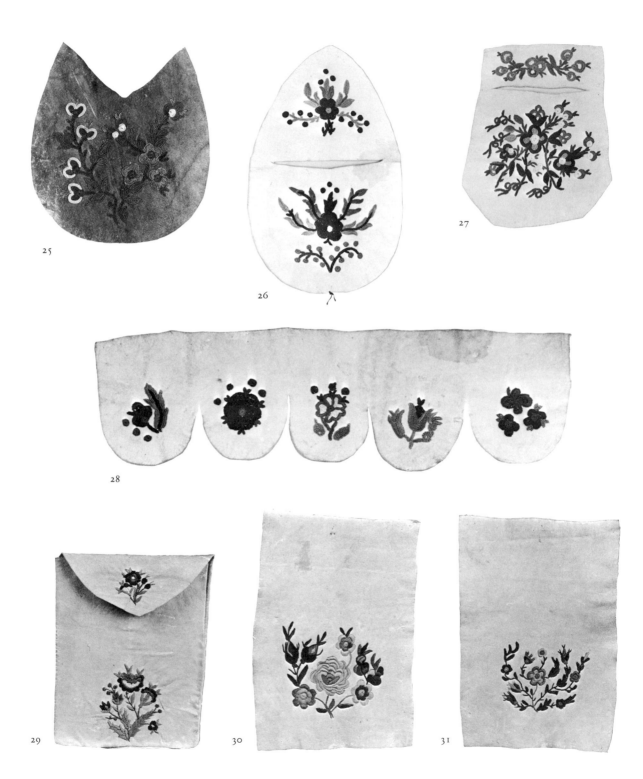

25

26

27

28

29

30

31

## 25 *Panel for Pocket or Purse*

Lake Winnipeg type, late nineteenth century
June Bedford collection

L: 13 cm  W: 11.5 cm

87–136

Smoked caribou hide, oval-bottomed, V-shaped upper edge, embroidered in chain and buttonhole stitch, in silk thread, in colors of green, red, blue, lavender, and tan. Evidence of paper support, now torn away, on back of hide.

## 26 *Panel for Wall or Watch Pocket*

Lake Winnipeg type, late nineteenth century
June Bedford collection

L: 21.5 cm  W: 13.5 cm

87–135

Unsmoked caribou hide, pointed oval, horizontal central slit. Embroidered in silk thread with floral sprays, chain stitch (buttonhole for berries), in greens, maroon, red, blue, and purple; remnants of paper support, now torn away, on back of hide.

## 27 *Panel for Purse or Wall Pocket*

Lake Winnipeg type, late nineteenth century
June Bedford collection

L: 15 cm  W: 12 cm

87–137

Unsmoked caribou hide, rectangular, with slit opening and lower corners cut off; embroidered in silk thread with floral sprays, chain stitch (buttonhole for berries), in purple, greens, blues, reds and pale peach faded to tan; evidence of paper support, now torn away, on back of hide.

## 28 *Band with Five Scallops*

Lake Winnipeg type, late nineteenth century
June Bedford collection

L: 8 cm  W: 38 cm

87–139

Scalloped strip of unsmoked caribou hide. Tiny floral spray embroidered in silk thread on each scallop using buttonhole and chain stitches. Thread colors: purples, maroon, greens, red, and blue; evidence of paper support, now torn away, on back of hide.

Embroidered scalloped bands longer than this were sometimes applied to either side of a jacket placket and along the cuffs.

## 29 *Parts for Small Purse with Flap*

Cree or Cree-Métis, late nineteenth century
Collected by Emma Shaw Colcleugh, Lake Winnipeg, Manitoba, 1888–94

L: 24.3 cm  W: 18.5 cm

57–326

*Cree embroidery, Lake Winnipeg country* (ESC: GL 44)

Single piece bleached caribou hide folded and sewn with thread along bottom and side to form rectangular pouch with flap; floral spray embroidered with silk thread in satin stitch on front and flap in shades of green and rose, blue, purple, buff, and a touch of orange.

This piece and the two following pieces lack precision and control of stitches, and were probably made by students.

## 30 *Embroidered Panel*

Cree or Cree-Métis, late nineteenth century
Collected by Emma Shaw Colcleugh, Lake Winnipeg, Manitoba, 1888–94

L: 28 cm  W: 19.5 cm

57–331

*Cree embroidery, Lake Winnipeg country* (ESC: GL 44)

Rectangular panel of bleached caribou hide, embroidered with silk thread in floral spray using buttonhole and chain stitches; thread colors: hot pink faded to light pink, plum to rose, salmon to buff, purple to lavender, maroon to dark rose; also shades of green and gold.

## 31 *Embroidered Panel*

Cree or Cree-Métis, late nineteenth century
Collected by Emma Shaw Colcleugh, Lake Winnipeg, Manitoba, 1888–94

L: 27.5 cm  W: 19 cm

57–330

*Cree embroidery, Lake Winnipeg country* (ESC: GL 44)

Rectangular panel of bleached caribou hide, embroidered with silk thread in floral spray using buttonhole and chain stitches; thread colors: buff, medium green, olive, blue-green, purple, lavender, plum faded to rose, pink faded to buff, shades of pink, red, and yellow-orange.

## The Norway House Style

Late in the nineteenth century a variation of the "Lake Winnipeg small flower style" developed in the communities at the north end of the lake. A logical outgrowth of the less flamboyant style popular farther south on the lake, it was produced in silk thread and occasionally in beads. The "Norway House style" appears on jackets, moccasins, handwear, as well as an assortment of "Victoriana". Many examples were collected at Norway House, but the style was also popular at Cross Lake and it was likely that it extended to other communities. Expanded rosettes, serpentine composite leaves and small multi-lobed buds dominate in the style. Large rosettes composed of many narrow elongated petals are expanded by the addition of one to three outer layers of unarticulated (scalloped) petals added around the outside. Color tones change gradually from a deep shade on the outside to pale on the inside. Most often red and orange shade down to pale pink; rose and lavender are sometimes also incorporated. In some cases there are two layers of this combination of articulated plus unarticulated petals, and the deep-to-pale color pattern is repeated with each. The rosette center is normally small and gold-colored.

Serpentine leaves constructed of thin green S-shaped elements laid along the sides of a similar but lighter or darker green central vein are prominent in this style. Layered scalloped lobes often wrap along one side and over the top of such leaves. Small buds with outer scalloped layers that wrap part way around the center are also common. These buds appear most often grouped in threes, and as on the rosettes, color is deeper on the outer layer, shaded to pale in the center. Blues and lavenders against a gold center are common for buds. A similar bud, in shades of pink but with articulated center petals is a less common variation. Curly wisps with short ends, and tendrils with two loops in alternate directions appear on some Norway House examples. In small designs such as those for a pocket, a purse, or a moccasin vamp, the design is usually a single rosette encompassed by symmetrically placed groups of buds and leaves. Larger designs such as those for jacket bibs include several rosettes and an active design field. Embroidery in the Norway House style is dynamic and fluid.

"Indian, north of The Pas, around 1930," wearing silk-thread embroidered jacket and hood; courtesy Manitoba Provincial Archives.

32

## 32 *Jacket*

Cree or Cree-Métis, Norway House style,
1890–1910
Collected by Robert Colonna at North Bay, Ontario,
1930
L: 93 cm
77–113C

Smoked moose hide, hand-pinked edges, hand-sewn seams, yoke with straight-cut fringes, front placket lined with printed cotton; embroidered with silk thread in buttonhole stitch. Front placket embroidered with large expanded rosettes and multi-lobed buds along a thick sinuous central stem edged with S-shaped leaves; back yoke with clusters of profile buds, some lobed, some petaled, curly wisps, and serpentine composite leaves; pockets with similar clusters. Silk thread in various shades of pink, rose, green, and lavender, blue, gold, purple, and black. Narrow commercial bead braid along tops of pockets and cuffs.

The Norway House embroidery style appears on several different types of jackets, including some with a separate rectangular or oval front bib. Compare with jackets: MMMN H4.12.127, collected at Norway House; MMMN H4.11.12, collected at Berens River Reserve; LFG 5549; GAI AP 2026, Cree.

32 back view

"Man with Dog, God's Lake." Courtesy Pitt Rivers Museum, Oxford.

Murray Chisholm Colcleugh and Charles Cuthbert Sinclair, ca. 1908, wearing silk-thread embroidered jackets in "Norway House style." Garbutt coll., courtesy Hudson's Bay Company Archives, MPA. See Notes, p. 154.

## 33 *Purse*

Cree or Cree-Métis, Norway House style, late nineteenth century

Collected by Emma Shaw Colcleugh at Fort Chipewyan in 1894.

L: 11 cm    W: 12.9 cm

57–443

*Pouch, Hudson's Bay Post, Fort Chipewyan* (ESC: GL 49)

Small, round-bottomed, flapped, of smoked caribou hide, lined with red silk. Sides machine-stitched together, no edge-binding. Embroidered florally with silk floss, buttonhole stitch, in rose, pink, green, gold, blue, and lavender, some colors now faded.

Chipewyan, Cree and mixed-bloods of both groups have lived at Fort Chipewyan for many years. The fort was also a stopover point for those on their way from Alberta and Saskatchewan into the Great Slave Lake area. It is not surprising that a pouch embroidered in a style characteristic of the Norway House area on northern Lake Winnipeg should have been available to Colcleugh at Fort Chipewyan.

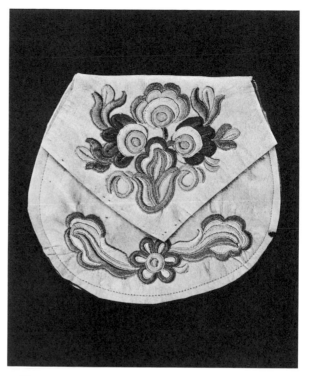

33

34

## 34 *Pocket*

Cree or Cree-Métis, Norway House style, 1890–1910

June Bedford collection

L: 28 cm  W: 18 cm

87–133

Six-sided; of bleached caribou hide with hand-pinked edges, machine-stitched to backing and lining of off-white plain-weave cotton. Embroidered with silk thread in buttonhole stitch with rosettes, leaves, curly wisps and floating berries. Thread colors: reds, pink, purple, plum, maroon, violet, blues, greens, and golds. Thin black ink lines of design occasionally show.

It was common for parts for a jacket (yoke, placket, cuffs, pockets) to be embroidered as a set. Some of these shapes could be used in other ways as well. This embroidered pocket could have been used as a jacket pocket (see cat. 32) or made into a pouch or wall pocket.

Compare with embroidered jacket parts APM H66.233.174, Darby collection, 1880–1910; and wall pouch MMMN H4.12.223, ca. 1910.

35

## 35 *Cushion Cover*

Cree or Cree-Métis, Norway House style,
1890–1910

June Bedford collection

L: 40.5 cm    w: 38.5 cm to 40.5 cm

87–132

Bleached caribou hide embroidered with silk thread in buttonhole stitch. Large central composite floral motif of rosette, buds and leaves, and narrow border of same. Thread colors: shades of red, pink, blue, green, lavender, purple and grey. Remnants of paper-support on back of hide.

Ornamented cushions, shelf valances, and wall pockets were used in native households as well as sold to visitors.

Compare with cushions MMMN H4.33.10, and GAI AP 2383, Cree, Bannerman collection.

## 36 *Moccasin*

Lake Winnipeg Saulteaux-Métis, Cree-Métis, 1909?

June Bedford collection

L: 25.5 cm

87–131

Single; pointed toe, of smoked hide, with T-shaped heel seam, straight central toe-seam; hand-pinked low cuff of lightly smoked hide; vamp of unsmoked hide bordered along upper edge with same, and along vamp edge with seven rows of thread-wrapped horsehair in aqua-faded-to-grey, red, pink, and maroon. Vamp embroidered with a crest in red, yellow, gold and aqua-faded-to-grey silk thread in buttonhole stitch; date 1606 in black thread in chain stitch.

The significance of the crest is unknown. The style of the piece is that prevalent around Lake Winnipeg at the turn of the present century. If the other (missing) moccasin contained a mirror image of the date on this piece, one could speculate that the moccasins were made to commemorate the opening date, 1909, of the Peguis Reserve on the southwestern shores of Lake Winnipeg in the Manitoba Interlake. The band had been located on Netley Creek along the Red River just north of present-day Selkirk since about 1790. At the

36

beginning of the twentieth century, developers and railroad interests wished to obtain the Netley Creek Reserve land, and largely through pressure from these interests the community was moved to the shores of Lake Winnipeg. Only the church, St. Peter's Dynevor, and a cemetery, in which rests the grave of Chief Peguis, remain at the original site.

37

## 37 *Gauntlets*

Cree or Cree-Métis, The Pas, Manitoba, early
twentieth century

Collected by Robert Colonna in The Pas, Manitoba,
1930

L: 39 cm    W: 23 cm

77–113

Smoked moose hide, embroidered with silk thread in
buttonhole stitch, lined with grey flannel, edged with
trimmed beaver fur. Large layered profile blossoms with
centers showing and expanded calyx and tiny pointed leaves

along edges, in graduated shades of rose, pink, orange and
lavender, with medium greens, chartreuse and blue.

Blossoms, expanded in profile rather than concentrically, show a variation of the concentrically expanded
motifs familiar on Norway House style examples, and
sometimes appear on gauntlets. The expanded calyx
and tiny pointed leaves are seen on other examples
from the northwest coast of Lake Winnipeg.

Compare with gloves: PS E27395, Cree, collected by Frank
Speck; LFG 3836, Cree-Chipewyan, Anderson collection,
1894–1901.

## 38 *Moccasins*

Cree or Cree-Métis, Norway House style, ca. 1900

Miriam Carreker-Burges Johnson collection,
acquired New Mexico, 1920–35

L: 25 cm   w: 14 cm

86–260

38

Soft sole, pointed toe; of tanned, smoked caribou hide, with
T-shaped heel seam and straight front seam. Double vamp
of smoked hide underneath and unsmoked hide above; low
cuff of unsmoked hide. Both upper vamp and cuff embroidered in silk thread, buttonhole stitch. Vamp embroidered
with central floral motif and wide border of repeated double
chevrons; cuffs with floral motifs, in red, orange, pinks,
greens, white, blue faded to grey, and purple faded to lavender.

Compare with moccasins: PRM 1942.6.203, collected by
Blackwood 1925; AMNH 50.2-946 collected at Fort Chipewyan before 1917; St. Boniface II–71, Cree; BM 2–3063.

## Athapaskan Embroidery

Floss embroidery has never been as important to Athapaskan people as
to Cree-speakers. It was encouraged at the mission at Hay River (1910–
1920) and was practiced at some of the Great Slave Lake posts at mid-
century. There is also a small body of work from the British Columbia
Kaska, Sekani and others, where thread seems to have been used when
beads were in short supply.

39

## 39 *Moccasins*

Eastern Athapaskan type, late nineteenth century

Collected by Emma Shaw Colcleugh, possibly at
Fort Simpson, 1894

L: 25.5 cm

57–536

Soft sole, pointed toe, of smoked moose hide, with T-shaped
heel-seam and central toe-seam. Seams sewn with sinew.
Double tongue (smoked moose-hide under, unsmoked
caribou-hide upper); upper embroidered with floral spray in
chain stitch; center of blossom in buttonhole stitch. Silk embroidery thread in pinks, red, greens, blue and yellow. Bundle
of horsehair, wrapped with medium- and light-blue silk
thread, and one row of lavender and pink (now faded) four-
quill plaiting bordering the tongue. Black-wool lower cuffs
with crenelated edge; hand-pinked high cuffs and thong ties
of unsmoked caribou hide. See cat. 40.

Compare with moccasins: AMNH 50–7983, collected by Alanson Skinner, 1911; and ROM 972.306.12, possibly Northern
Manitoba, received 1922.

## 40 *Moccasins*

Central Subarctic

Collected by Emma Shaw Colcleugh at Fort
Simpson, 1894

L: 23.5 cm

57–581

*Three pairs moccasins, Fort Simpson, Mackenzie River*
(ESC: GL 46)

Soft sole, pointed toe, smoked hide, with T-shaped heel-
seam and central toe-seam. Seams sewn with sinew. Tongue
of unsmoked caribou hide embroidered with floral spray in
buttonhole stitch, stems in chain stitch. Silk floss, now faded
to shades of lavender, pale salmon, blue, light green and tan.
Three rows of wrapped horsehair in yellow, red and olive
green, and a border of purple two-quill plaiting edge the
tongue. High cuffs and thong ties of unsmoked caribou hide.

Although Colcleugh notes three pairs of moccasins collected at Fort Simpson, there are five in the collection and
only one (57–581) was noted as Colcleugh collection when
given a Haffenreffer Museum number. It is not clear which
of the remaining pairs (57–360, 57–536, 57–538, 57–566)

were collected at Fort Simpson, but all are of a type that could
well have been made there.

During the second half of the nineteenth century the
Hudson's Bay Company carried horsehair dyed in several colors. It was used to form the delicate border
along the seam where the tongue (vamp) of a moccasin
was attached to the body. Several strands of horsehair
laid along the seam were wrapped with a single strand.
The wrapping process took place as the border was
applied. At regular intervals the wrapping strand pen-
etrated the hide to form an attaching stitch. This horsehair technique replaced an earlier one in which porcupine quills were wrapped over a split bird-quill.

Frank Russell identifies a very similar pair of moccasins as "silk-worked moccasins from Grand Rapids, an
excellent example of métis art." He speaks of another
pair he collected at Fort McPherson as "made after a
métis pattern by the way of the Eskimo interpreter"
(1898: 172). It is unclear whether "métis pattern" refers
to the cut of the moccasin, the floral embroidery, or
both.

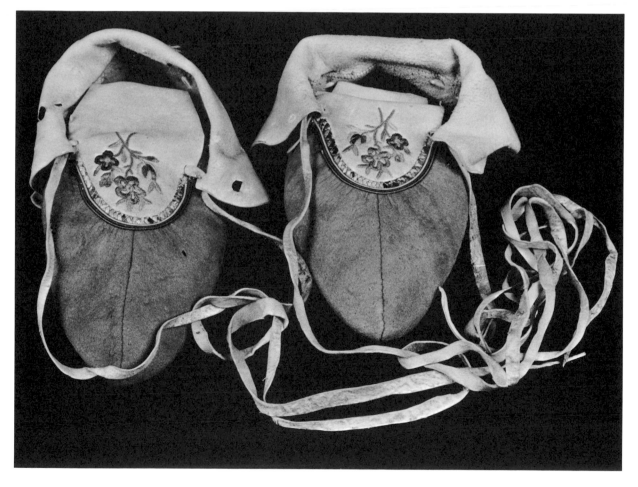

40

## 41 *Moccasins*

Dogrib, late nineteenth century

Collected by Emma Shaw Colcleugh at Fort McPherson, 1894

L: 23 cm

57–537

*Slippers made of reindeer skin, embroidered by a Dog Rib woman, wife of the trader at Fort McPherson, the most northern post of the Hudson Bay's Company, Peel River* (ESC: GL 35)

Soft sole, pointed toe, lightly smoked caribou hide; tongue and crenelated cuff of untanned, sun-bleached hide. Seams sewn with sinew. Tongue embroidered with silk thread in open chain stitch, with delicate floral spray of tiny buds, leaves and rosettes in pale salmon, blue and greens; cuffs with same, in band layout along a stem, but in satin stitch. Faceted, polished-iron beads form center of rosette petals and stem projections. Two rows of wrapped horsehair of natural and blue, and a band of four-quill plaiting in salmon, green, lavender, black and natural edge the vamp. Vamp lined with caribou hide. Ankle binding and pull-on tabs of silk ribbon in salmon color.

Tanned, unsmoked hide can be bleached even whiter by hanging it in the bright March and April sun that reflects off the snow. It is sometimes used as a contrast with darker, smoked hide. The two different thread-embroidery techniques used on this example demonstrate how technique affects the look of identical motifs. Satin stitch enhances the sheen of floss and the delicacy of motifs; chain stitch subdues the sheen and imposes onto motifs an even thickness of repeated contours. The addition of beads to thread embroidery is unusual on Subarctic examples.

Colcleugh's information on this pair of moccasins punctuates the complexities involved in understanding Subarctic embroidery. The maker was a Dogrib woman married to a Hudson's Bay trader who was most likely a non-Indian, but Colcleugh calls her Dogrib rather than métis. The woman happened to be living at Fort McPherson when the moccasins were collected, but she may have learned to embroider elsewhere, probably in a community on Great Slave Lake, and likely at a mission school, because by the late

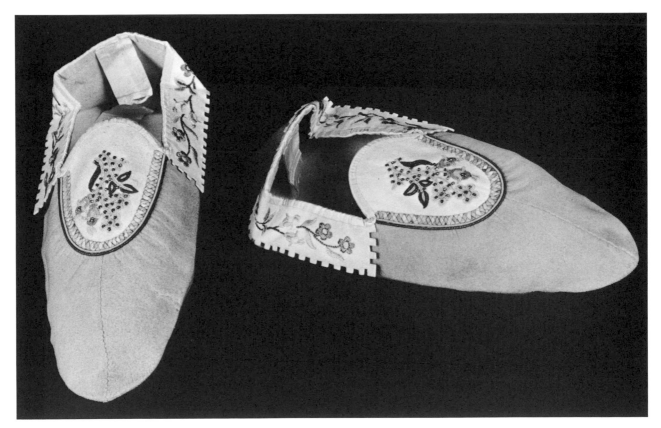

41

nineteenth century Hudson's Bay men usually sought wives among native or métis women with some education.

Compare with moccasins: MAI 18–8894, called Sekani; MMMN H40.769, Donald Campbell MacTavish collection, Central Subarctic, second-half nineteenth century.

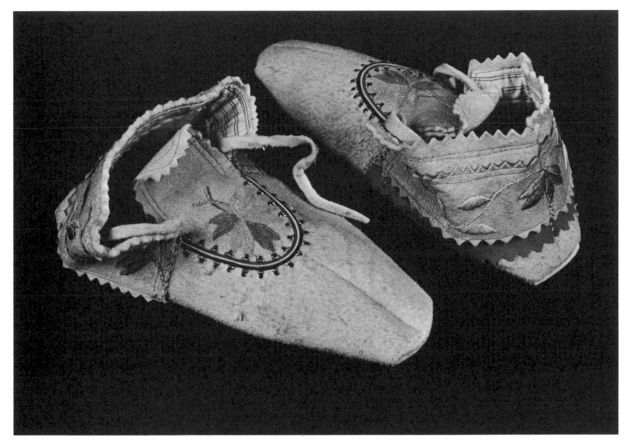

42

## 42 *Moccasins*

Sekani type, Cordillera, 1920s

Rudolf F. Haffenreffer Sr. collection

L: 24 cm    W: 13 cm

57-564

Soft sole; smoked moose hide with T-shaped heel and toe-seams. Long oval tongue hand-pinked along upper edge; low attached cuffs of hand-pinked moose hide, machine-sewn over hand-pinked red wool insert, and lined with cotton ticking. Tongue embroidered with five-part leaf using red, grey and gold single-strand thread in chain stitch. Cuffs embroidered with leaves and profile foliate forms in red, grey and gold floss in satin stitch.

These moccasins resemble thread-embroidered examples collected from the Sekani in the Liard-Frasier region in the 1920s, sharing a blunt toe (with a T or a straight seam), similar motifs and layout in vamp and cuff embroidery, and the use of accents of metal beads along the horsehair vamp edging. Single-strand embroidery using a single thin strand of thread (sometimes sewing rather than embroidery thread) has a thin, open look. It is sometimes found on Sekani, Kaska and Chilcotin work. The layered cuffs of these moccasins are unusual.

Compare with NMM VI-M-11, Sekani, McLeod Lake, 1924 and BCPM 4477, Sekani, McLeod Lake, 1920s.

# Beads

## 43 *Cartridge Bag*

Naskapi, probably early twentieth century

June Bedford collection

Bag: L: 23 cm  W: 18 cm  Strap: L: 45.8 cm  W: 1.3 cm

87–124

Round-bottomed; red wool stroud, lined and backed with tan and orange plaid fabric, edged with wool worsted braid faded from magenta to pink-tinged grey; strap and upper edge of pouch bound with red stroud; front panel embroidered with glass seed-beads, in bilaterally symmetrical floral design with geometric border; colors: opaque white, milky white, aqua, teal blue, light green; translucent royal blue, red, dark green; sinew-strung, thread-couched.

This pouch is the typical shape used by the Naskapi. Earlier pouches tend to have wider geometric borders and very simplified, angular foliate motifs. Painted cartridge pouches use the same border design, and similar double curves, but are more geometric in the central pattern. The color preference for pink, aqua and white, the layout, and the unarticulated rosettes, particularly the central star-centered one, on this type Naskapi bag demonstrate it to be an eastern relative of the James Bay Cree style.

Since the earliest historic period, the Montagnais-Naskapi people have inhabited the land mass east of Hudson and James bays in present-day Newfoundland and Quebec. Belonging to the northern or Cree branch of the Algonquian language family, these people spoke dialects of Cree and were subdivided by their location in three drainage patterns, with the Montagnais in the south, along the St. Lawrence River and Gulf; the Naskapi in the north at Ungava Bay and the North Atlantic; and the East Cree to the west, along the coast of James and Hudson bays. The East Cree were variously known as James Bay, East Main, and Mistassini Cree (Rogers & Leacock 1981: 169). Due to these Cree-Montagnais-Naskapi ties, it is not surprising to find a variant of a style popular at James Bay among the Naskapi farther east.

Compare with pouch, BRM 1921.10.4, east coast Hudson Bay, received 1921; and cartridge pouch, MAI 16-2358, collected by Frank Speck from Barren Ground band of Naskapi, Labrador with similar bead design but longer, undecorated thong straps; and shot pouch with carrying band, ROM 958.131, Barren Ground Band Naskapi, pictured in Burnham 1981: 32.

43

## 44  *Tobacco Pouch*

Labrador: Montagnais or Inuit, first half twentieth
century

Rudolf F. Haffenreffer Sr. collection

L: 13 cm    W: 10 cm

57–373

Sealskin; oval fold-over flap, thong closure, lined with muslin, thread-sewn; glass seed-beads in opaque pink, black,
white, yellow, blue; translucent yellow, green, clear and red;
sinew-strung in lazy stitch, between edges of skin cutouts in
leaf and border design.

Both this pouch and the following one have been
used to carry tobacco. They have a strong aroma, and
show heavy wear, with most of the seal fur lost.

Compare with tobacco pouch, MAI 22-5293, Romaine band,
North Shore Montagnais, Quebec, coll. by Stiles, 1957;
beaded sealskin tobacco pouches, NMM-III-C-262, III-C-130,
III-C-260, Montagnais, coll. by Speck, Seven Islands, Lake St.
John; and man's roll-up sealskin tobacco pouch, NMM IV-B-
176, Inuit, coll. by Speck, Aillik Bay, Labrador, 1914.

44

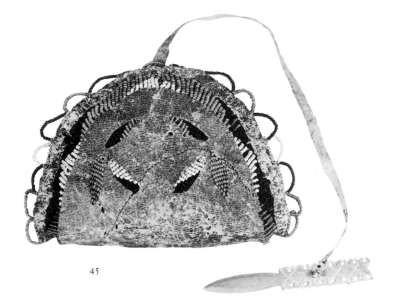

45

## 45  *Tobacco Pouch*

Montagnais or Inuit, Labrador Peninsula, first half
twentieth century

Rudolf F. Haffenreffer Sr. collection

L: 14.5 cm    W: 9 cm

60–4641

Sealskin; oval fold-over flap; lining of printed cotton paisley;
carved bone pipe cleaner and tamper attached to thong serving as closure; glass seed-beads in opaque pink, yellow, blue,
white; translucent red, dark green, yellow, clear and blue;
sinew-strung in lazy stitch between edges of skin cutouts in
leaf and border design; scalloped edge-beading. For comparative pieces, see cat. 44.

## 46 *Woman's Hood*

East Cree, James Bay type, second half nineteenth century

June Bedford collection

L: 65.5 cm (54 cm + 11.5 cm fringe) w: 27 cm

87–121

Rectangle of midnight navy stroud seamed down the back, lined with printed cotton fabric. Tassel of mixed silk thread in greens, gold, blue-green and purple at hood point. Hood beaded in three bands of floral motifs emanating from the lower hood corners, the outer narrow bands with almond-shaped buds alternating along a leafed stem, the central wider band with leaves, leafed stems, unarticulated rosettes and profile blossoms in a patterned alternation along a serpentine stem; two-beaded edging. Sinew-strung, thread-couched glass seed-beads in opaque white, green, teal, aqua, pink; translucent red and clear. Fringes along lower edge of seed-beads strung to create pattern of horizontal lines; tassles of red double-twist wool crewel yarn.

The early hoods (ca. 1840s) from the James Bay area are characterized by three bands (the center one usually wider), each with a full but delicate patterning of leaves and flowers repeated along a serpentine stem. Typical are the pairs of small almond-shaped leaves on either side of the stems ("leaf stems"), rosettes with unarticulated petals, almond-shaped buds and several profile bud forms. White, crystal, aqua and pink usually dominate against a navy or black wool ground. Tassel-ended bead fringes with the colors arranged to form a patterning of horizontal bands hang at the bottom. A thick tassel of silk thread usually hangs from the peak of each hood.

This hood shares the basic characteristics of the earlier type: design configuration, main motifs, color preferences and fringe configuration, but there are also differences which date it a bit later in the century. The design demonstrates artistic license: the central band is wider than usual, and the beadworker has filled in

"Cree, Albany." Courtesy Smithsonian Institution, National Anthropological Archives.

"The Indian women in this photograph are wearing beaded hoods, the back of which nearly touched the ground when they were standing." Fort Albany, James Bay, 1865. Courtesy Public Archives of Canada.

the rosettes, added lobes to the almond-shaped buds, and used far more green than on most hoods. The beads are also slightly larger than on earlier examples.

The floral style of early James Bay hoods appears also on octopus and panel bags from the mid-nineteenth century (see Chapter III).

Hoods were a necessary winter head and shoulder covering in the North. Worn by both men and women, many variations were in use by the late eighteenth century. In the Northeast, hoods were conical, either peaked with straight sides (Micmac, 1775, HMA 64–923) or peaked with rounded sides (Penobscot, 1860, coll. Michael Johnson, Walsall, UK). Hoods with single and double peaks were in use in Red River in the 1820s, and were recorded by Peter Rindisbacher (see painting "A Cree Hunter and His Family at Fort York," Public Archives of Canada). A rectangular hood, usually of red wool decorated with an appliquéd navy stripe, was used by Great Slave Lake–Mackenzie River Region Athapaskans in the nineteenth century.

This particular style of hood seems to have been prevalent around the Fort Albany area of James Bay in the early- to mid-nineteenth century, and to have been worn by women. The extreme length of the James Bay style hood, fully covering the wearer's back, would have helped to protect the neck and shoulders from wet snow and icy winds. It would be interesting to know more about the occasions on which they were worn, and whether they played a societal role other than as practical and beautiful head-coverings.

Compare with hoods: BirM Museum 63'61, received ca. 1890; NMM III-C-512, Tête-de-Boule, collected ca. 1890 at la Tuque, Quebec. Also earlier examples: NMM II-D-572 coll. after 1805 at Moose Factory; NMM III-D-60, mid-nineteenth century, Moose Factory; APM H64.64.34; LFG 60-59; BirM 1'75.

46

47

## 47 *Firebag*

Cree or Cree-Métis type, third quarter nineteenth century

Rudolf F. Haffenreffer Sr. collection

L: 24.5 cm   W: 17.5 cm

60–4586

Round-bottomed pocket of black wool broadcloth, lined with cotton twill and bound with navy silk ribbon and single-beaded edging (yellow, white); red and white wool yarn pompons. Front of pouch and back extension densely and precisely beaded with fluid floral sprays in opaque pinks, greens, crystals, aqua, blue and yellow; glass seed-beads strung on sinew and couched with thread.

Compare with firebag MCC M973.68.3, MacLean collection, possibly from Fort Chimo, which shows a similar evenness and precision in the use of tiny seed-beads.

## 48 *Firebag with Woven Panel*

Cree or Cree-Métis type, mid-nineteenth century

HMA purchase 1987

L: 43 cm including fringe   W: 19 cm top panel, 31 cm bottom panel including fringe

87–142

Black wool broadcloth pouch, beaded on both sides in symmetrical floral sprays with delicately detailed motifs, above bead panel woven in geometric pattern; striped cotton lining. Pouch edged with black silk ribbon and white two-beaded edging. Warp and weft threads of woven panel extend to become bead-strung fringes with tassels of red wool. Glass seed-beads sinew-strung and thread-couched; colors are opaque greasy yellow, blues, white, pink, greens; translucent dark green, plum, blue, orange, lavender, gold and crystal. Four beaded rosettes at top corners of bag reinforce and decorate areas where grosgrain-ribbon carrying straps are attached to inner side.

The complexity of the lower woven panel and the small beads date this to the mid-nineteenth century.

Decorated pouches were used by nineteenth century Subarctic Indian and métis men to carry shot for their guns, hold flint and steel for fire-making, and safeguard precious pipe tobacco. In different regions they have been variously called shot pouches, firebags, and tobacco pouches. They were also used by non-Indians (see p. 185).

48

This type of bag was illustrated in a sketch by Frank Blackwell Mayer in 1851, entitled "Winter dress of Red River half-breeds."

## 49 *Firebag with Woven Panel*

Cree or Cree-Métis type, mid-nineteenth century

June Bedford collection

L: 22 cm top + 14.5 cm woven panel + 7 cm
tasseled fringe w: 18.5 cm + 7 cm side fringes

87–120

Midnight-navy wool broadcloth pouch, with rectangular loom-woven panel fringed on three sides, attached to bottom. Pouch lined with striped cotton fabric, bound with black silk ribbon and white two-beaded edging. Pouch loosely beaded on both sides with stylized symmetrical foliate spray of tiny motifs. Glass seed-beads, sinew-strung and thread-couched: opaque pinks, greasy yellow; semi-translucent medium blue; translucent red, milky white; opaque white and mustard. Lower panel woven on thread in three rows of repeated rectangles with inner motifs, using beads of the same colors. Fringes of dark blue, white, translucent red, medium blue, pink and black seed-beads strung to create a pattern of horizontal lines; wool crewel-yarn tassels at bottom.

This bag retains but simplifies the floral configuration of the James Bay floral style (see fig. III-1). Motifs are now small and stylized, at the ends of spindly stems, and colors are limited. The floral design shows the simplifications and stylizations that studies in visual perception predict will occur when complex designs are reproduced from memory.

Compare with octopus bags: MMMN H40.0.735, Cree, Mac-Tavish collection, 1860s–1903; PH 56-14 10/44018, received 1859; MAI 19-6214, purchased in London, called Tahltan, Alaska.

Egerton Ryerson Young, a Methodist missionary in Norway House and Berens River, Manitoba in the 1860s and 1870s, wearing a woven panel bag (from Young 1893).

49

50

## 50 *Panel Bag*

Northeast coast Lake Winnipeg Cree or Cree-Métis, circa 1900

HMA purchase 1987

L: 44 cm    W: 17.5 cm

87–148

Oval-topped pouch of black wool broadcloth with floral beadwork on both sides; woven bead panel in geometrical pattern hangs below; purple cotton lining. Pouch bound with traces of red silk ribbon and white two-beaded edging. Fringes of seed-beads strung on extensions of cotton warp threads of woven panel, and finished with tassels of red-orange wool yarn. Pouch motifs arranged differently on each side, with opaque white, medium blue, pink, yellow; cornalines; translucent light and dark rose, medium and dark green, yellow, crystal and dark blue glass seed-beads thread-strung and couched through paper. Paper pulled away to reveal wool ground.

Certain motifs are characteristic of this "Lake Winnipeg cascading lobe style": a flat-topped bell with single-line inner color change, a rosette with a pointed leaf behind each petal, cascading petals and teardrop shapes (often pink) wrapping along a rosette or stacked leaves. The style was popular for garters, legging strips and moccasins and also appears on tea cosies, ornamental panels and an assortment of other items.

At least fourteen bags with one or both sides identical or nearly identical in design to this bag are known. The colors vary but the motifs and their placement are the same. The use of a drawn pattern laid on top of the wool, then beaded through, may have encouraged multiple use of the same pattern, although nowhere else in the repertoire of Cree beadwork-through-paper is there such a large body of so closely related pieces. For each bag, two patterns were chosen from the several available and one used for each side. The geometric woven panels on some of these bags are elaborate; others, such as this one with its tiny geometric motifs dotted on a white ground, are far simpler (see discussion Chapter III).

Documentation on most pieces in this style is seldom specific but what little there is reflects the inter-tribal interaction in this region as it points primarily to the Cree-speaking communities of Norway House and Trout Lake, Manitoba but also to the Saulteaux-speaking communities of Island Lake and Berens River, Manitoba and Big Trout Lake, Ontario (see fig. III-11).

The following bags have the same floral design as cat. 50 (but variations in colors) on both sides: GAI AP 962 and AP 558; same on one side and slightly different on the other: GAI AP 1978, MMMN H4.0.738, CMC V-Z-2; slightly different on both sides: MAI 17-6924, Swampy Cree, collected at Trout Lake, Manitoba by A. Irving Hallowell, 1930; MAI 14-7431; MMMN H65.235.44 and H4.0.739.

## 51 *Wall Pocket*

Saulteaux type, late nineteenth century

Rudolf F. Haffenreffer Sr. collection

L: 28 cm    W: 17 cm

60–4587

51

Black velvet; pockets opening in two directions, lined with patterned cotton; edging and suspension loop of purple silk (now faded). Embroidered with floral sprays. Sinew-strung, thread-couched glass seed-beads in opaque yellows, blues, pink, white, green, and orange; translucent yellow, greens, crystal; white-core rose.

The flamboyance of the lower design and the use of black velvet ground are characteristic of late-nineteenth century bandolier bags from the Great Lakes Ojibwa. Touchwood Cree beadwork, which also sometimes uses a velvet ground, has a similar buoyancy.

## 52 *Octopus Bag*

Lake Winnipeg Saulteaux or Cree type, or Métis of either, east coast Lake Winnipeg, second half nineteenth century

June Bedford collection

L: 36 cm + 8 cm tassels   w: 21 cm

87–118

52

Black broadcloth, bound with black silk ribbon, white two-beaded edging; body and tabs lined with navy cotton. On each side, two small hexagonal mirrors set into rosettes of teal and rose-colored silk ribbon. Short strap of red wool-worsted braid attached on one side of underside to back shanks of mirrors. No evidence of shoulder strap; sewing at bottom of pouch body now missing; yarn fringes in blue-green, red and magenta. Bag embroidered on one side with unarticulated rosette against a large leaf, on the other with three rosettes grouped against several veined leaves. Glass seed-beads in translucent and opaque greens, pinks and golds; translucent red and teal; opaque pale blue and aqua; white-core rose.

The Ojibwa-speakers (sometimes called Saulteaux) who lived on the eastern coast of Lake Winnipeg in communities such as Berens River and Island Lake, intermarried with Cree from surrounding areas. Cree and Saulteaux influences combine on this octopus bag, suggesting that it was made in the eastern Lake Winnipeg area. The unarticulated rosette, descendant from the James Bay Cree style, joins with the flamboyant leaf typical of the Ojibwa, both on a Cree bag form.

Compare with octopus bag MCC 10072, Wabamum, Alberta, 1912.

## 53 *Octopus Bag*

Central Subarctic, Cree or Cree-Métis type, second
half nineteenth century

June Bedford collection

L: 35.5   W: 19 cm

87–116

Black broadcloth, unlined; bag bound in brown velvet ribbon,
tabs in purple silk, both with two-beaded edging. Tabs attached at bottom, no evidence of tassels. Beaded spiral circles
edged with tiny triangles where cord strap would attach, but
no evidence of cord. Both sides beaded in asymmetrical floral
sprays; center tabs on both sides with alternating tight spirals, outer tabs on one side with rosettes connected by
straight hair stems, on the other, with almond shaped motifs
connected by serpentine hair stems. Glass seed-beads in
opaque and translucent greens, blues and reds, white-core
rose, greasy yellow, yellow-orange, milky white, opaque
white, translucent taupe, and metal beads of polished, faceted
iron (now rusted) and faceted brass (somewhat deteriorated),
sinew-strung and thread-couched.

The vase design that appears occasionally on octopus bags is here but a reference. Hairs edging some
of the bud motifs are unusual but do occur elsewhere.

53

54

## 54 *Octopus Bag*

Cree or Cree-Métis type, Central Subarctic, second
half nineteenth century

June Bedford collection

L: 34 cm plus 1.5 cm hide tabs   W: 21.2 cm where
tabs attach

87–117

Black wool broadcloth lined with teal blue silk (mostly gone),
bound with purple silk ribbon and two-beaded outer edging.
Sewing at lower edge of pouch where tabs begin now missing. No evidence of tabs having ever been attached at bottom.
Both sides heavily beaded in seed-beads of slightly varying
sizes, thread-strung and thread-couched over paper. One
side beaded with large multi-layered central rosette, pointed
leaves, smaller rosettes and buds; outer tabs with rosettes
connected by double hair stems, inner tabs with hummingbirds connected by hair stems. Reverse beaded in asymmetrical sprig of multi-layered rosette with leaves, and
profile blossoms and buds emerging from the top and sides;
outer tabs with hummingbirds connected by double hair
stems, inner tabs with rosettes and buds alternated along
curving hair stems.

Compare with octopus bag ROM 969.336, Grand Rapids, Ontario; for bead design, with leggings DAM B-ce-15, East Cree.

## 55 *Jacket*

Cree, Northern Ojibwa, or Saulteaux area, Central Subarctic, circa 1900

HMA purchase 1984

L: 76 cm   W: 46 cm

84–77

Tanned moose hide, made into a jacket by splitting a shirt of the English hunting style down the middle of the front. Set-in sleeves, stand-up collar, pockets; beaded back yoke, front bib, and cuffs; sinew-sewn seams. Bib and cuffs edged with short fringes; yoke and pockets with long fringes. Collar and placket edged with navy wool worsted braid (now faded to brown) sewn on with tan thread. Sinew-strung, thread-couched floral sprays of unarticulated rosettes, multi-part serpentine leaves and tendrils in opaque pink, light green,

dark and light blues; translucent maroon, rose, dark green and gold; white-core rose. Synthetic buttons.

The frontiersman shirt, also called an English hunting shirt, was used across the north but was particularly popular at the turn of the century among Athapaskans living along the Upper Yukon River (Duncan 1989). The unarticulated rosettes, such as on this shirt, are found on material from the Cree, Northern Ojibwa and Saulteaux areas. As with some other such shirts (see HMA 87–128), an owner has transformed it into a jacket. One can speculate that as cloth shirts, which were both washable and replaceable, became more readily available, some hide shirts were converted into the more versatile jacket form.

55

## 56 *Man's Leggings*

Cree or Cree-Métis type, late nineteenth, early twentieth century

June Bedford collection (formerly Hooper, Britain)

L: 44 cm  W: 19.5 cm  FRINGES: ca. 25 cm

87–127

Smoked caribou hide, sewn with sinew and thread; straight-cut fringes inserted into hide binding at top. On each legging a narrow vertical strip backed with paper, embroidered with beads, lined with muslin. Strips embroidered with floral stem in thread-sewn glass seed-beads in opaque pink, medium green, and white; translucent greens, pink, red, gold, rose; white-core rose. Repeated pairs of faceted iron beads edge beaded strips.

Short, decorative hide leggings were worn over cloth trousers, especially by métis employees of fur trading companies in order to protect their expensive cloth trousers from wear (Conn 1982: 143). They were made by wives or commissioned from other native or métis women, and appear in collections from the Cree, Cree-Métis, Ojibwa, and Ojibwa-Métis of Manitoba and Saskatchewan, and the Sioux-Métis of North Dakota.

Compare with leggings: Oregon Historical Society 1959.35.3, and cat. 57 for a longer pair constructed from short fringed ones with extensions added along the lower edge; "half-breed" leggings of deerskin, RHF 1881.3.59, coll. Terry's Landing, Manitoba Territory 1879; leggings with fold-over self-fringed top and vertical quilled strip down center of leg, Yanktonai Dakota, RHF 1881.3.57.

56

John McKay, a Métis of Cree and Scottish descent, wearing undecorated short hide leggings over cloth trousers. Taken at Red River, Manitoba by H. L. Hime, Hind Exploring Expedition 1857–1858. Courtesy Smithsonian Institution, National Anthropological Archives.

## 57  Man's Leggings

Cree or Cree-Métis, Central Subarctic, circa 1885

Part of the outfit of a Cree chief, collected by James Houston in Alberta, 1975

L: 76 cm    W: 30 cm

80–168

Constructed by attaching a pair of shorter hide leggings above an extension of red wool stroud to which have been added panels of solid beadwork. Upper section of tanned, smoked deer hide, pieced with buffalo hide in the back; seams thread-sewn. Hide fringes attached with thread along bottom and sides of floral panel beaded on black wool. Long straps of hide for tying to belt. Floral panels (once edged with red wool worsted braid) with large, flamboyant blossoms with leaves, in sinew-strung and thread-couched glass seed-beads in opaque pink, green, aqua, gold, yellow and white; translucent greens, gold, pink, red; semi-translucent milky white; teal blues; white-core red. Lower geometric panels of white, aqua, black, and greasy yellow seed-beads, sinew-strung and thread-couched onto thick, dark-tanned hide. Stroud has been repaired by a former owner.

These leggings illustrate a pragmatic solution to a need for a pair of long leggings. They have been constructed from a pair of Cree half-leggings that have been turned upside down (the fringes would originally have hung from the top: see cat. 56. The lower beaded panels may have come from leggings or gauntlets made by a Plains Cree.

Compare with leggings, Oregon Historical Society 1959.35.3.

57

58

## 58  *Model Baby Carrier*

Cree or Ojibwa, Manitoba or Ontario, circa 1900

Rudolf F. Haffenreffer Sr. collection

L: 34 cm   W: 28 cm   DEPTH: 23 cm

60–4604

Front panels of mossbag of dark green wool broadcloth bound in brown worsted braid (now faded), lined with heavy tan cotton twill. Bag embroidered with rosettes and thistles in sinew-strung, thread-couched glass seed-beads: beads are opaque golds and pinks; translucent green, dark blue, red, crystal and charcoal; white-core rose; brass faceted beads, now corroded. Beaded panels mounted with thong stitches onto U-shaped inner wooden frame secured by seven rawhide knots to rectangular wooden board painted brown; scalloped top and oval cutout. Wooden protector bar attached to cross bar attached to back, held in place by hide thong. Hanging strap of commercial braid with black and crystal beads woven in a zigzag pattern. Strap lined with bias-cut striped light-weight fabric and tied on with hide thongs.

Both the Cree and the Ojibwa made model cradles like the larger ones in which they carried their babies (see fig. IV-4). Little girls carried their dolls in them. On this model the protector bar is large in proportion to the back panel, and the bag is truncated in length. The use of the board as a backing was not common west of Manitoba. In Saskatchewan the Cree, like the Athapaskans, placed their babies in soft moss bags without boards (Brasser 1987).

Compare with board baby carrier, Amerind 1209.

"Woman carrying baby. Chippewa, Saulteaux, Long Lac, Ontario."
Courtesy Museum of the American Indian, Heye Foundation.

"Woman and child. Northern Saulteaux, Fort Hope, Keewatin."
Photo by Alanson B. Skinner, 1910–1913. Courtesy Museum of the American Indian, Heye Foundation.

## 59 Trade Beads

European, probably early-to mid-nineteenth century

Collected by Emma Shaw Colcleugh, Winnipeg, Canada, 1888–94

BEAD DIAM: 0.8 cm  STRAND LENGTH: 140 cm

57–392

*Beads used in the early days of barter by the Hudson's Bay traders. Found in an old warehouse in Winnipeg and given me by one of the old-timers in the Company's service* (ESC: NB 94)

Three strands large, drawn glass tubular beads with unmodified ends, six-sided, corners ground off, translucent deep blue; strung on cloth.

These early cornerless hexagonal beads have variously been called "Russian beads," "Ambassador beads," and "Hudson's Bay beads." Highly desired by the native people of the Alaskan coast and northwestern interior, they were circulated in trade by the Russian trading colonies in Alaska; however, there is no evidence to support a Russian origin. A smaller size of this bead has been found on Bohemian sample cards from Jablonec that date to 1870; the large ones might also have been manufactured in Bohemia. Trade lists have shown that the Russians bought many of their goods from American and British traders. By 1811 Russian traders were buying from the American Fur Company of John Jacob Astor, and by 1839 from the Hudson's Bay Company (Francis 1988: 39ff). It is likely that the major fur-trading companies supplied these large beads to the Russians for their trade, as well as directly supplying the native populations of the Northwest, western Subarctic and Plains with beads in exchange for beaver pelts, bison hides, and other goods.

59

## 60 *Firebag*

Great Slave Lake-Mackenzie River Region,
Athapaskan or Athapaskan-Métis type, late
nineteenth century

Collected by Emma Shaw Colcleugh at St. Peter's
Reserve, Red River, Manitoba, 1888–94

L: 26.7 cm  W: 16.3 cm

57–453

*Half-breed Fire bag. St. Peter, Red River, Manitoba*
(ESC: GL 23)

Black velvet bordered with black silk ribbon, white two-beaded edging. Beaded on both sides with floral sprays, one issuing from cup-like vase, in sinew-strung, thread-couched glass seed-beads in pinks, white-core rose, greens, blues, reds, mustard, yellow, milky translucent white, translucent gold, and faceted brass and faceted polished iron beads, the latter mostly rusted. Fringes of round blue, black and bronze faceted beads strung on cotton thread, ending in large pressed black beads. Holes for braided silk thread strap (missing) outlined with thread in buttonhole-stitch.

Firebags were used by men for carrying flint and steel for fire-making and later for carrying shot and in some areas, tobacco. An ornamented firebag was a possession of value and intense pride. In general, central Subarctic firebags show less wear than those from farther west, and were probably carried more for show than use.

The motifs, varied motif size, color shading, and placement of metal beads on this bag are all typical of the Great Slave Lake-Mackenzie River Region style, as is the preference for black velvet. The large center rosette with the center broken by segmenting so as to maintain a balance of internal scale is most often seen on dog blankets of the region. That the bag was acquired at Red River is not unusual because some of the métis of the Great Slave Lake area had relatives there. Employed as boatmen along the waterways between Lake Winnipeg and Great Slave Lake, métis and their possessions moved about over a wide area. Colcleugh may have obtained the bag when she attended the "Treaty Day" at St. Peter's Reserve in 1888. Such social gatherings attracted native and métis people from many places.

Compare bags: AMNH 50-3930, Mackenzie River, collected by Stone before 1902; GAI AC 115, Slavey, Goodsell collection; McC M3342 Loucheux, Fort McPherson; NMM VI-Z-210, Fort Resolution, collected by P. W. Bell, 1860–68 (Thompson 1983: 39).

60

## 61 *Tobacco Pouch*

Great Slave Lake-Mackenzie River Region
Athapaskan or Athapaskan-Métis type, late
nineteenth century

Collected by Emma Shaw Colcleugh at Fort
McMurray, Athabasca River, 1894

L: 18 cm   W: 13 cm

60–4589

*Tobacco pouch, French half-breed, Fort McMurray*
(ESC: GL 13)

Two panels of black velvet, lined with cotton twill, bound with red ribbon; silk thread drawstring and tassels. Beaded on both sides with floral sprays, one issuing from pitcher-type vase, in sinew-strung, thread-couched glass seed-beads, in opaque greens, pinks, blues, yellows, milky whites, white-core rose, and translucent gold; faceted, polished iron (now rusted) beads.

The beading is typical of the Great Slave Lake-Mackenzie River region, but the pouch differs from most of the region's tobacco pouches in that it is constructed without a narrow side strip connecting the front and back, and the drawstring is placed in the upper edge binding rather than in a channel sewn below the upper edge. Cree, Chipewyan, and métis of both groups lived at Fort McMurray. The bead motifs and color choices are similar to that of cat. 60, suggesting that both may have been embroidered by the same woman.

Frank Russell (1898: 174) who collected a similar pouch (UI 10,888) at Fort McPherson between 1892–94, speaks of tobacco pouches and firebags together, saying "Each of these contains flint, steel, touch-wood, a small quantity of plug tobacco and a medium-sized pocket knife."

Compare also with bags: BrM 1949.AM.6.5, Heard Collection, 1889–96; BrM Q.83.AM.292; LFG 4033, Yellowknife, received in 1921 from Anderson; McC M4984, Dogrib(?), Learmont collection.

61

## Items Made for Sale to Visitors

An examination of the Colcleugh and other museum collections make it clear that in nineteenth century Athapaskan communities there were fewer items designed specifically for sale to visitors than in communities around Lake Winnipeg; most Athapaskan bead embroidery was made for Athapaskan use. A limited number of small wall pockets and watch pockets such as cats. 62, 63, 64 are an exception.

62

## 62 *Watch Pocket*

Hare or Hare-Métis, 1890s

Collected by Emma Shaw Colcleugh at Fort Good Hope, 1894

L: 14 cm    w: 11 cm

57–452

*Watch pocket Fort Good Hope, Mackenzie River where it crosses the Arctic circle, ornamented by beads and quill work* (ESC: GL 29)

Small; black velvet bound with cerise silk ribbon and two-beaded edging, lined with cotton. Strip of violet, yellow, green and natural porcupine quills woven on thread and attached to hide. Glass seed-beads in opaque pinks, yellow, mustard, greens, blues; white-core rose; translucent gold, and faceted, polished iron beads (now rusted), sinew-strung and thread-couched in a Great Slave Lake-Mackenzie River Region style floral design. The combination of quill and beadwork is uncommon in this area.

63                                                    64

## 63 *Watch Pocket*

Slavey or Slavey-Métis, 1890s

Collected by Emma Shaw Colcleugh at Fort
Simpson, 1894

L: 12 cm   w: 10 cm

60–4588

Black velvet, bound with pink silk (now faded) and outer
two-beaded edging, lined with cotton, backed with wool.
Beaded on one side in Great Slave Lake-Mackenzie River
Region style with sinew-strung, thread-couched glass seed-
beads in blues, pink, white-core rose, yellow, mustard, green,
white, clear; faceted, polished iron beads (now rusted).

Compare with watch pockets: NLM no number, Slavey, Hay
River, 1903–09; GAI AC 378, Slavey, Hay River, 1896–1908,
Rusler Collection.

## 64 *Watch Pocket*

Slavey or Slavey-Métis, 1890s

Collected by Emma Shaw Colcleugh at Fort
Simpson, 1894

L: 15 cm   w: 11 cm

57–449

*Watch pocket, Fort Simpson* (ESC: GL 30)

Black velvet bound with red silk and two-beaded edging,
lined with cotton, backed with wool. One side beaded in
Great Slave Lake-Mackenzie River Region style with sinew-
strung, thread-couched glass seed-beads in opaque pinks,
greens, blues, clear, yellow; white-core rose; faceted brass,
and faceted, polished iron beads (now rusted).

The motifs on this tiny pocket are unusual in the use
of split color on some petals.

## 65 *Woman's Leggings*

Great Slave Lake-Mackenzie River Athapaskan or
Athapaskan-Métis type, late nineteenth century

Obtained by Rev. Frederick Hugh Tatum in Canada
while serving as an incumbent to the parish of St.
Luke at Broadview, Saskatchewan. HMA purchase
1987.

L: 36.5 cm    W: 49 cm

87–149

Rectangular, with notches at the lower corners, of "super
fine" (very fine melton) black wool broadcloth, lined with
muslin, bound with black silk ribbon and single-beaded inner
and two-beaded outer edging, both in white seed-beads.
Wool extensions along upper edge may have been added
later. Ornamented with a band of white triangles below a
symmetrical floral spray of sinew-strung, thread-couched
glass seed-beads in opaque pinks, greens, blue, yellow,
white, and lavender, and translucent greens, crystal, red and
light blue; cornalines; faceted brass and faceted, polished
iron beads.

Elaborately embroidered leggings were worn on
special occasions such as weddings and New Years'
dances. The decorated area, only around the cuff,
showed discreetly below the hemline of a woman's
dress.

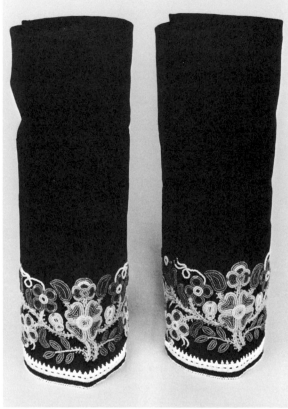

65

66

## 66 *Garter*

Great Slave Lake-Mackenzie River Region
Athapaskan or Athapaskan-Métis, late nineteenth
century

June Bedford collection

L: 36 cm  W: 4.5 cm

87–125

Midnight-blue stroud edged with plaid cotton fabric and
white, thread-sewn two-beaded edging; beaded in Great

Slave Lake-Mackenzie River style with sinew-strung, thread-
couched glass seed-beads in pink, crystal, teal, red, greasy
yellow; translucent pink, green, and gold; remnant of yarn
pompon of pink and red wool attached directly to hide; black
elastic band.

Athapaskan garters are far less common in collections than Cree ones.

## 67 Moccasins

Hare or Hare-Métis, late nineteenth century

Collected by Emma Shaw Colcleugh at Fort Good Hope, 1894

L: 24 cm

57–534

*Slippers made of moose skin, Fort Good Hope, Mackenzie River* (ESC: GL 45)

Soft-sole, pointed toe, of tanned smoked moose hide with T-shaped heel seam and straight front seam. Black velvet vamp edged with four rows of horsehair wrapped with horsehair dyed gold, lavender, red and green. Symmetrical floral design on vamp in sinew-strung, thread-couched glass seed-beads in greens, pink, mustard, yellow, aqua; white-core rose; transparent gold; faceted brass and faceted, polished iron beads (now rusted). Crenelated red-wool stroud cuffs attached at ankle with chartreuse silk ribbon. Loops of black wool twill braid attached at inner back seam to help when pulling the moccasin on.

Pointed-toe moccasins were at one time widespread in the eastern Athapaskan area. The Kutchin called them "sharp moccasins." In the twentieth century they have been replaced by a soft-sole moccasin with a large tongue and no center toe seam.

Athapaskan women have often referred to certain motifs by using identifying names descriptive of forms they resemble. Elderly women of Fort Simpson, southeast of Fort Good Hope, remember the double-circle bud being called "spider bump" and the tiny stem projections "pickerel guts" (Duncan 1982). Kutchin bead-workers call the same motifs "beaver castor" and "mice running" (Duncan and Carney 1988).

Compare with slippers, UBC A2.18

67

## Ornamented Sled Dog Gear

A set of "garnished" dog blankets or "tapies" (tupies) and ornamented standing irons allowed a dog runner to flash into a post in a cacophony of color and sound. Blankets were either beaded or embroidered with wool or floss. Beaded examples are more common in museum collections, and most come from the Great Slave Lake-Mackenzie River area, although paintings by Peter Rindisbacher and Paul Kane and old photographs picture them in use among the Cree.

Louis Mercredi, a Chipewyan-Métis, ran dogs for the Hudson's Bay Company for many years beginning about 1910, carrying district managers from post to post around Great Slave Lake. He sometimes used sets of ornamented blankets. His first set was made by his first wife and later sets were bought from other people. All were embroidered with wool rather than beads which were "too expensive." In 1982 Louis, then in his nineties, talked about dog running and fancy dog gear (Mercredi, pers. comm. 1982).

I used to travel about forty miles sometimes, you know, in crossing (Great Slave Lake) . . . . a dog pulling a passenger, you cannot go more than five miles an hour or six. (In a day) thirty-five, forty miles, that's the most. Forty-five the most. That's when they have good going.

You don't use all the time the dog blanket on the dog. When they go into town, you want to decorate yourself and you decorate the dogs. You want to put a different handkerchief on your neck. On the dog you have a blanket, too! Then, when you leave there, then after you're gone, leave town, well, then you take them off and put them in the bag again. So you take it to the next town. But the standing iron stays there (on the dog).

Nineteen-twenties—them days everybody had dogs. That's a car. Wherever they go, they've got five dogs or four dogs. If they're big dogs they'll use four. If they're small dogs, well, they'll use five. They used to be proud. . . . of a team of dogs. Like if you have a good car you're proud of your car. You shine it up all the time. Well, if a guy had a team of dogs he used to buy nice new traces, they don't patch up a harness at all. It's got to be new ones in the fall.

You don't use the blankets all the time. . . . too heavy. If the dog sweats with the blanket over him, then he's going to stop, then he gets cold. Then he can't lay down and curl up with his blanket on him, so we generally take the blanket off, so when we stop, why it can curl up and warm itself up.

"Dog team and carriole, Fort Chipewyan, Treaty Number 8." C. C. Sinclair coll. 1898. Courtesy Manitoba Provincial Archives.

The standing iron, an iron projection attached to the round, hide-covered neck piece of the dog harness, rose above the animal's neck. Most were wrapped or plaited over with multicolored yarn and topped with a multicolored yarn pompon. Ribbons and fox tails were often attached to flutter in the wind. Mercredi depended on his dog Stanley who wore a standing iron ornamented with multicolored ribbons about a foot long.

Stanley had it on. When I traveled on a meat leg, that's my compass. See when I leave the camp I know where north and east is and stuff like that. Then I know it, what it is, it's gonna blow from the east. But when I leave the camp and I don't know where I'm supposed to go, well I follow that ribbon. (The ribbon blows) toward me, see? I go in too much, well, it goes in too, instead of going away from it. So I gotta straighten up my dogs and go this way a little more.
  You can tell right away when you're blown off the compass. Any way, your ribbon moves, this way or that way, see you got to judge yourself to guide your dogs. . . . They don't believe me but that's my belief and I never got lost on a leg. Doesn't matter how stormy it is. You couldn't see anywhere at all except the ribbon there.

69

68

## 68  *Sled Dog Blanket*

Great Slave Lake-Mackenzie River Region Slavey
or Slavey-Métis type, fourth quarter nineteenth
century

Collected by Emma Shaw Colcleugh at Fort
Simpson, 1894

L: 45 cm  w: 45 cm

60–4527, 61–453 (bells)

*Very old beaded dog blanket like those in use through all
the Mackenzie district* (ESC: NB 178); *Dog blanket used
for the sledge dogs in the north* (ESC: GL 1)

Floral sprays of buds, bells, berries and blossoms emerging
from a large rosette in each corner. Designs on two front and
two rear corners alike. Beaded in glass seed-beads strung on
sinew and couched with thread onto black wool, in opaque
pink, light and medium green, light and medium blue, white,
yellow, pearl; translucent pinks, crystal and yellow; faceted
brass and faceted, polished iron beads (mostly rusted).
Bisecting center strip of scalloped, crenelated green wool
fabric over red wool fabric; center strip bordered with black
wool-twill braid and white single-beaded edging. Large
sleigh bells on commercial leather strip now detached from
central strip. Blanket bordered with red wool twill braid and

white single-beaded edging; remnants of wool yarn fringes
in blocks of reds, yellows and blues border blanket and central strip. Blanket backed with buff plain-weave fabric.

Of conventional form and in beading typical of
others from the Great Slave Lake-Mackenzie River
region, this blanket had been well used by the time that
Colcleugh acquired it. Worn away fringes are common
on heavily used blankets. Other blankets of the set to
which this belonged would have had identical fringes
and center handling, and related but different floral
designs on each. When worn, the unfringed area in the
center of one side of the dog blanket fell along the
animal's neck and the bells crossed over its back. Large,
heavy bells such as these or a smaller, lighter type were
common. Blankets were tied to the dog harness by
means of thongs attached to circles of hide on the
underside corners.

Compare with turn-of-the-century sets and single blankets:
AMNH 50-3921–3924, Mackenzie River; MᶜC 927.1.8.1–2,
Mackenzie River; MᶜC 955X 111.1–4, Dogrib or Slave, Great
Slave Lake; MAI 22-4523; LFG 4135–4136, Great Slave Lake-
Mackenzie River area.

## 69 Pompon From Standing Iron

Great Slave Lake-Mackenzie River Region Slavey or
Slavey-Métis type, late nineteenth century

Collected by Emma Shaw Colcleugh at Fort
Simpson, 1894

L: 22 cm plus ribbons 25cm   W: 6.5 cm

57–299

*Pompon used to ornament dog harness* (ESC: NB 179);
*Ornament used on the dog sledge* (ESC: GL 2)

Wool yarn in red, maroon, lavender, purple, grey and white
(discolored to yellow), tufted onto stuffed cotton form and
wrapped around lower section of iron rod with attaching
crescent. Twelve navy, yellow, maroon and pale and medium
green silk ribbons tied on with hide thong.

While the blanket lay sparkling but static on the sled
dog's back, the puff and flutter of color of the standing
iron rose from the harness neck-piece, bouncing to the
gait of the running dog, in cadence with the rhythmic
jangling of his harness and blanket bells. The dog runner's whip was also ornamented, usually with a carved
and painted handle hung with ribbons.

Standing-iron pompons are elongated or spherical;
the iron piece for connection to the harness varies in
configuration.

Compare with other examples: McC 927.1.7, Todd collection,
and 966 XI11.5–6; LFG HBC 38–101 A–E; and several at NLM.

## 70 Pouch, Camera Case

Great Slave Lake-Mackenzie River Region
Athapaskan type, circa 1900

June Bedford collection

L: 23.5 cm   W: 16 cm   D: 3.5 cm

87–126

Sealskin (hair now gone) sewn with sinew and lined with
white duffle. Skin loops at side for attachment of a carrying
strap. Decorative panel, bead-embroidered in the Great Slave
Lake-Mackenzie River Region style, bound in brown
polished cotton and attached to the front. Remnants of ermine edging. Floral beadwork in glass seed-beads in opaque
medium green, pinks, gold, greasy yellow, blues, teal, white;
two shades white-core rose; translucent green, gold; faceted
brass and faceted, polished iron beads.

This case was probably constructed on the lower
Mackenzie, by a woman who had access to both
sealskin and Athapaskan beadwork typical of the region. The thick duffle liner would have helped protect
a camera from the lens condensation and brittleness of
film that are a problem when photographing at below-
zero temperatures.

Compare with more recent camera case of same size and
shape, which contains Jiffy Kodak camera, PWNHC 986.51.4
A & B.

70

## 71 *Octopus Bag*

Great Slave Lake-Mackenzie River Region
Athapaskan type, 1870
Collected by Emma Shaw Colcleugh, 1894
L: 48 cm   W: 25.5 cm

57-462

*Firebag given me in 1894 by an old Hudson Bay trader for
whom it was made by an Eskimaux woman 24 years
previous* (ESC: GL 9)

Tabbed; beaded on both sides with related symmetrical floral
arrangements of rosettes, berries and occasional buds on
each side issuing from a tiny vase. Glass seed-beads in
graduated shades of pink, green and blue; crystal, dark red,
white-core rose, translucent yellow, faceted brass and faceted, polished iron beads, sinew-strung and thread-couched
onto black wool broadcloth. Navy ribbon border with sinew-
strung, two-beaded edging; loops of large black seed-beads
and grey-white pony beads at ends of tabs; cotton print
pocket and tab lining.

The tabbed bag, called an octopus bag in reference
to its four pairs of tabs, was popular among the Cree
and Cree-Métis particularly during the second half of
the nineteenth century. It was introduced by them
across the Northern Plains, and by the 1880s had
reached the Tlingit of the Northwest Coast. Just a few
octopus bags can be associated with the Athapaskans
(see Chapter III).

Style characteristics suggest that this bag was made
by a woman working in a combined Athapaskan-Cree
tradition. It is unique in several ways. Compared to
Woodland Cree octopus bags with rounded tops, it is
unusually long in the body. The beading combines
meticulous precision and dominance of small, similar-
scale motifs, both characteristic of much Cree work,
with the use of metal or red beads at the center of the
outer color layer on petals and at the tips of tendrils, a
trait typical of Athapaskan beadwork of the Great
Slave Lake-Mackenzie River Region. Red beads replacing metal ones appear on other lower Mackenzie
River examples from the same period. The emphasis
on a few simple repeated motifs rather than a range of
different ones constructed by elaboration of elements
onto a core element is more typical of Athapaskan
work peripheral and west of the Great Slave Lake Region. The importance of darker blue beads here is unusual, although they appear also on a group of pieces
collected in the same area slightly later (Conroy collection, 1911, NMM).

71

Cree wives of Hudson's Bay personnel were instrumental in the introduction of floral seed-bead embroidery to Fort McPherson, and Hudson's Bay wives
socialized and sewed together (Duncan and Carney
1988). The maker of this bag could have been the
Eskimo wife of a Hudson's Bay man who joined other
Hudson's Bay wives in sewing together or, more
likely, a Loucheux woman.

Compare with octopus bags NMM VI-Z-196, ROM 969.336; and
MAI 19-6592 (called Woodland Cree, purchased London, no
information) for bag proportions, and with the range of Great
Slave Lake-Mackenzie River Region beadwork for floral patterning.

## 72 *Smoking Cap*

Great Slave Lake-Mackenzie River Region, Athapaskan or Athapaskan-Métis type, late nineteenth century

June Bedford collection

H: 8 cm   DIAM: 14.5 cm

87–122

72

Black velvet lined with quilted black fabric. Remnants of flour-and-water paste used for drawing on design. Glass seed-beads, both sinew- and thread-strung, and thread couched, in pinks, white-core rose, translucent red, translucent and opaque greens and blues, pearl white, greasy yellow and translucent milky white; faceted brass and faceted polished iron beads. Top of hat beaded with large central rosette surrounded by smaller rosettes, leaves and buds on "hair stems;" sides with two leafed rosettes alternated with rosettes with projecting stems with berries. Twist of two strands of beads along upper seam.

The mixed scale of motifs and color accents in the outer petal color layer on the rosettes of this cap are characteristic of Great Slave Lake-Mackenzie River Region Athapaskan beadwork.

The man's embroidered smoking cap was popular in Victorian times. Patterns for them appeared in women's magazines and were available from Briggs Transferring Papers. Subarctic women enjoyed ornamenting clothing for their men and produced a variety of headwear for them.

Smoking caps were also used by the Northern Ojibwa. Cree and eastern Athapaskan versions were thread-embroidered or beaded with multi-colored floral designs. A version beaded solely in metal beads developed among the Kutchin (Duncan 1989).

Compare with smoking cap NMNH 221376, west coast Hudson's Bay, before 1903.

"Fort Good Hope Indians and Hudson's Bay Company interpreters." Photo by Elizabeth Taylor, 1892. Courtesy James Taylor Dunn.

## 73 Baby Belt

Probably Slavey, late nineteenth century

Collected by Emma Shaw Colcleugh at Fort Simpson or Fort Norman, 1894

L: 110 cm   W: 8 cm at widest section

57-465

*Fort Norman, Mackenzie River. Strap used by the Louchoux women as blanket support for holding child* (ESC: GL 14); *Louchoux Indian carrying strap. Used by Indian women of different tribes to help support the weight of the child they carry on their backs. Fort Simpson-Mackenzie River 1894* (ESC: NB 202)

Tapered at ends, of navy wool fabric beaded in pattern of pointed-petal rosettes alternated with pairs of leaf and bell forms, four alternately facing spirals at either end. Glass seed-beads in opaque white, blues, pink, yellow, mustard; white-core rose; translucent green; strung on sinew, couched with thread.

The people of both Fort Norman and Fort Simpson are Slavey. At one time baby belts were widespread in the Great Slave Lake-Mackenzie River region. A few are made by Slavey women today (see cat. 152) and they were definitely used in Slavey communities at the turn of the century. Colcleugh's association of the baby belt with the Loucheux (Eastern Kutchin) is interesting, however, in that most photographs showing them in use are of Kutchin women (in the 1920s and 30s) and today it is Loucheux women who still make them for use (Duncan 1989).

The design on this belt, with its large simplified motifs and fat colored point accents suggests that it was made by a woman who was not in close contact with the prescribed version of the regional style. Nor is it typical of Loucheux work. Alternating tight spirals such as those used here are common on Great Slave Lake area leggings, particularly from the Dogrib, and unusual on baby belts.

Compare with baby belts: AMNH 50-3905, Liard River, 1902; GAI AP 2539, called Cree-Ojibwa(?); APM H73.55, for spirals.

Mother with child supported by carrying belt, Fort McPherson, Northwest Territories, 1928. Photo by Lachlan T. Burwash. Courtesy Public Archives of Canada, Ottawa

74

## 74 *Moss Bag for a Doll*

Central Subarctic Athapaskan or Athapaskan-Métis type, late nineteenth century

June Bedford collection

L: 29.5 cm   W: 13.5 cm

87–123

Black wool broadcloth lined with plain-weave cotton and bound at edges with blue silk ribbon; tanned hide thongs. Floral stem on each side of sinew-strung and thread-couched glass seed-beads: pinks, greens, crystal, dark blue, translucent blue, white-core rose. No evidence of use.

Small babies were diapered with moss packed into a soft tanned-hide diaper, then laced snugly into moss bags. The bags were stabilized by the insertion of something stiff into the backs. A moss bag, with baby, could then be carried on the mother's back, using a cord which lay over her shoulders (Krause, pers. comm. 1982). The Cree sometimes used the bag with a cradleboard (see cat. 58) similar to that more common among the Ojibwa. The design on this small-sized bag is simpler than would be found on a full-sized bag (see fig. I-12).

Compare with moss bag: NLM uncatalogued, Hay River.

## 75 *Tobacco Pouch*

Loucheux or Eskimo, Lower Mackenzie River, late nineteenth century

Collected by Emma Shaw Colcleugh at Fort McPherson, 1894

L: 18.5 cm   W: 8.5 cm

57–371

*Tobacco pouch, Eskimaux, Fort McPherson, Peel River, Mackenzie Delta* (ESC: GL 15)

Hide embroidered solidly in lazy stitch on lower half of both sides. Pattern of concentric U's formed with sinew-strung glass seed-beads in pink, teal blue, and small amount of navy, black, white. Large seed- and pony-sized teal blue and white-core rose beads attached with sinew to form three-beaded edging around pouch and upper beaded extension; looped edging at opening; hide strip separating upper edging into two sections.

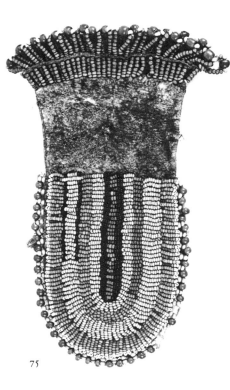

75

The few pouches of this type which have been collected come from the lower Mackenzie River and are called Athapaskan. An elderly Kutchin woman recognized the type in 1982 (Duncan and Carney 1988). But Colcleugh's Eskimo attribution suggests examining whether pouches of this type may be Eskimo rather than Athapaskan. The bead pattern is unlike that of other Kutchin work. Although the pony bead ornament of early tunics from the Kutchin provides a precedent for the use of lazy stitch, the stitch appears in seed-beads only on this type of pouch. There are, however, western Eskimo women's headpieces constructed of long vertical strands of beads arranged to create horizontal color bands and strung separated at intervals with narrow horizontal hide strips, similar to those used here. Since the Mackenzie River Athapaskan are known for their beadwork and the Eskimo of the area are not, such pouches collected from the region have been thought to be Athapaskan; however, they could have been Eskimo-made.

Compare with similar bags: MAI 19-687, Athapaskan; McC ME 930.1.21, Kutchin; LMA 2-65025.

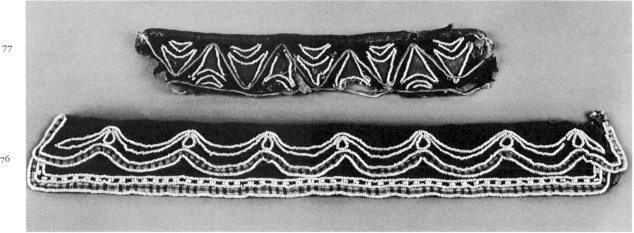

77

76

## 76 *Game Bag Fragment, Appliqué*

Dogrib, late nineteenth century

Collected by Emma Shaw Colcleugh at Fort Rae, 1894

L: 46 cm   W: 5 cm

57–515

*Band for ornamenting Dog Rib game bag (babiche destroyed by squirrels)* (ESC: GL 18)

Strip of red wool broadcloth appliquéd with black wool broadcloth cut in an open pattern of double triangles alternately reversed; triangles outlined in aqua and yellow glass seed-beads strung on sinew and couched with thread. Remnants of double row of narrow blue wool-worsted braid along upper edge and of interwoven red wool and tan cotton thread outlining triangles and along lower edge.

The width of the band and remnant of upper border on this strip are typical of front ornamental bands of Eastern Athapaskan babiche game-bags. Appliqué cutwork on babiche bags is rare (see also BCPM 6575); it appears mostly on Slavey tunics, collars, and firebags from the last quarter of the nineteenth century (Duncan 1980, 1989). The alternated triangle pattern on this remnant is unusually intricate for cutwork, but maintains the zigzag common on babiche-bag upper bands.

## 77 *Cuff Fragment, Appliqué*

Dogrib, late nineteenth century

Collected by Emma Shaw Colcleugh at Fort Rae, 1894

L: 39.5 cm   W: 5 cm

57–369

Red wool fabric appliquéd in scallops onto black velvet; lower edge bordered with blue-and-white checked cotton fabric. White seed-beads sinew-strung and thread-couched along all cut edges.

The length of the fragment and its finished stepped edges suggests that this was the lower portion of a legging. The scalloped cutwork with beaded loops is more complex than usual.

## 78 *Pouch and Strap*

Liard-Fraser Region Sekani type, Cordillera, early twentieth century

Rudolph F. Haffenreffer Sr. collection

Pouch: L: 20.5 cm  w: 17 cm  Strap: L: 56 cm w: 4.8 cm

79–62

Canvas and black wool twill, bound at edges with red stroud, printed cotton and silk ribbon; some single-beaded edging in yellow and white. Strap of red stroud bound with black-twill fabric and yellow thread-sewn, single-beaded edging of glass seed-beads; backed with faded-red polished cotton. Pouch and strap embroidered with sinew-strung, thread-couched seed-beads in opaque medium blue, yellow, greasy green, pink, with some translucent gold, translucent dark red, and opaque teal, aqua, white and milky white. Pouch central design of rosette with symmetrically projecting buds, profile flowers, and background elaboration. Strap design of tripartite foliate forms alternated with diamonds along a serpentine stem with tiny projections.

This bag shares characteristics of others from the Liard-Fraser Region. Several background materials are combined, and parts are pieced, showing economic use of sparsely available fabric. Colors are limited and stylized floral motifs are created in a free, exuberant fashion. Most characteristic is the background elaboration, where foreground motifs such as stems have suggested random non-representational contour filling-in of background space.

Compare with firebag NMM VI-M-4, Sekani, Bear Lake, collected by Teit, 1915, and firebag LFG 47-23, Liard-Fraser Region, early 20th century, for contour-filling of background; for motifs suggesting other motifs, compare with firebag NMM VI-M-2, collected 1924 by Jenness from the Sekani at Fort Grahame. See also flapped bags BCPM 10478, Sekani; BCPM 7916, MAI 1-885, collected from the Tahltan; LFG 4062 (HBC 45-79).

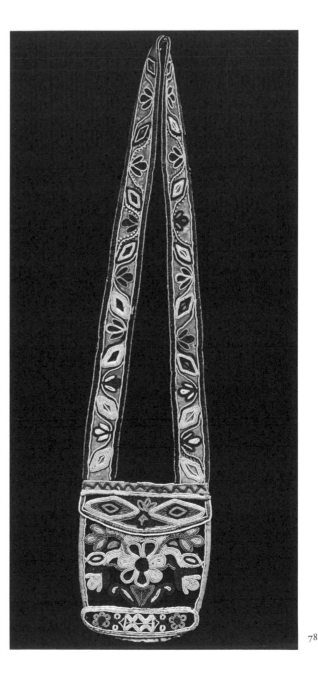

78

79

## 79 *Firebag with Woven Panel*

Cree-influenced, probably central or southern British Columbia, second half nineteenth century

June Bedford collection

L: 18 cm top, 13.5 cm woven panel, 9 cm fringe
W: 16.5 cm

87–119

Rectangular, of red broadcloth on one side, black on the other, with rectangular woven panel attached at bottom. Pouch lined with blue-green corded fabric; pouch and sides of woven panel bound with black silk ribbon on one side, blue on the other; with white two-beaded edging. Fringes of thread-strung glass seed-beads with red wool yarn tassels. Pouch beaded with eagle, deer and floral motifs on one side, and floral spray of large unarticulated rosettes, smaller round blossoms and stylized leaves on the other. Thread-strung and couched seed-beads in black, white, greens, greasy yellow, greasy green, blues, teal, aqua, pink, white-core rose, clear and translucent burgundy. Thread-woven panel of white, teal and white-core rose seed-beads forming symmetrical geometric design. No evidence of the strap usual on such bags.

The animal forms (most common on Plateau beaded bags), the exuberant experimentation with motifs and color within motifs, and the use of small triangles of beads to edge some of the motifs point to central-southern British Columbia as the most likely place of origin for this bag. Cree bands moved into British Columbia in the nineteenth century and influenced bead styles of other groups (see Chapter III). Cree-type bags were made by Thompson River, Nicola and Tahltan people in British Columbia, by some Plateau groups, and by the Tlingit of the coast. In this example a basic bag form introduced by the Cree has taken on regional characteristics.

Compare with bags: BCPM 15133; LMA 2–19525, collected 1869 by Dr. Edward Mallock in the Fort Garry area.

## 80 *Octopus Bag*

Cree influenced, Liard-Fraser Region Athapaskan or
Plains Cree, late nineteenth century

Collected by Emma Shaw Colcleugh, 1894

L: 23 cm   W: 13.7 cm

71–5007

*Used by a French Half-breed, Fort Simpson* ( ESC: GL 12)

Tabbed; beaded on both sides in different but similar bilaterally symmetrical designs of a central rosette with peripheral
rosettes, teardrop and U-shaped buds. Body of black wool
fabric bordered with maroon cotton-twill fabric and white
two-beaded edging; beaded zigzag band outlining tabs. Glass
seed-beads in semi-opaque blue-grey; opaque pinks, white,
medium blue, aqua; white-core rose; opaque and translucent
golds, reds and green, and polished iron beads, strung and
couched with thread. Tabs and pocket lined in cotton.

This bag is unusual in having three rather than the
usual four tabs on each side and in the geometric bead
patterning outlining the tabs. This, along with the im-
precise beading, the simplified semi-floral motifs, and
the addition of extra stem sections and of "hairs" to
motifs as well as stems, suggest that the bag was made
in the Liard and Fraser rivers region or bordering
Plains Cree area by a woman who had not been trained
directly in the more elaborate floral styles typical of
woodland Cree and Cree-Métis octopus bags (see also
Chapter III). That it was collected from a French half-
breed in Fort Simpson is not unusual, as both métis
and their possessions moved about a great deal
through activities in the fur trade and river-portering
system.

See cat. 78 and Duncan 1989 on Liard-Fraser beadwork
style and the relation of Beaver, Sekani and Kaska to the
Cree. Three-tabbed bags are very rare: compare with UMP
NA5800, called Alaskan Tanana, ROM HD 8615, and LFG 4087;
and for the zigzag pattern outlining the tabs, with MAI 10-
4321. Each of these bags is unique in different ways.

80

81

## 81 *Knife Case*

Tutchone, Upper Yukon River, Cordillera, late
nineteenth century
Rudolf F. Haffenreffer Sr. collection
Case: L: 28.5 cm   w: 8 cm   Strap: L: 68 cm
01–1435

Smoked moose hide; trapezoidal metal protector folded over
at case bottom. Front side of case beaded with checked horizontal band above vertical stylized foliate motif based on
central of three parallel lines. Greasy yellow, translucent
green, translucent pink-core, clear, black, and metallic
copper-coated glass seed-beads sinew-strung and thread-
couched. Two-beaded edging in pink and aqua along bag
and strap.

Typical of Upper Yukon knife cases from the late
nineteenth century, but more elaborate than usual, this
case has a solidly-beaded band across the top rather
than a sparser, more open pattern, and foliate forms
elaborating the usual vertical central bead line.

Compare with collection of Upper Yukon knife sheaths at
LMA; MAI 23-3093, Tanana; sheath worn by Dandy Jim,
Tahltan, in photograph (Helm 1981: 464).

## 82 *Gold Poke*

Upper Yukon River Athapaskan type, Alaska
Plateau, late nineteenth century

Rudolf F. Haffenreffer Sr. collection

L: 17 cm   W: 7.5 cm

57–491

Tubular, round-bottomed, of smoked moose hide, seams
sewn with sinew; lined with printed cotton; thong ties. Border of loose cross stitch in yellow and magenta thread below
opening. Both sides beaded with symmetrical stylized floral
motifs along thick central stems, using dark blue, white,
translucent pink, and faceted gun-metal iridescent glass seed-
beads, sinew-strung and thread-couched.

Late in the nineteenth century, in response to a series
of gold rushes, Indian women in the Yukon Territory
and northern British Columbia beaded "gold pokes"
for carrying gold dust. If the prospector did not return
"down below" a rich man, he could at least bring home
a token of his time up north. The motifs on this poke
show the horizontal color-splitting characteristic of
Yukon-Tanana Region designs and the freedom of design and execution typical of gold pokes.

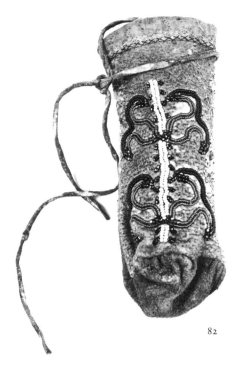

82

Compare with collection of Upper Yukon pokes, LMA and
McBride Museum, Whitehorse, Yukon Territory.

83

## 83 *Wall Pocket*

Yukon-Tanana Region Athapaskan type, Alaska
Plateau, early twentieth century

HMA purchase 1983

L: 34.5 cm   W: 20 cm

83–31

Elongated, of smoked moose hide, with two pockets lined
with black-and-white printed cotton; hanger of blue-grey
silk (tattered). Two-beaded edging in teal beads. Symmetrical semi-floral designs of central rosette or split bell with
almond-shaped leaves, three-petal centerless rosettes,
widely spread split bells, wisps and stacked leaves. Seed-
beads in opaque aqua, medium blues, pink, white and gold;
white-core rose; translucent lavender, dark green and chartreuse; semi-translucent teal and milky clear. Occasional faceted bugle bead.

At the turn of the century, wall pockets were important in both native and non-native households where
drawer space was scarce. A plain one might hang above

the wash basin to hold combs and brushes. A fancy one in the main room brightened the wall and held letters and other miscellany. This pocket exhibits characteristics typical of the Yukon-Tanana Region: beadwork couched on hide with open background, a limited number of repeated simple stylized floral motifs, especially teardrop-shaped buds and centerless rosettes, a skeletal stem network, solid-color or outlined and filled motifs, color seldom shaded on motifs, controlled color palette, color accents at points of wisps, and tiny petals (in this case, in pink and blue rather than the more common brass).

Compare with wall pocket ASM II-C-66, Han, Eagle, Alaska, 1906–14; wall pocket MAI 21-3089, Tanana, Nenana, collected between 1900–40; moccasins MAI 21-7881 and 21-8029, called Takutine (probably referring to the Tutchone), received 1951.

## 84 *Belt*

Yukon-Tanana Region Athapaskan type, Alaska Plateau, late nineteenth, early twentieth century

HMA purchase 1983

L: 96 cm    W: 7.5 cm

83–29

Lightly tanned moose hide, lined with black-and-white printed cotton, edged with loosely sewn two-beaded edging on thread. Floral design (symmetrical from center) of three separate foliate combinations of leaves, rosettes, wisps, tendrils and berries, on either side of a central rosette. Double-thread-strung, thread-couched glass seed-beads in opaque pink, green, greasy yellow, aqua and faceted black; translucent blues, dark red, dark green and chartreuse; also round brass and faceted metallic-coated glass beads.

This belt shares the style characteristics typical of Yukon-Tanana Region beadwork (see cat. 83). The tiny beads allow a lyric delicacy.

84

## 85 *Belt*

Yukon-Tanana Region Athapaskan type, Alaska Plateau, late nineteenth, early twentieth century

HMA purchase 1983

L: 74 cm   W: 4.5 cm

83–30

Heavily smoked moose hide lined with cotton muslin, three-beaded edging of medium blue seed-beads. Floral design (symmetrical from center) of simple centered and centerless rosettes, split bells, buds and leaves, in opaque dark and light blues, pink, green, greasy yellow, white and translucent dark green seed-beads; silver-colored round beads; round and faceted brass beads.

Motifs connected with a serpentine stem are more common on narrow belts from this area than are the discrete segments of cat. 84. The single-line stem is unusual, probably dictated by the narrow belt width.

Compare with belt BM B2214, Athapaskan.

85

## 86 *Arm Bands*

Probably Kutchin, Cordillera, Alaska, 1920–40

Collected by Mr. and Mrs. Walter Clarke in Oklahoma, 1940s

L: 29 cm   W: 5.5 cm

72–2186

Constructed of two pieces of smoked moose hide, unlined. Embroidered with glass seed-beads in faceted pink color-core; opaque green, blues and white; translucent reds, dark green, and orange; copper-colored; and faceted polished iron beads; all thread-strung and couched into symmetrical designs of rosettes, buds and leaves. Looped edging of thread-strung beads.

The pink color-core beads used here were especially popular at Fort Yukon, Alaska for a decade or so starting in the 1920s. They are particularly vulnerable to fading.

86

## 87 *Bag*

Athapaskan type, Cordillera, circa 1900
Rudolf F. Haffenreffer Sr. collection
Pouch: L: 11 cm   W: 11.5 cm   Strap: L: 9.5 cm
60–4597

Round-bottomed; lightly smoked hide, lined with white flannel. Embroidered with glass seed-beads in translucent green and dark red, thread-sewn and couched: on pouch, outlined simplified floral motifs, similar on back and front but in opposite color placement; on strap, zigzag; two-beaded edging.

Although simple outlined foliate forms similar to these are found on small items sold to visitors along the Alaskan Inside Passage by the Tlingit at the turn of the century, this small bag is not quite like Tlingit examples. The bag shape is unusual, and the motifs are particularly open and angular. Color is split across the horizontal axis of the motifs. The combination of characteristics suggests that this bag was probably made in the Cordillera, the region bordering the coast, in British Columbia or the southern Yukon Territory. The onslaught of gold seekers in the region late in the nineteenth century provided a market for such mementos.

87

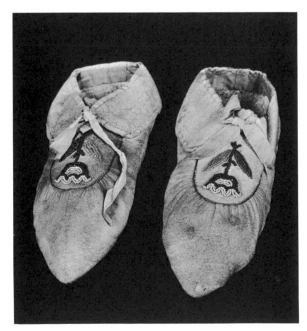

88

## 88 *Child's Moccasins*

Western Subarctic, late nineteenth, early twentieth century
Rudolf F. Haffenreffer Sr. collection
L: 18 cm   W: 8 cm
60–4631

Soft sole; pointed toe, T-shaped heel seam and straight center seam; hide vamp beaded with tulip-shaped flower in tiny, faceted pink, red, and blue and translucent yellow glass seedbeads, sinew-strung and thread-couched. Cuff lined with blue polished cotton; cuff binding and ties of pale pink silk.

Children's moccasins are often difficult to attribute specifically, since the vamps on them are usually too small for more than a very simple design.

## 89 *Baby Moccasins*

Yukon-Tanana Region Athapaskan type, Cordillera, 1890s

Collected by Emma Shaw Colcleugh in 1898

L: 8.5 cm   W: 4 cm

60–928

*Baby slippers sent me from the Klondike (1898)*
(ESC: GL 43)

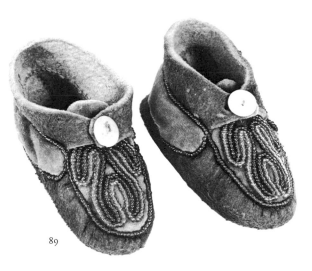
89

Soft sole, rounded-toe, of smoked moose hide, with cuff and large vamp of caramel-colored velvet; embroidered in abstract curvilinear pattern in thread-sewn translucent yellow, pink and taupe seed-beads; pearl and bone button closures.

The Klondike gold rush especially affected the Athapaskan-speaking Han of the Dawson area in the Yukon Territory. Wage employment was available for some men, and an increased market for curio items also gave women an opportunity to earn money.

# Babiche

## 90 *Game Bag*

Dogrib, late nineteenth century

Collected by Emma Shaw Colcleugh at Fort Rae, 1894

L: 20.5 cm   W: 39 cm

57–514

*Dog Rib game bag (Great Slave Lake)* 1894
(ESC: NB 141)

Folded rectangle of lightly tanned, netted babiche attached with narrow hide insertion strips to side panels of smoked moose hide faced with black wool broadcloth. Band encircling opening, made of double-layered tanned hide sewn together at top with sinew in overcast stitch. Front band ornamented with three horizontal zigzags of purple and natural quills sewn with sinew in two-thread zigzag technique and placed to form diamonds. Upper edge of front band bordered with narrow strip of black wool edged along the bottom with medium blue glass seed-beads, sinew-strung, thread-couched, and along the top with orange and natural quills wrapped over a thong.

Netting of undyed babiche in simple (buttonhole) looping, broken by single and three-part extension bands created by addition of extra twists to the babiche. Extension band babiche colored with ochre and black before netting. Remnants of tassels of red (from unraveled fabric), green and blue wool yarn attached with hide thongs on front along three sides of the bag and just above first single extension band. Side attachment loops of hide and three sets of hide tie thongs on opposite sides of upper bands.

The babiche bag was usually worn slung over the the back or shoulder, with the ornamental side showing. A piece of birch bark inserted inside kept the wearer dry. The open netting of the babiche allowed air to circulate around the fish or small game being transported (Lafferty, pers. comm. 1982).

The greatest number of babiche bags of this cut come from the Dogrib. Most have geometric ornamentation. Shape, side bands (usually with insertion

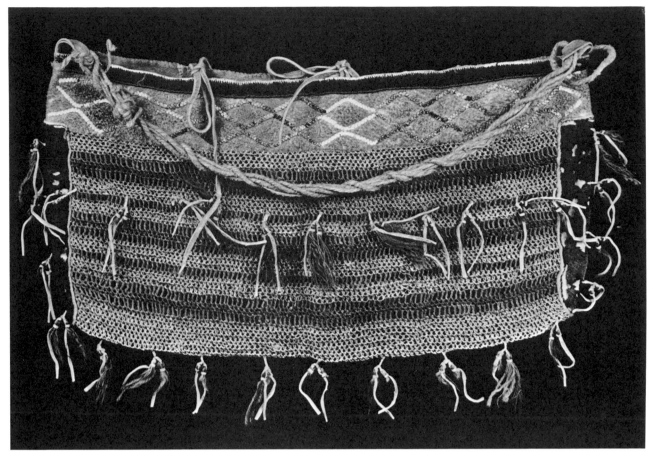

90

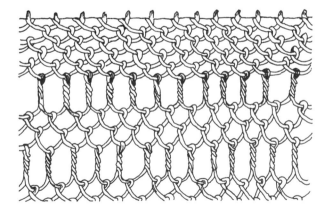

Detail of single and multiple-twist looped netting.

strips), netting technique with colored extension strips, thong-tied yarn tassels and front band ornamentation on an applied band of hide or fabric are characteristic. A single zigzag formed with flattened folded quills or narrow wool worsted twill braid (sometimes called llama braid or military braid) is the most common ornamental motif on Dogrib bags. Loops, lobes or leaves sometimes elaborate the sides of the zigzag. The triple zigzags forming diamonds on this bag are unusual.

There are also a few babiche bags embroidered with beads or thread in the Great Slave Lake-Mackenzie River floral style. These come from the Slavey, Hare, Chipewyan and Kutchin, rather than from the Dogrib.

See Burnham 1981:4; Emery 1980:31, figs. 9, 11; and compare with RSM 1951.387, Fraser River area; LFG C63.1.8; UI 10831, Russell collection, 1890s; NMM VI-E-35, all ornamented with folded quills. On some mid-nineteenth century examples (RSM 481.8 and 559.22 [pictured in Clark 1974a, fig. 92] and 558.45) quills are wrapped around a fillet of sinew or thong and bulge slightly away from the hide.

91

# 91 *Game Bag*

Dogrib, late nineteenth century

Collected by Emma Shaw Colcleugh at Fort Rae, 1894

L: 25 cm    W: 36 cm

61–44

*Dogrib game bag, made from babiche, Great Slave Lake* (ESC: GL 17)

Knotted rawhide babiche, attached to wide upper band of thick, smoked moose hide; two-color bands of deep grey-brown babiche incorporated; holes cut at intervals along upper edge of upper band to allow thong lacing; hide attachment loops at corners.

This simple bag is typical of a type better known in a western Athapaskan (primarily Pacific drainage) version that is often taller than it is wide. Typical of the type is the tubular shape in a continuous mesh construction connected at the bottom and the use of rawhide babiche knotted in double loops pulled tight. Upper rawhide bands are the same on both sides, undecorated and pierced for a thong lacing. Examples from the Alaska-Canada border area sometimes incorporate occasional trade beads or bird claws (ptarmigan?) into the mesh.

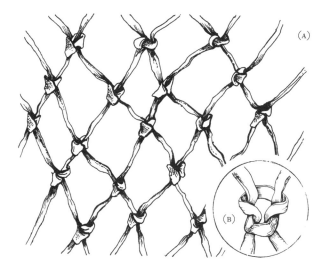

Detail:
(A) knotted babiche    (B) knot made of double loops of babiche

Compare GAI AC 173, 1880s, Antrobus collection and AC 281, Yukon area; DMNH 11509, Alaska; NMNH 248,443, Stikine River Tahltan, received from G.T. Emmons 1907; NMNH 166967, Porcupine River, collected by J. Henry Turner.

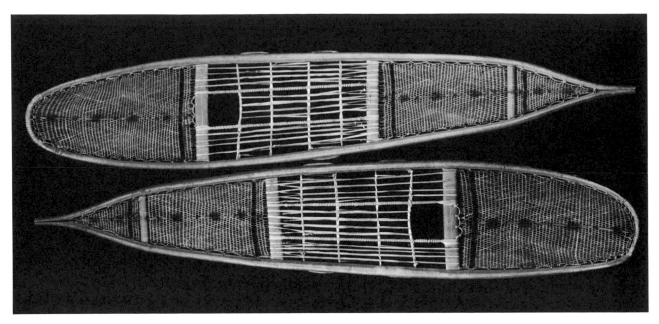

## 92 *Snowshoes*

Loucheux (Eastern Kutchin), late nineteenth century

Collected by Emma Shaw Colcleugh, Fort
McPherson, Mackenzie River, 1894

L: 108 cm   W: 21 cm

83–455

*Loucheux Indian snowshoes from Fort McPherson, the most
northern Post occupied by the Hudson's Bay Company*
(ESC: GL 95)

Steam-bent birch frame curves up slightly to rounded toe;
tail short; hexagonal babiche lacing, finely spaced, forms
mesh forward and rear; center of babiche has widely spaced
rectangular openings; clusters of blue seed-beads strung in
groups of three in center of forward and rear lacing, which
also bears remains of purple paint motif; remains of red
mineral paint on wood frame.

The shape of snowshoes varies greatly depending
on the type of terrain they are meant to track, and on
local styles. The nearby Ojibwa used pointed-toe
snowshoes, in Labrador the rounded "bear-paw" type
was popular, and in the northern forests the Athapaskans used this narrower style, which allowed the
wearer to move swiftly through the woods without
catching his snowshoes in the underbrush.

This pair lacks the harness for attaching the snowshoe to the foot. The fine hexagonal lacing of the forward and rear sections is created by wetting the babiche
so that it is flexible, and then lacing it in a triangular

pattern. These decorative areas are often executed by
women, while men prepare the stronger central section
which bears the weight of the foot.

For diagrams and description of construction, see Helm 1981:
382: fig. 12, Kutchin snowshoe, NMNH 230427; Steinbright
1983: 37–47; Burnham 1981: 6. Compare with snowshoes,
ROM 22198, Kutchin; also UI 10848, coll. by Russell
(1898:183) who calls these "the most skillfully made of any
that I have seen in the North."

A Chipewyan creation story told to Father Emile
Petitot (1838–1916), an Oblate priest who lived among
the Hare people at Fort Good Hope and recorded much
of the oral history of the Mackenzie River Athapaskans,
affirms the importance of snowshoes to the first man
and the antiquity of the division of labor by gender in
their construction (Petitot 1976:1):

### *The First Man*

In the beginning, man did not exist.
Then suddenly there was man, it is said.
Who made man?
We do not know.
When winter came, man made himself some snowshoes.
"How am I going to do it?" he wondered.
He did not really know, but he cut down a birch tree and
eventually made a frame.
The following day he put in the bars and they were almost
complete.

"How will I do the lattice work?" he thought, for he had no woman to do it for him.

He lay down his tent to sleep and when he awoke in the morning he saw that his snowshoes had been partially laced.

"Who could have laced my snowshoes while I was asleep?" he said to himself, for there was no one else around.

The next night he again lay down to sleep and in the morning he saw that a little more of the lattice work had been done.

"Now who has done this?" he thought.

He looked up at the tent roof and saw a partridge flying away.

"Ah! It must have been the partridge!" he thought.

Again the next night the man went to sleep and at daybreak there were the snowshoes almost completely laced and again

he glimpsed the partridge flying away.

"I know what I shall do," he said to himself. That evening he covered the top of the tent with a skin.

Then he lay down to sleep.

When he awoke next morning the snowshoes were complete and were lying beside him.

The partridge thought, "I must fly away quickly," but the tent top was blocked up and she could not escape.

The partridge was turned into a beautiful woman with long silky hair.

The man and woman slept together, of course, and in time they had many children.

We are their descendants.

That is the end of the story.

## 93 *Chair*

Made in Oblate Mission, Fort Good Hope, Mackenzie River, latter nineteenth century

Collected by Emma Shaw Colcleugh, Fort Good Hope, 1894

L: 47 cm   W: 50 cm   H: 92.5 cm

00–10152

Birch wood frame; constructed with wooden pegs; painted with rust-red mineral paint; two back slats; four dowels connect legs that are hand-carved in the round, and form seat frame; seat laced with babiche (twisted strips of hide) in hexagonal lacing in same technique as snowshoes (cat. 92).

This chair was probably made at the Oblate Mission at Fort Good Hope under the direction of priests who may have learned the chair-making craft in Quebec. It seems likely that the idea for the babiche-webbed seat was taken from snowshoes made by native Hare Indians.

Because of a need for furniture at the early mission stations, local native craftsmen and mission staff often cooperated in making chairs and other necessities. Sister Flore Pierson of Fort Providence recalled that when she was stationed at Fort Good Hope in the early 1970s, Father La Batte tried to encourage a revival of babiche chair-making as it was done in the old days, using babiche and local wood. She recognized a photograph of this chair as similar to those that she had learned to make. "We thought if we could get this back into style, it would be a livelihood for a couple of families there. We examined an old chair there and tried to get the pattern . . . and we did get it. . . . we tried different ways, and we finally had it. But it didn't

Detail of babiche netting technique used in both snowshoes and chair seat

93

catch hold . . . anyway, we had lots of fun" (Pierson, pers. comm. 1985).

Similar chairs are in the Mother House of the Grey Nuns, Montreal; MMMN; LFG; and PWNHC 979.10.72, from the Old Mission at Fort Rae.

# Birch Bark

## Birch Bark: Its Place in the Subarctic

Life in the Subarctic boreal forest in pre-contact and historic times was heavily dependent upon the bark of the white birch (*Betula papyrifera*). It was used in transportation, shelter, carrying and storing food and household objects, and possibly as part of a sacred complex common to the circumboreal region (Butler 1957: 49–56; Webber 1978: 57–61). The importance of birch bark in this area compares with that of bison rawhide in the Plains, and there are similarities in the folded construction of containers from both materials. The Plains Indians relied on the American bison for food, shelter, clothing, transportation, utensils and fuel, and considered this animal, so necessary to their survival, as a sacred part of their ceremonies for each year's world renewal. Of similar importance among Subarctic forest inhabitants was the indispensable birch tree. It supplied material for canoes, wigwam coverings, cooking utensils, cradles, pipes, rattles, bedding, torches, raincoats, animal calls and firewood. Because it contributed in so many ways to their daily living, birch became a part of the northern peoples' mythology.

Among the Montagnais and neighboring Subarctic and Northeastern peoples, the cosmic tale of *How The Summer Birds Were Stolen and Brought North* describes a northern country bound in perpetual winter until birds, which had been confined in birch-bark cages by the people of the South, were freed by an expedition from the North. As the birds flew north they brought with them the first changing season, creating warmth and plant life in all its nurturing and medicinal qualities. According to Montagnais Chief Joseph Kurtness, who told the tale to Frank Speck in 1925, this was the origin of birch-bark containers in the North, and it explained their decoration with floral and figurative designs that were representations of the summer birds and their associates, the edible and medicinal shrubs and plants (Speck 1937: 113).

Because of the fragility of bark, there is little evidence in museum collections to point to aboriginal use. However, recent archaeological investigations in the North American Arctic and Subarctic show that sewn birch bark has been used for roof covers, cache covers, house partitions and small and large containers for at least the last 2000 years, including straight-cut birch-bark fragments edged with rows of

"Cree Indian settlement on the Jack Fish River, Lake Winnipeg, 1884." Note two kinds of bark shelter and a bark canoe. Photo by T. C. Weston, courtesy Peabody Museum, Harvard University.

stitching-holes excavated from an Ipiutak site at Point Hope, Alaska, dating 2,000 years ago (Webber 1978: 61; Larsen 1948: PL.23, fig. 7–8).

Bark containers were most successfully made in early spring in the northeastern Woodlands and Subarctic, and in late spring in the western Subarctic where the winters were longer. The winter bark from the white birch was cut, without injuring the cortex, and peeled from the tree in rectangular sheets, from which an appropriate pattern for a desired container would be cut.

If the container was to be decorated, the inner surface was moistened and darkened with water or with a wash of boiled willow bark, so that the surface bark was softened and more easily scraped away.

If the decoration was with motifs based on a cut-out pattern or template, such a template might be cut from another piece of birch bark and laid on the surface of the larger piece of bark that formed the container. The edge of the pattern would be outlined with a knife tip. According to Speck (1937) the use of bark cut-outs as decorative patterns among the Montagnais-Naskapi may have evolved from modifying scraps left over from the birch-bark sheet out of which a container pattern was cut. Sources of new ideas for patterns may also have evolved from bitten birch-bark designs that were created by elderly women as entertainment for children.

The area surrounding the cut-out pattern was scraped with a knife so that the moistened, dark layer was removed and a lighter under-layer exposed. The design under the cut-out then stood out dark against a light background. This is known as a scraped-away or positive design and was the more usual method in use by the Montagnais-Naskapi in the Eastern Subarctic. Negative designs were achieved by scraping a design free-hand into or through the dark bark layer, so that the design stood out lighter than the background. This method was common among Athapaskan groups, as well as among the Penobscot and Micmac. Some groups, including the Lake Winnipeg Saulteaux and Ojibwa and sometimes the Montagnais-Naskapi, practiced both negative and positive methods for creating design (Speck 1937: 71–73). Contemporary bark containers made by Athapaskan craftsmen in the Nelson-Liard area also use a combination of positive and negative design techniques (see cat. 175), as well as decoration with a kind of quill embroidery, here called quill insertion (see cats. 176 and 177).

The containers were usually folded and cut along scored lines and sewn with black-spruce root (*picea mariana*). The rims were often reinforced with a thin hoop made from a flexible wood splint.

94

## 94 Storage Container

Montagnais-Naskapi, late nineteenth century

Collected by Emma Shaw Colcleugh, Lake St. John, Quebec, 1895

L: 57 cm   W: 25.5 cm   H: 23.5 cm

OB–65

*Birch bark "rogan" made by Indian woman at Lake St. John. Finished for me while I waited*
(ESC: GL 143, NB 143)

Oblong, constructed from a single piece of birch bark, cut and folded; rough, outside white bark forms interior of container; smoother, darker inner bark forms outside of container. Y-shaped seams at two ends stitched with spruce root, open stitching. Rim reinforced with flat, wide wood splints lashed with spruce root. Exterior sides and ends decorated with linear zigzag and triangle designs, achieved by two scraping techniques: the background around a cut-out pattern is scraped to expose the lighter bark layer underneath (positive technique); and a free-hand design is scraped directly into or through the surface so the motifs are light

(negative technique). Bottom unscraped; scored at folds and half-way up interior sides.

Among Subarctic peoples large storage containers might be fashioned from birch bark or from the leg skins of caribou or moose (see cat. 114). Some distinguishing features characterize eastern or Algonquian birch-bark containers from western or Athapaskan ones; in this example, Algonquian characteristics include the vertical grain of the bark, and the absence of cutout reinforcement below the rim (Whiteford, pers. comm. 1988). In general, Algonquian peoples preferred to scrape away the background rather than the design itself, although here both positive and negative techniques were used.

Compare with similar form of large elongated container or "wigwamatew," Beothuk, c. 1827, British Museum 6975 (Webber 1978). The Lake St. John Band calls these by a special designation, *mi' ctebustc'la'gan*, or "big container" (Speck 1937: 58). For similar line design, compare meat pail, Montagnais, CMC III-C-168, pictured in Speck 1937: PL.XX: A.

## 95 Bowl or Dish

Montagnais type, late nineteenth century

Collected by Emma Shaw Colcleugh in Saskatchewan, 1888–94

L: 19.5 cm   W: 18 cm   H: 9.5 cm

71–5044

*Birch bark basket, stencil ornament, Saskatchewan*
(ESC: GL 115)

Rectangular base, oval top, constructed from a single piece of birch bark, folded and cut; light, outer surface of bark forms interior of container; smoother, darker inner bark forms exterior; four seams stitched with spruce root; rim reinforced with wood splints wrapped with spruce root. Rim stitches of alternating lengths on two sides on which grain of bark is parallel to the rim; in even lengths on two sides in which grain is vertical. Exterior decorated on four sides in paired variations of double curve; design delineated by scraping away background around a template to reveal a contrasting lighter layer of inner bark; X-design on base is scraped into the bark in negative technique, with remainder of base unscraped.

The alternating length of stitch-holes serves as a safeguard against horizontal splitting of the bark between stitch-holes.

Algonquian peoples of the Eastern Subarctic applied

95

stylized plant designs to birch bark in various bilaterally symmetrical arrangements. The design on this container is a variation of the "double curve" common to Algonquians in both Woodlands and Subarctic regions and possibly predating contact. A bark template was often used to establish the outlines of the motifs. Stylized bilateral plant designs may also be seen in contemporary Cree birch-bark bitings (see cats. 170–173). In Algonquian mythology these forms represent the important herbal and medicinal plant life brought to the North by the Summer Birds. Although collected in Saskatchewan this basket shows design characteris-

tics more typical of Quebec and Ontario (see Conn 1979: 69, figs. 64, 65).

Compare with food dish, Chicoutimi, MAI 15-3296, pictured in Speck 1937: PL.XX e, and bowls, dishes, PL.XIX c-h.

96

## 96 *Food Dish or Pan*

Northern Algonquian, first quarter twentieth century

Rudolf F. Haffenreffer Sr. collection

D: 39 cm    H: 14 cm

01–1719

Square base, outcurving rim; constructed of single piece birch bark, scored, cut, folded, straight side-seams stitched with spruce root; rim reinforced on outside with wood splint attached with peeled spruce root in open stitching, repaired by replacement with string; alternating-length stitch pattern on two sides where grain of bark is horizontal to rim to prevent splitting along stitch-holes; even stitching on two sides with bark grain running perpendicular to rim.

## 97 *Food Dish or Pan*

Eastern Algonquian type, first quarter twentieth century

Rudolf F. Haffenreffer Sr. collection

D: 33 cm    H: 8.5 cm

OB–62

Square base, circular outcurving rim, constructed from single piece of birch bark, scored, cut, folded and sewn; outer surface of bark forms interior of bowl but both inner and outer surfaces have been scraped to create light, smooth texture; four seams stitched with spruce root; flat rim of wood splints wrapped with spruce root; rim stitches applied in alternating lengths on two sides on which grain of bark is horizontal; in

97

97 bottom

even lengths on sides with vertical grain; geometric designs of circles, stars, and lines on sides and bottom of dish, achieved through scraping away background from around template in positive technique.

Although the history of this container is unknown, it is very similar to the bark dishes once used among the Montagnais-Naskapi, which were decorated on the bottom and sides and which have been documented for "special occasion" use. Sometimes they were gifts from a female relative to a young girl to bring her the blessings of health and long life. Often they were used by successful hunters when eating game, with a representation of the game animal or of a spiritual helper applied as design. Meat dishes were referred to in a spiritual way as "my dish," implying that they were regarded as ceremonial utensils whose use was connected with the prayer processes involved in obtaining and consuming food through spiritual intervention (Speck 1937: 59–60).

Compare with dishes decorated on bottom and sides pictured in Speck 1937: PL.XIX g, h, and PL.XX c.

## 98 Container with Lid

Algonquian, Manitoba, probably Lake Winnipeg
Saulteaux or Swampy Cree, late nineteenth century

Collected by Emma Shaw Colcleugh in Manitoba, 1888–94

D: 19 cm    H: 14 cm

OB–63

*Covered birch bark box, Indians near Lake Winnipeg*
(ESC: NB 145)

Birch bark, inner layers; a single piece scored, cut and folded to form eight-sided container with circular top and octagonal base; side-seams stitched with spruce root in running stitch; rim composed of bark strip attached to upper, inner sides with long bird-quill stitches; around strip on outside is lip of wood splint wrapped with bird quills dyed green and purple (faded). Lid of birch bark with "sawtooth" edging, folded

98

over bark strip and stitched down with spruce root and bird quill; lined with thin layer of bark.

The bark strip attached to the side pieces at the top provides necessary reinforcement in holding the eight sides firmly together in a circular form. The attachment is effectively hidden by the decorative bird quill lip. This construction is typically Subarctic, developing in the birch-bark areas of southern Manitoba and Ontario.

Compare with similar six-, eight- and nine-sided birch-bark containers with central quill-wrapped wood splint lips and sawtooth lid-edgings: MAI 18-2774, called Chipewyan; MAI 3-7801 Ojibwa; MAI 2-5130, called Athapaskan; and four-sided container, UI, Cree, coll. by Frank Russell in Grand Rapids, Manitoba, 1892.

## 99 *Container with Lid*

Algonquian, Central Subarctic or Woodland, third quarter nineteenth century

Collected by Emma Shaw Colcleugh in Ontario, circa 1875

D: 14 cm   H: 11 cm

61–81

*Covered birch bark box ornamented with porcupine quills, Lake Huron Indians* (ESC: GL 117)

Single piece of birch bark, inner layers; scored, cut, and folded to form six-sided container with circular top and hexagonal base; six side-seams stitched with spruce root in zigzag stitch; rim composed of bark strip attached with spruce-root stitches to upper inner sides of container; wood splint wrapped with spruce root circles bark strip on outside. Birch-bark lid with sawtooth edging folded over bark strip and stitched with spruce root. Porcupine quills in floral pattern, dyed green, red, purple, blue, inserted through bark on sides of box and on top of lid. Paper lining glued on.

99

This box and cat. 100 are constructed in the same manner as cat. 98, with porcupine-quill floral designs added as decoration. Floral-quillwork insertion on birch bark is frequently found on Ojibwa objects from the time period in which this box was collected. Quill decoration such as this is typical of southern Ojibwa or Chippewa work, but the bark container itself was constructed in a Subarctic form. Mid- and late-nineteenth century Ottawa quilled flowers on birch bark also show some similarities to the flowers on these examples.

This floral style in quillwork can be compared with Algonquian floral beadwork and silk thread embroidery on hide and cloth from the southern Manitoba and Ontario area, both Swampy Cree and Ojibwa (Lake Winnipeg Saulteaux). The large central flower superimposed on a surrounding leaf, the buds, circular berries, spurred stems, and overall symmetry bring to mind both bead (cat. 54), and silk (cats. 16, 24) floral designs of the region. The style, which shows strong European influence, is very different from earlier geometric and curvilinear decoration on birch bark, both incised and executed with quills.

Compare with floral quillwork on birch-bark model canoe, MAI 3-6402, Ojibwa; quilled-birch boxes, MCC A6086, Manitoba Cree and RSM 1871.18, North American Indian, Red River District.

## 100 *Container with Lid*

Algonquian, Central Subarctic or Woodland, fourth quarter nineteenth century

Rudolf F. Haffenreffer Sr. collection

D: 18 cm   H: 9 cm

OB–24

Single piece birch bark, inner layers; scored, cut and folded to form six-sided container with circular top and hexagonal base; six seams sewn with spruce root in tiny zigzag stitch; rim composed of bark strip attached to upper, inner sides with dyed-bird-quill stitches; wood-splint lip wrapped with bird quills, dyed green, red, and purple covers stitches on outside of strip. Lid of birch bark has sawtooth edging, folded over a bark strip, then stitched down with spruce root. Porcupine-quill insertion in floral design on lid and sides in brown, red, green, purple, natural; cloth lining.

The fact that the interior of the box is completely lined with cloth suggests that it may have been made for use as a sewing basket. Compare with cat. 98 from Lake Winnipeg area for construction.

100

101

## 101 *Tray*

Algonquian, Central Subarctic or Woodland, Cree or Ojibwa

Collected by Emma Shaw Colcleugh, northern shore of Lake Superior, 1875

L: 30 cm   W: 22 cm

61–90

Birch bark, oval, two layers, stitched with spruce root; willow rim-splint, rim wrapped with spruce root and purple-dyed and natural-color porcupine quills; decorated on upper side with purple-dyed porcupine quills, sinew-sewn, in zigzag design around edge.

The tray is similar in construction to the lidded bark containers, cats. 98, 99, 100. Trays, plates, dishes, cups and cooking vessels were made from birch bark throughout the Subarctic. Similar use of spruce-root rim-stitching can be found among many northern Athapaskan groups (compare plate, Koyukon, NMM 73-46-1).

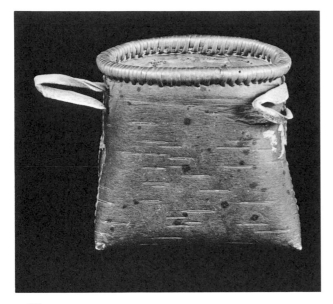

102

## 102 *Container*

Athapaskan, late nineteenth century

Collected by Emma Shaw Colcleugh in Great
Slave Lake, Mackenzie River area, 1894

L: 13 cm    W: 9 cm    H: 13 cm

71-5045

*Small birch bark rogan. Very fine specimen, Athapascan*
(ESC: GL 120; NB 151, 152)

Oval top, rectangular bottom, constructed of a single piece
of birch bark, folded and cut; outer bark used as interior
surface of basket; rim reinforced with wood splints wrapped
with spruce root stitched to horizontally-grained bark sides
in alternate up-and-down pattern; squared Y-shaped seams
on sides covered with spruce root in chain-stitch; two moose-
hide loops on sides.

For use and comparative example, see cat. 103.

## 103 *Container*

Athapaskan, late nineteenth century

Collected by Emma Shaw Colcleugh in Great
Slave Lake-Mackenzie River area, 1894

L: 10.5 cm    W: 9 cm    H: 12 cm

57-202

*Small birch bark rogan. Very fine specimen*
(ESC: NB 151, 152; GL 121)

Oval top, rectangular bottom, constructed from a single piece
of birch bark with exterior of bark forming interior of container; folded and cut, with squared Y-shaped side-seams
stitched with spruce root in chain stitch; rim reinforced with
wood splints, tightly lashed over spruce root in stitches of
alternating length through horizontal bark grain; two moose-
hide loops attached at sides.

Colcleugh frequently referred to a birch-bark container as a "rogan." The same term was used by
Elizabeth Taylor, the only white woman tourist to pre-
cede Colcleugh down the Mackenzie River. In 1892
she described rogans as "water-tight vessels of birch
bark, beautifully stitched with roots, and trimmed
around the opening with colored porcupine quills.
They are of all sizes, holding from a pint to a gallon"
(Taylor 1894–5: 127). "Rogan" is probably a seventeenth century borrowing in old Ojibway from the
French *ouragan* or *oragan* meaning birch bark. In old
Algonquian *roggin* meant dish or plate (Goddard, pers.

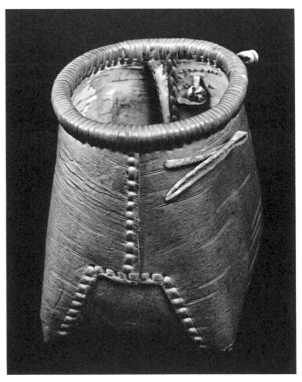

103

comm. 1989). Larger versions of this type of vessel are
often used by women and children to gather berries.

Compare with berry basket, Slavey, 1962, NMM VI-N-52.

## 104 *Pail*

Northwestern Athapaskan, late nineteenth century

Collected by Emma Shaw Colcleugh, 1894

L: 13.5 cm   W: 12.5 cm   H: 11 cm

OB–25

*Birch bark basket* (ESC: NB 149)

Oval top, rectangular bottom, constructed of a single piece of birch bark, cut and folded in wing shape; lighter exterior of bark forms interior of container; smooth, brown, inner surface of bark forms exterior of container; Y-shaped side seams stitched with spruce root, some in chain stitch; rim dips on sides, is reinforced on inside with wood splints wrapped with spruce root, stitched so that, below the rim, triangular patterns are created on both the inside and outside surfaces of the horizontally grained bark; natural black- and red-dyed horse hair plaited with spruce root forms checkered pattern on rim surface; exact, meticulous stitching.

This kind of pail was often used by women and children for gathering berries. Originally a thong carrying-strap would have made it possible for the container to be attached to the belt in order to leave the hands free for picking the fruit. A larger bark container with similar triangular-rim design, although of cut bark rather than of spruce-root stitching, was collected from the Dogrib at Fort Resolution, Great Slave Lake by J. A. Mason in 1913 (NMM VI-E-42) and functioned as a vessel for collecting urine for use in the preparation of skins.

Compare with pail, NMM VI-B-132, Carrier, collected by H. I. Smith, 1922; containers with curved rims, DAM 1950.100.68, 1950.101, Kutchin, Yukon and Alaska; and woman's berry basket, H: 14 cm, NMNH 381.2621, Carrier, coll. by Julian H. Steward, Ft. St. James, BC, 1940.

104

# Antler, Bone, Stone

105

## 105 *Drinking Tube*

Northern Athapaskan, Cordillera and Alaska
Plateau, late nineteenth, early twentieth century

Rudolf F. Haffenreffer Sr. collection

L: 33 cm    DIAM: 1.7 cm

60–4716

Swan-wing bone incised with chip marks at regular intervals
along one side; hollow.

The drinking tube was used by young women during their isolation on the occasion of first menses, in order that their lips not touch their drinking water. Both Athapaskan and Cree people believed that the general well-being of the group was protected by observing certain food and touching taboos. Because menstruation was considered to be a particularly dangerous period, both for the individual and for the group, women were separated from men's hunting and food-gathering activities at this time, in order that they not offend the spirits of the game animals nor adversely affect other natural phenomena such as the weather. A close relationship was seen between female physiology and the forces of nature. In some communities a girl would wear a special hood to hide her face and prevent eye-contact with males. In others, she might be pegged to the ground so that she did not accidentally stray near a game trail. A young woman's first seclusion became a training period during which she was taught the social restraints and ritual behavior needed to control the natural power inherent in her body, and in order to prepare her for adult female responsibilities (McClellan and Denniston 1981: 385). She also developed patience and diligence as she practiced the domestic skills necessary for her later marriage. Articles in the *Subarctic* volume of the *Handbook of North American Indians*, based on more extensive monographs, detect some regional differences in puberty practices (see Honigmann, McClellan and Denniston, and Tobey, in Helm 1981).

Compare with drinking tube, Tahltan, Cordillera, NMM VI-O-57 a, b, pictured in Honigmann 1981: 728: fig. 9.

## 106 *Netting Needle*

Northern Athapaskan type, possibly Kutchin or
Southern Tutchone, late nineteenth century

Rudolf F. Haffenreffer Sr. collection

L: 9 cm    W: 1 cm

85–3

Bone, caribou or moose; pointed at both ends with hole in
center.

Used in working the lacing of snowshoes such as
cat. 92.

Compare netting needle, NMM VI-Q-129, Southern Tutchone, pictured in McClellan and Denniston 1981: 382: fig. 12 i; FMNH 270118 a, b, Alaskan Athapaskan, pictured in VanStone 1986: fig. 28 e.

106

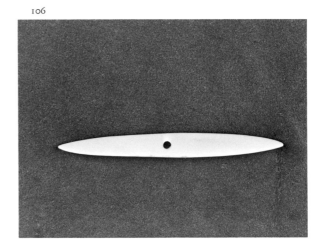

## 107 *Ladle*

Northern Athapaskan, early twentieth century

HMA purchase 1984

L: 32 cm   W: 16 cm

84–65

Moose antler; handle incised with circle-dot design with red and dark-blue ink-lined perforations; file marks on exterior of bowl.

The history of this ladle is not known. Similar large, decorated ladles were used by the Athapaskan Tutchone of Yukon Territory for ceremonial grease drinking (McClellan 1981: 503: fig. 7). The circle-dot design decorating the ladle is one of both universality and antiquity. It has been found on objects in the Arctic, Africa and Australia, among other places. It has been interpreted by some as symbolic of man's relationship to the universe around him, and it may impart ceremonial significance to an object. A compass-type tool was used to create the design.

Compare with decorated spoons of sheep horn and wood, Upper Tanana, Alaskan plateau, Hood Museum of Art: 30-2-4624, 30-2-4626-7, coll. 1929.

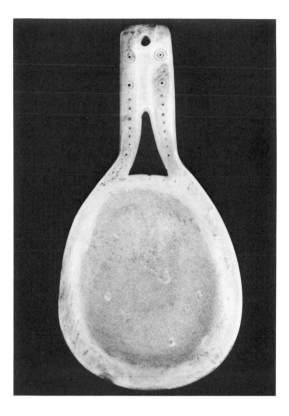

107

108

109

## 108 *Sap Scraper*

Northern Athapaskan, possibly Chilcotin or Carrier, British Columbia, late nineteenth century

Rudolf F. Haffenreffer Sr. collection

L: 17.5 cm   W: 4 cm

86–63

Caribou antler, carved in double-ended bow shape; incised with crossed lines and circles.

Sap scrapers were used to collect the inner or cambium layer of the bark of black pines (jack pines), which provided a source of food.

Compare with sap scraper collected from the Chilcotin in 1897 (Teit, 1909: 780); sap scraper collected from the Carrier, NMM VI-B-299.

## 109 *Awl*

Subarctic, nineteenth century

Rudolf F. Haffenreffer Sr. collection

L: 12.5 cm   W: 2.3 cm

86–65

Split leg bone, possibly deer, tapered to a point.

Prior to the introduction of steel needles by traders, awls were used throughout the Subarctic in the process of stitching hide clothing and bark equipment. When sewing hides, a woman would first make a hole in the hide with a bone awl, or later, an iron awl, and then push sinew thread through it. When making bark containers, the awl would be used to pierce the stiff bark in order to insert a spruce-root lacing.

Carved
Stone
Pipes

Carving, whether in stone, antler, bone, or wood, has been an art practiced largely by men in the Subarctic, as they used the natural materials around them to produce the necessities for survival: utensils, tools, weapons, and ritual objects.

In the southern Subarctic, aboriginal smoking has ancient roots. A catlinite pipe of platform style has been found at the Michipicotan site on the northeast coast of Lake Superior, dating to the Terminal Woodland Period, circa AD 600–1600 (Wright 1981: 91–93). Pipe-smoking was not an aboriginal practice in the northern Subarctic, however, since the climate was too severe for tobacco to have been a part of the natural environment. Ironically, tobacco was introduced to Europe and Asia from North America, and re-introduced to the far North by way of a long-existing trade between Asia and Alaska. In protohistoric times, before 1800, annual trade fairs were held in the Yukon Delta, among other places, and here tobacco from Asia was traded for Alaskan furs and objects made of wood (Hosley 1981: 546). In historic times the importance of tobacco to Alaskan Eskimos and Indians continued. Russian trader Hieromonk Illarion wrote: "It is impossible to achieve anything with the savages if there is no tobacco. Tobacco to a savage is the same as bread is to a Russian" (ID 1862, in Oswalt 1980: 97).

Aboriginal pipe-bowls were carved from soft stone, either black steatite, diorite, chlorite or slate, or red clay slate, commonly known as catlinite. They were fitted with stems of reed, bone or wood in varying

110

## 110 *Pipe Bowl*

Algonquian

Collected by Emma Shaw Colcleugh, who received it as a gift in 1888 from the Honorable Horace Belanger, chief factor of Cumberland House, Saskatchewan

L: 9.5 cm    H: 10.5 cm    DIAM: 4 cm

61–420

*A very old stone pipe made by the Indians around Cumberland House* (ESC: NB)

Modified Micmac: black-green stone, unusually large orifice: tapered borings; bowl set upon highly ornate stem base with single large and 10 small perforations in center of base, used for attaching bowl to stem with skin thong of ornamental quillwork.

The Indians around Cumberland House in 1888 may have been Plains Cree or Plains Ojibwa to the south, Western Woods Cree to the east and west, or Northern Ojibwa or Saulteaux to the east.

lengths. The native artisan drilled the bore to the desired size with a bow or other type of stone drill. A variety of stone tools were used for reaming, scraping and gouging in order to enlarge the drill bores. A gritty, abrasive stone might be used as a chisel or scraper to smooth the pipe's surface, after which it would be polished with sand or talc, using buckskin or perhaps simply rubbing it with the hand (West 1970: 1: 334).

Pipe-smoking had ritual, economic and social importance. Among some hunting people, such as the Montagnais-Naskapi of Ungava Bay, Quebec, smoking items were part of a man's spiritual hunting equipment and were used to improve his luck in obtaining food animals (Speck 1935: 219). Records of Hudson's Bay Company factors along the shores of Eastern James Bay describe both the act of pipe-smoking and gifts of tobacco and pipes as important in maintaining good trade relationships between the English and the Cree during the nineteenth century: "Plugs of tobacco were given along with the credit. When he arrived at the post, each native trapper was given a quantity of grain. . . . some tobacco, and a pipe and on departure these gifts were repeated" (Francis and Morantz 1983: 146). For the many native and métis voyageurs, who paddled canoes and carried packs along the fur-trade river routes, the pipe provided comfort and solace during long, cold journeys. The northern pipe was usually small, in order to be easily carried and conveniently tucked away during these journeys. Older women also smoked small pipes simply for pleasure.

111

## 111 *Pipe Bowl*

Cree or Chipewyan, nineteenth century
Collected by Emma Shaw Colcleugh, Norway House, Manitoba, 1888–1894

L: 6.2 cm W: 2 cm H: 8.5 cm DIAM BOWL: 3.5 cm
60–918

*Old stone pipe from the northwest of Lake Winnipeg*
(ESC: NB 96)

Steatite; rectangular platform base; tall, narrow bowl, slightly flared; two lines incised horizontally across sides of platform; beveled drill cavity, cone-shaped; smoke-blackened, tar-coated bore.

The platform style of pipe was in use from East to West across the Subarctic. This particular style is called Modified Micmac after the Micmac people of Lower Canada, the St. Lawrence valley, and the Maritime Provinces, among whom this pipe form was in general use at the time of first contact with Europeans (West 1970 I: 28; II: 823, PL. 171: fig. 1).

### 112 *Pipe Bowl*

Cree, late nineteenth century

Collected by Emma Shaw Colcleugh, Lake
Winnipeg, Manitoba, 1888–1894

L: 5 cm  H: 5 cm  DIAM BOWL: 2.5 cm

60–919

Steatite, mottled black-green, polished; oblong bowl, small
platform, narrow, tapered stem; unused.

This stone bowl is carved in imitation of European
clay pipes. Colcleugh called this a "squaw pipe;" its
small size is characteristic of pipes favored by older
women.

112

113

### 113 *Pipe*

Cree, late nineteenth century

Collected by Emma Shaw Colcleugh, Cumberland
House, Saskatchewan River, Saskatchewan, 1888–
94

L: 6.5 cm + 5 cm wood stem extension  H: 5 cm
DIAM BOWL: 2.5 cm

60–920

Steatite, black; elbow-type pipe bowl with small base protru-
sion; stem carved in rings at end where tapered wood stem
fits inside stone stem; wood stem attached with string to
stone pipe; smoke-blackened bore.

Colcleugh called this a "squaw pipe." In the Subarctic and Northern Woodlands, many pipes had string
attachments that served to keep the two small pipe
parts from getting separated and lost. This was particularly useful to smokers who travelled by canoe and
York boat on the waters of the river transport system.

Compare pipe, RSM 558.15, Dogrib, coll. by Ross, 1859, pictured in Clark 1974a: cat 202.

# Hide, Birdskin

## 114 *Storage Bag*

Western Kutchin, 1910

Made by Martha John Charlie, of Old Crow, Yukon Territory, about 1910, for her husband John

HMA purchase from Eunice Carney, Kutchin, 1986

L: 101.5 cm    W: 91.5 cm

86–66

Made of the skin from thirty moose legs, tanned, with hair left on, sewn together in strips with sinew in an overcast stitch; attached to hand-pinked upper strip of tanned moose hide; bottom of raw moose hide, only partly de-haired; drawstring of caribou hide.

Eunice Carney inherited this bag from her mother, who was born in the 1890s. She said that such bags were used to store tanned and smoked moose or caribou hides that would later be made into footwear and jackets for the family. "It is a beautiful bag, nicely made and almost indestructible, with hair matched, and it will keep for years. It is a one-of-a-kind bag now, because the younger Indian women are not in the least interested in making something like this" (Carney, pers. comm. 1986). Eunice particularly wanted the bag to be preserved in a museum.

Compare with "deer shank bag" (of caribou) RSM 558.46, Dogrib, received from B. R. Ross 1860.

114

## 115 *Drum*

Montagnais-Naskapi, first quarter twentieth
century

Rudolf F. Haffenreffer Sr. collection, acquired in
1927, Hamilton Inlet, Labrador

D: 58.5 cm, head   W: 10 cm, frame

84–28

Single head; made of whole young caribou hide held between
two wooden ring frames; babiche lashings colored red-violet;
loose end of lashing forms handle by which drum is held;
frames are steamed and bent, painted on top and bottom
surfaces with red-violet commercial paint, and held together
with string, wood pegs and lead inserts; eight tin disks set
into frames as rattles; bird-quill snares attached to babiche
resonator stretched across head on both sides; native repair:
patch in head, double-sewn.

Rituals surrounded the caribou hunt, as survival depended on its success. It was believed that the herds
were ruled by a giant caribou who lived in a cave in
the mountains to the east. Unless the slaughtered
caribou were treated in certain ritual ways, the overlord
would not again release the herds to the Naskapi hunters (Rogers 1969: 42). Hunting songs were sung by
older men to the accompaniment of the drum's beat.
In these songs help was sought from spirits who had
knowledge of the future to ensure the successful pursuit of caribou.

Compare with drum photographed by William Duncan
Strong, 1928, Naskapi, Davis Inlet band, FMNH 61540, pictured in Helm 1981: 734: fig. 16. See also painting of a drum-
mer on meat tray (cat. 179), probably relating a drumming
to a successful hunt followed by feasting on meat.

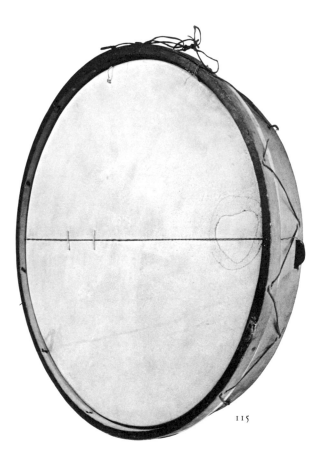

115

## 116 *Swan's Foot Tobacco Pouch*

Dogrib, late nineteenth century

Collected by Emma Shaw Colcleugh on Great
Slave Lake, probably at Fort Rae, 1894

L: 11 cm   W: 14 cm

57–442

*Tobacco pouch made of the skin of a swan's foot, Dog
Rib Indians, Great Slave Lake (unfinished)*
(ESC: GL 41)

Constructed from the two sides of a swan's foot, split; opening edged with moose hide; sinew-sewn.

Animal bodies or parts form convenient natural containers and were used by Subarctic native people for
making a variety of bags. The swan's foot bag was
durable and waterproof, ideal for keeping tobacco dry,
and of a convenient size and shape in its natural form.
Often the claws of the bird were retained as decoration.

Compare with NMNH 381477; a more elaborate bag (UI 9614)
collected by Frank Russell at Herschel Island from the Rat
(Porcupine River Kutchin) in the 1890s; and LFG HBC 427,
collected 1880s at Fort Chipewyan (pictured Rogers and
Smith 1981: 145, fig. 15 b).

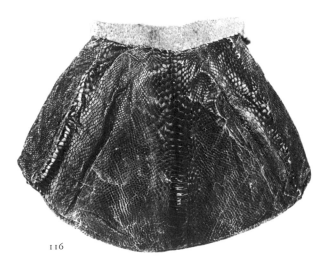

116

PART II    The Contemporary Collection

# Porcupine and Bird Quills

Porcupine
Quill
Weaving

The contemporary weaving of porcupine quills continues an ancient Athapaskan art with replacement of certain materials. Although some changes have been made—from birch-bark to cardboard spacers on the looms, from natural to commercial dyes, and from sinew to thread—the resulting woven designs show remarkable continuity with the past. They favor continuous repeated geometric motifs of diamonds, chevrons and zigzags. For a description by Ross of mid-nineteenth century weaving, see page 144.

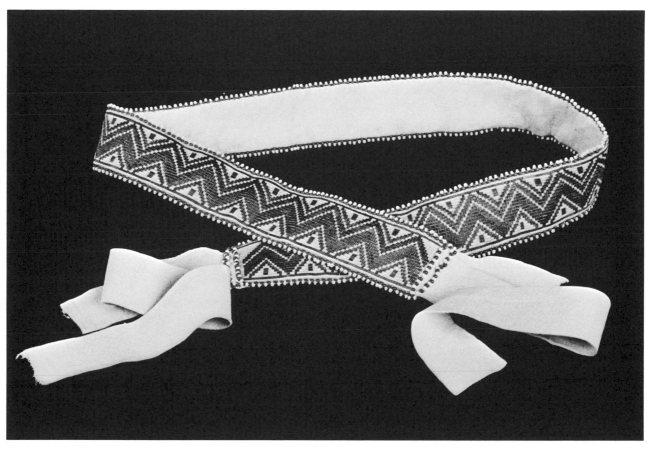

117

## 117 *Baby Belt*

Slavey

Made by Rosa Minoza, Fort Providence,
Northwest Territories, 1986; commissioned by
HMA

L: 143 cm    W: 4.5 cm

87–143

Porcupine quills woven on cotton thread warp and weft using
bow loom; loom-work backed with pair of native-tanned,
bleached, caribou-hide strips, extending beyond quillwork;
quill design in continuous zigzag with small rectangles filling
triangular negative spaces, in commercial dyes of blue, violet,
red, green, on natural ground; two-beaded edging of opaque
red and white glass seed-beads.

In the northwestern Subarctic women traditionally
carried their babies on their backs, supported by a
strong hide belt or carrying strap. This custom is continued today only among the Kutchin. Although
Slavey in Fort Providence no longer use the belts, the
memory remains and occasionally an example, such as
this one, is re-created.

The quality of this belt equals those made in the
1890s and collected by Emma Shaw Colcleugh (see
cat. 3 A–H). It took Rosa Minoza most of the winter to
make it. Memoree Philipp of Fort Providence, who
served as liaison between the Museum and the artist,
doubted that many more of these would be made, as
none of the younger women of Fort Providence wanted
to do it, and the older ones no longer had sufficiently
strong eyesight to execute the intricate quill-woven
designs.

Compare with Memoree Philipp collection of quill-woven
belts, Slavey, Fort Providence, 1970s, PWNHC, Yellowknife.

## 118 *Burden Strap*

Slavey

Made by Elise Gargan, Fort Providence,
Northwest Territories, 1984

HMA purchase 1987

L: 69 cm    W: 4.5 cm

87–144

Porcupine quills woven on cotton thread warp and weft using
bow loom; three-beaded edging of color-lined pink and green
seed-beads; backing of thick, native-tanned and smoked
moose hide extending 14 and 7.5 cm at ends; quill design a
continuous zigzag in three-color rows of purple, pink, blue,
red, greens, yellow (commercial dyes), separated by rows of
undyed quills.

Made for use as a burden strap worn across the
forehead. The heavy moose-hide ends would have
been fastened to the straps of a game bag carried by a
hunter across his shoulders and back.

Elise Gargan, who was born in 1926 near Fort Providence, said: "No one ever taught me to work. I
watched others and then I'd try. If I didn't sew something properly I'd undo it and try again until I could
do it. If you keep on trying eventually you'll succeed"
(Slavey Research Project 1987: 22).

118

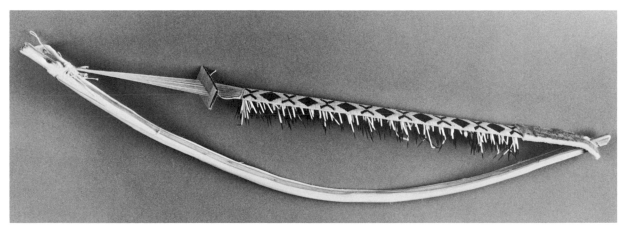

119 (C)

# 119 *Quill Bow Looms*

Slavey

(A) 85–637   (B) 85–638   (C) 85–639

(A) Made by Dora Minoza, Fort Providence, Northwest Territories, 1985, for Hail and Duncan. L: 46 cm W: 5 cm H: 6 cm. Peeled willow strung with cotton thread; porcupine quills woven on cotton warp and weft in pattern of parallel red and yellow zigzag lines on natural ground; partially completed; end-tab of commercially tanned hide, commercial dyes, cardboard warp spacer.

Dora Minoza made this on request, between noon of one day and 9:30 the following morning. Because of the need for haste she used whatever materials were at hand: a granulated-sugar box-top for the cardboard warp spacer, and commercial rather than native-smoked hide. Dora, born in 1923, learned quill-weaving on her own by watching other women work, as her mother was blind and could not teach her.

(B) 85–638 Made by Dora Minoza, Fort Providence, Northwest Territories, 1985; collected by Hail and Duncan. L: 43 cm W: 6 cm H: 9.5 cm. Peeled willow; strung with cotton thread; porcupine quills woven on cotton warp and weft in pattern of blue diamonds, green and yellow chevrons on natural ground; partially completed; smoked moose-hide end-tab; cardboard warp spacer, commercial dyes.

(C) 85–639 Made by Christine Minoza, Fort Providence, Northwest Territories, 1985; collected by Hail and Duncan. L: 47 cm W: 5 CM H: 8.7 cm. Peeled willow; strung with cotton thread; porcupine quills woven on cotton warp and weft in pattern of green diamonds, lavender chevrons on natural ground; partially completed; cardboard warp spacer, smoked moose-hide end-tab; commercial dyes.

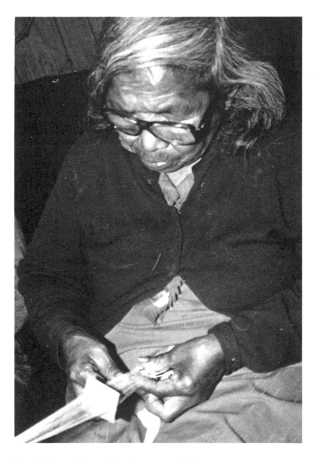

Dora Minoza, Slavey, Fort Providence, Northwest Territories, weaving quills on a bow loom, 1985, cat. 119 (A).

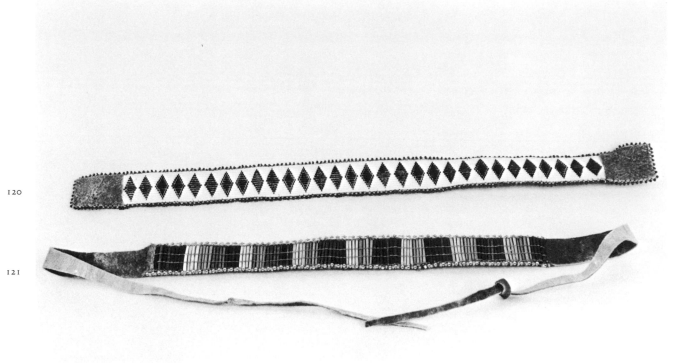

120

121

## 120 *Band*

Slavey

Collected by Hail and Duncan, Fort Providence, Northwest Territories, 1985

L: 47 cm    W: 3 cm

85–640

Porcupine quills woven on cotton thread warp and weft using bow loom; backed with canvas and red stroud; end-tabs of smoked moose hide; two-beaded edging in alternating translucent red and opaque green glass seed-beads; quill pattern a series of diamond shapes in blue, red and yellow on natural ground; commercial dyes.

## 121 *Band*

Slavey

Made by Mary Madelaine Nadu, Fort Providence, Northwest Territories, 1984

Collected by Hail and Duncan, Fort Providence, 1985

L: 30.5 cm + two 38 cm ties    W: 3.5 cm

85–643

Bird-quill sections laid side by side and twined together at regular intervals with orange cotton string in banded color pattern: blue, brown, yellow, pink, commercial dyes; smoked moose-hide backing and ties; two-beaded edging of alternating color-lined blue and opaque orange seed-beads.

Possibly intended as a choker. The decorative use of bird quills among Northern Athapaskans has a long history.

Compare with quilled band, NMM VI-N-23, collected Hay River, 1924, pictured Helm 1981: 343, and GAI AC 207 (Duncan 1989, fig. 2.7), both used as baby-carrying belts; and William Dall's 1870 illustration of Kutchin man wearing bird-quill head-band (Duncan 1987: fig. 28).

## 122 *Band*

Slavey

Collected by Hail and Duncan, Fort Providence, Northwest Territories, 1985

L: 19.5 cm     w: 3 cm

85–642

Porcupine quills woven on cotton thread warp and weft using bow loom; backing of white stroud; end-tabs and ties of smoked moose hide; single-beaded edging with white glass seed-beads; quill pattern of continuous diamond shapes in alternate red and green with yellow and blue interiors on natural ground; commercial dyes.


## 123 *Band*

Slavey

Made by Anastasia Bonnetrouge, Fort Providence, Northwest Territories

Collected by Hail and Duncan, Fort Providence, 1985

L: 28 cm + 20 cm ties     w: 4 cm

85–636

Porcupine quills woven on cotton thread warp and weft using bow loom; backed with native-smoked hide; two-beaded edging in translucent green and milk-white seed-beads; quill pattern of continuous stepped, checkered diamonds in red, pink, violet, green and yellow commercial dyes on natural ground.

This more complex pattern is reminiscent of nineteenth-century bands. The small size makes this piece suitable for the tourist market and for decorative use as a wristlet, arm band or choker.


## 124 *Band*

Slavey

Made by Dora Minoza, Fort Providence, Northwest Territories

Collected by Hail and Duncan, Fort Providence, 1985

L: 16.5 cm + two 19.5 cm ties

85–641

Porcupine quills woven on cotton thread warp and weft using bow loom; backing and ties of commercial hide; end-tabs of smoked hide; two-beaded edging in alternating color-core rose, translucent blue seed-beads; quill pattern of alternated diamond and chevrons in purple, green and yellow on natural ground; commercial dyes.

122                                 123                                 124

## 125 *Gun Case*

Slavey

Quill-weaving by Dora Minoza, Fort Providence, Northwest Territories, 1986–7, commissioned by HMA.

L: 74 cm    W: 18 cm

87–145

Tapered cylinder of native-tanned and smoked caribou hide decorated with two bands of porcupine-quill loom-weaving on cotton thread; two-beaded edging of red seed-beads; flat fringing attached under bands; open end of case pinked; circular piece inserted at muzzle end; hand-sewn seams; quills commercially dyed yellow, blue, dark red; woven in non-traditional pattern.

This gun case does not replicate earlier styles of functional gun cases. It is small and short and was possibly intended for a lever action carbine. There are no carrying straps. The quill-work pattern is a variation on a late-nineteenth-century Central Plains beadwork pattern that has somehow come to the attention of the weaver, possibly through an actual beaded object from the Plains, or through a craft book or museum catalogue. Design ideas have spread through time and from one area to another through the movement of goods, even though the artists themselves may not have left their home communities.

Compare bead design known as "rabbit's ear" on girl's leggings, Central Plains, HMA 57–519.

## 126 *Moccasins*

Great Slave Lake-Mackenzie River Region
Athapaskan

HMA purchase, Northwest Territories Native Arts
& Crafts Society, Yellowknife, 1987

L: 22 cm  W: 10 cm  H: 16 cm

87–228

Soft sole, of smoked moose hide, front seam, pointed toe;
T-shaped heel-seam; seams sinew-sewn; ankle cuff of red
stroud; high ankle-wrap of smoke-tanned caribou with long

wrap-around thong ties; inserted vamp of black velvet edged
with two-quill diagonal plaiting with superimposed quills in
contrasting colors, in commercial dyes of orange, dark purple, wine red; porcupine quills outlined with red thread in
chain stitch; inner sawtooth line of quills folded alternately
up and down; quills sinew-sewn.

A very nice example of the persistence of old
techniques and styles.

Compare with Mackenzie River Athapaskan moccasins made
a hundred years earlier, cats. 8 and 9; and GAI AC 39, Slavey,
Fort Providence, made in 1966 by Angelique Nadley.

126

## 127 *Mukluks*

Slavey

Made by Mary Agnes Bonnetrouge, Fort Providence, Northwest Territories, 1985

Collected by Hail and Duncan, Fort Providence, 1985

L: 28 cm   W: 19 cm   H: 33 cm

85–645

Soft sole, of smoked moose hide, gathered into large vamp, T-shaped heel-seam, caribou fur in leg area, moose-hide fringing at tops. Seams sinew-sewn; vamp, of porcupine quills in a floral motif, in two-quill plaiting, edged in twisted (one-thread, one-quill sewing, or simple line) technique, superimposed on background of natural quills in multiple-quill plaiting with border in geometric design; quills commercially dyed in colors of red, blue, yellow and green; blue and brown yarn-ties, cotton lining.

Mary Agnes Bonnetrouge, Slavey, working on porcupine-quill projects in her home in Fort Providence, Northwest Territories, 1985.

Warm and cheerful, decorated mukluks are popular among both native and non-native people for winter dress occasions in the North.

127

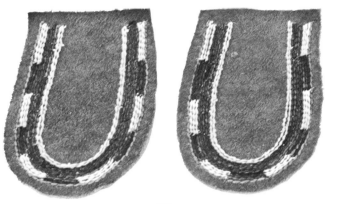

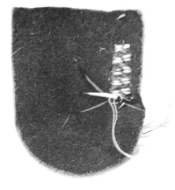

128

129

## 128 *Quilled Moccasin Vamps*

Great Slave Lake-Mackenzie River Region
Athapaskan

Collected by Hail and Duncan, Hay River,
Northwest Territories, 1985

L: 12 cm    W: 7.4 cm

85–666.5

U-shaped; commercially-tanned hide; edging of eleven rows
of porcupine quills, twisted over cotton thread and sewn to
hide in bar-pattern in alternating blue, rose, pink, natural
white; commercial dyes.

Twisted (also called simple line) quillwork has a
wide distribution. Rows of it appear on some of the
earliest moccasins, trousers and gloves from the Western Athapaskans. The technique was also important in
the Eastern Woodlands. It appears on pouches and
moccasins from the eighteenth and nineteenth centuries.

## 129 *Quilled Moccasin Vamp*

Slavey

Work in progress by Mary Agnes Bonnetrouge,
Fort Providence, Northwest Territories, 1985

Collected by Hail and Duncan 1985

L: 10.5 cm    W: 6.5 cm

85–657

U-shaped; smoked moose hide; porcupine quills; four-quill-
plaiting in red-and-white geometric pattern forms band 1 cm
wide around edge; cotton thread.

Agnes, born in 1916 near Horn River, west of Fort
Providence, was working on this vamp when interviewed (see below).

Close-up of Mary Agnes Bonnetrouge's hands, working on
porcupine-quill project in her home in Fort Providence, Northwest
Territories, 1985.

# Moose and Caribou Hair

**Twisting and Tufting**

Twisting moose and caribou hair for decorative use is an old Athapaskan art. Tufting these hairs is a new Athapaskan art form that came into existence shortly after the first World War among the Slavey of Fort Providence in the Northwest Territories. According to Sister Beatrice Leduc of the Order of the Grey Nuns, the inventer of the craft was Mrs. Boniface Laferte, later Lafferty (nee Madeleine Bouvier), of Indian and French descent. Mrs. Laferte had been one of the first pupils of the Grey Nuns of Montreal at the Sacred Heart Convent in Fort Providence. Because many commercial materials such as silk and beads that were used in hand embroidery were unavailable during and after the first World War, Mrs. Laferte had the inspiration to imitate with moose hair a type of work called "punch work," made with wool, that she had seen done by one of the Sisters for the bishop's chair and kneeler in the church (and now in the Northern Life Museum, Fort Smith, Northwest Territories). Many years later Mrs. Laferte taught her craft to her two daughters-in-law, one of whom is Mrs. Joe Lafferty (Celine Laviolette), now of Fort Simpson, and to a number of other women. In 1931 Sister Beatrice Leduc was transferred from Fort Chipewyan to Fort Providence. "It is then that I became interested in moose-hair craft of which I had never heard before. . . . I asked Celine if she would be my tutor and I started taking lessons. . . . From then on, year after year, I taught it to groups and groups of our students from Providence, Simpson, Wrigley, Norman and Liard. . . . When I was transferred to Fort Resolution in 1941 I also taught it to our girls of St. Joseph Convent, from Resolution, Hay River, Yellowknife and Fort Rae. . . . Countless are the pieces of work that came out of our sewing clubs; gloves, mitts, slippers of moosehide and bleached caribou skin; fancy decorating and ornamental articles, some of which were offered to high dignitaries, even to His Holiness Pope Pius XII" (Leduc 1925–1963).

This twentieth-century use of moose hair differs from the moose-hair embroidery developed by the Ursuline Sisters and their students, the Hurons of Lorette, near Quebec during the eighteenth century. The earlier form involved threading a needle with moose hair and sewing with it, employing a satin stitch and tiny French knots, or couching over

## 130 *Barrette*

Slavey, 1985
Collected by Hail and Duncan, Fort Providence,
Northwest Territories, 1985

L: 12 cm   W: 6 cm

85–655

Smoked moose hide with hole at either end, wooden dowel
inserted; two-beaded edging in translucent blue glass seed-
beads; backed with navy stroud; upper surface embroidered
with moose-hair tufting in white, red, orange four-petal
flower, four green leaves.

a small bundle of threads, to create complex delicate floral designs on
black-dyed hide or fabric. This work, sold to visitors, provided income
for the convent during difficult financial periods. (See Turner [1955] for
illustrations of these sewing techniques and the later tufting techniques.)

The moose hair suitable for tufting is taken from the center back of
the moose during the winter months of December through March, when
it has grown six to eight inches in length. The white hairs are hand-
picked from the hide, as cutting them would destroy the best portion.
According to Sister Beatrice Leduc (1925–63): "How many times were
we offered by hunters of the village to go and pluck the hair from hides
of animals they had killed; it was hard and dirty work; we would come
back home with painful blisters on our fingers. . . . selection of the
longest and whitest almost one by one, how many hours did I spend in
that selection?"

The hairs are washed, sorted and dyed, using natural dyes made of
barks, berries and leaves, commercial powdered dyes, and crepe paper
and medicine gin pill (for blue). After slowly drying, the hairs are ready
for sewing.

In preparation for the tufted design, a pattern is drawn freehand on
hide or stiffly backed velvet with a small sharpened stick dipped in
flour-and-water paste. A small bundle of fifteen to twenty hairs is held
onto the pattern with a loop-stitch taken over the hair approximately a
quarter inch from the end. The stitch is pulled tight and knotted on the
back side of the backing material so that the moose hair stands upright
in a tuft. The long end of the bundle is cut off about a quarter to a half
inch from the stitch, making the hair form into a bristly tuft. The motif
outline is completely filled in with similar sewn bundles. With scissors
the hairs are sculpted into smooth hemispheres. This technique is used
for the petals of floral patterns. Stems of flowers are created with an

over-sewn line, in which diagonal thread stitches are taken around slightly twisted bundles of hair (Cohen 1977).

In recent years caribou hair has also been used for tufting. It creates a finer, softer tuft than moose hair, as the caribou hair is thinner. Sometimes both kinds of hair are used on one piece.

The moose-hair tufting that began at Fort Providence was practiced by Athapaskan women for a decade or so after World War I, although they never preferred it to embroidery with beads or silk. In the 1960s the craft was again revived, and has been particularly popular since then at Fort Providence, Jean Marie River and Fort Resolution. Red Willows Crafts, a native-owned shop in Fort Providence, today sells tufting on hide in the form of barrettes, purses, moccasins, and unfinished squares of tufting on velvet designed to be framed. Tufting on velvet is particularly popular. The bristly sheen of the petals contrasts with the soft pile of the velvet, creating a pleasing textural effect in the resulting floral picture.

131

## 131 *Moose-Hair Picture*

Slavey, 1985
Collected by Hail and Duncan, Red Willows Crafts, Fort Providence, Northwest Territories, 1985
L: 26 cm    W: 19 cm
85–653

Black velvet backed with canvas; tufted moose hair in three-flower pattern; twisted moose-hair stems; hair dyed orange, light grey-green, rust.

This combination of a traditional material and a new technique has resulted in an art form that has become popular among both native and non-native people. Framed and protected with glass, this embroidery becomes an attractive piece for display in the home. Similar pictures are also made using dyed and folded porcupine quills.

Compare with picture, TM1983.37, Slavey, Fort Providence, 1982; DAM F-SL-1, Slavey; selection of examples in MMMN, DAM, GAI, PWNHC.

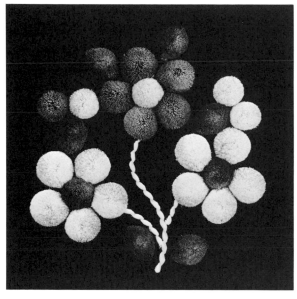

132

## 132 *Moose- and Caribou-Hair Picture*

Slavey, 1985

Collected by Hail and Duncan, Red Willows Native Crafts, Fort Providence, Northwest Territories, 1985

L: 25 cm   w: 21 cm

85–652

Black velvet backed with canvas; embroidered in three-flower pattern: central rust-colored flower tufted of moose hair, two side-flowers tufted of natural color (grey-white), brown and yellow-dyed caribou hair; stems of twisted caribou hair.

133

## 133 *Moose-Hair Picture*

Slavey, 1985

Collected by Hail and Duncan, Fort Providence, Northwest Territories, 1985

L: 22 cm   w: 21 cm

85–654

Black velvet embroidered with twisted moose hair in three-flower, five-petal pattern; pink and white petals, yellow centers, green leaves.

Intended to be framed under glass and used as wall art.

134

## 134 *Moccasins*

Slavey, 1985

Collected by Hail and Duncan, Fort Providence,
Northwest Territories, 1985

L: 25 cm   W: 13 cm

85–647

Soft sole, of moose hide, heavily smoked, rounded toe, T-shaped heel-seam, white stroud vamp embroidered with floral design in rose and yellow five-petaled flower and green leaves of tufted moose hair; blue, three-petaled flower of tufted caribou hair; beaver-fur cuff.

Caribou hair is finer and softer than moose hair. The artist apparently liked the variation in texture that resulted from combining the two materials in one embroidery.

Sister Flore Pierson, a Grey Nun who has lived in the North since 1943, observed, "I was surprised to see that they were putting tufting on slippers, because it doesn't work. At Fort Good Hope they didn't put tufting on moccasins and gloves because it didn't wear well. That's why they made pictures out of it" (Pierson, pers. comm. 1985). Perhaps those who buy fancy tufted moccasins today are not planning to wear them in the wet snow but to keep them as mementos and art pieces. The popular use of tufting for pictures is a good example of a change in the form of a native-crafted object to accomodate both native tastes and an outside market.

## 135 *Child's Mukluks*

Slavey

Made by Mary Agnes Bonnetrouge, Fort
Providence, Northwest Territories, 1985

Collected by Hail and Duncan, Fort Providence,
1985

L: 19 cm   W: 10 cm   H: 19 cm

85–646

Smoked moose-hide lowers, rounded toe; leg area of smoked caribou with wide fringing around top, caribou-fur strips sinew-sewn on calf area; inserted smoked-caribou vamps decorated with twisted moose hair in pattern of five-petal flower and leaves; flower is pink with white outline, yellow center; leaves green with yellow outline; artificial dyes; wool-blend green-and-black plaited-yarn drawstring around top cuff with tassled ends.

135

# Threads

## 136 *Dog Blanket*

Chipewyan-Cree-Metis

Made by Maria Houle, Fort Chipewyan, Alberta, 1985; commissioned by HMA.

L: 39 cm    W: 36cm+9 cm fringe

85-891

Blue stroud machine-sewn to canvas backing; pinked edging; border of fringed acrylic yarn in white, maroon, pink, red except in center front; pinked oval of red stroud appliquéd at the center serves as backing for bells attached to harness leather, secured with three hide loops; floral corner motifs in yarn embroidery, motifs on two front, two rear corners alike; colors: pink, purple, yellow, greens, lavender, maroon. Circle of white hide appliquéd on underside at each corner, with thongs for attachment to dog harness (bells are HMA 61–453).

Dog blankets have been used by dog-team drivers since the nineteenth century, but are rarer today. In earlier days when dogs were the main source of transport in winter, a good team was a Northerner's pride and joy. Old men's eyes sparkle when they remember their dog teams and describe how they used to dress them with colorful blankets and noisy bells. Today most native people have sold their dogs because they are expensive to feed and are not needed in the age of snowmobiles and cars, but dog races are still an annual event at The Pas, Manitoba and other places. A century earlier, Emma Shaw Colcleugh experienced the thrill and color of riding in a dog sleigh at The Pas (see Chapter II).

Dog blankets were usually made in matching sets of two, four or six, depending on the number of dogs in a man's team. According to older drivers, the blankets were put on the dogs just before they arrived in a settlement, so that the team might make a joyful and showy entrance.

Compare with dog blanket collected by Colcleugh in 1894 from Fort Simpson, cat. 68; dog blankets: NLM 70.13.1–5, Dogrib, 1903.

136

## 137 *Dog Whip*

Great Slave Lake-Mackenzie River Region
Athapaskan, 1980s

Collected by Barbara Hail from Agnes Mercredi
Williams, Chipewyan-Métis, Yellowknife,
Northwest Territories, 1987

L: 152 cm    W: 32 cm

87–222

Wool-acrylic-blend yarn plaited and wrapped around stick
handle from which extends long plaited rawhide whip; round
balls of yarn pile at each end of handle and on base of whip;
yarn pompons; colors: red, blues, green, white, yellow,
brown, tan, pink.

Agnes Mercredi Williams explained that the yarn
balls and brightly colored pompons were to keep the
whip visible if it dropped in the snow. Dog whips of
this type were common to Athapaskans who ran dogs.
Osgood (1931: 65) believed the yarn-ornamented dog
whip to have been introduced to the Lower Mackenzie
by métis.

Compare with whip: CMC VI-E -48, Dogrib, circa 1940.

137

Team of huskies carrying the mail between forts Resolution and Providence, Winter, 1926–27. Tom Troues and his forerunner, J. Lafferty,
wear mukluks; their dogs are dressed up in blankets. Courtesy Oblate Archives, Fort Smith, NWT.

## 138 *Mukluks* (A) *and Duffel Liners* (B)

Chipewyan-Métis, 1980s

Made by Bernadette Mercredi, Fort Smith, Northwest Territories, 1987

Collected by Barbara Hail from Agnes Mercredi Williams, daughter of maker, Yellowknife, Northwest Territories, 1987

L: 26 cm   W: 11 cm   H: 31 cm

87–223

(A) Soft sole, body and thong ties of native-smoked moose hide; top of white and navy stroud; acrylic-yarn embroidery on vamp and leg-upper in floral pattern in graduating tones-pink, burgundy, lavender, purple, blue, with green leaves and stem; machine-stitched cotton rickrack and seam-binding encircles top; drawstring around top formed of plaited yarn with fringed ends; white rabbit fur sewn to central portion of leg-upper. (B) Liners of green wool duffel.

Bernadette Mercredi presently resides in a nursing home in Fort Smith, but lived earlier in Fort Chipewyan, and before that in Fond du Lac, northern Saskatchewan. According to her daughter Agnes, she is known particularly for her floral embroidery in graduated color combinations. Also a skilled bead-worker, Bernadette has made each of her married children and their spouses a matching set of bead-embroidered gauntlets as a special gift.

138 A & B

139

## 139 *Crow Boots*

Chipewyan-Cree-Métis

Made by Maria Houle, Fort Chipewyan, Alberta; commissioned by HMA, 1985

L: 25.7 cm   W: 11 cm   H: 22 cm

85–894

Soft sole, native smoke-tanned moose hide, rounded toe, T-shaped heel-seam; large vamp, upper and lower cuffs of white wool stroud embroidered with floral design in buttonhole, chain and stem stitches using synthetic yarn in greens, hot pink, purples, and yellow. Front-opening, with plaited yarn ties, round pompons in light green, yellow, pink, white. Vamp and tongue one piece; edge of tongue and cuffs bordered with white rabbit fur; lower cuff pinked; lined with pink cotton-blend cloth.

White fur is commonly used on women's moccasins; brown fur, especially beaver, is preferred for men's. Like other soft-sole footwear, the "crow boot" can be worn outside when temperatures are below freezing and the snow is dry.

## 140 *Moccasins* (A) *and Purse* (B)

Chipewyan

Made by Judith Buggins, Yellowknife, Northwest Territories, 1987; commissioned by HMA through NWT Native Arts and Crafts Society.

(A) L: 27 cm    H: 20 cm

87–290

Soft sole, of sun-bleached, smoked caribou hide, pointed toe, T-shaped heel-seam; seams thread-sewn; four rows of dyed horsehair wrapped with silk thread cover vamp seam; high ankle wraps, ties, pinked cuffs and wraps; vamp and cuffs embroidered in small-flower pattern with silk thread in colors of pink, cerise, yellow, greens, blue; embroidery backed with plastic and thin cotton cloth; outline of floss design pre-drawn on hide.

(B) L: 17 cm    W: 17 cm

87–291

Sun-bleached smoked caribou hide, satin lining, shoulder strap, thread-sewn; front embroidered with sil thread in small-flower pattern: royal blue and turquoise flowers, yellow centers, veined green leaves.

Many older women who had learned as children to embroider with very fine silk thread complained in 1985 that since the 1940s, they had not been able to obtain real or "thin" silk. Since silk is once more available from Chinese markets, and since some women expressed a desire to work with the fine silk again, the Haffenreffer Museum obtained some for this purpose, and it was distributed to several silk embroiderers in 1987.[1] These moccasins and the accompanying purse are the first pieces embroidered with the Chinese silk to come back to the Museum.

Judith Buggins is seventy-four years old. She was born in Rocher River near Fort Resolution, but did not attend the mission school there. She says that her embroidery skills were "self-taught," that is, she learned, starting in her late teens, by watching others, and developed her own personal style. She remembered the old way of making pointed-toe moccasins, with the vamp edged with a ribbing of horsehair wrapped with silk thread and embroidered with silk in a small-flower design. She enjoyed selecting favorite shades of silk threads from among the multiple colors available in

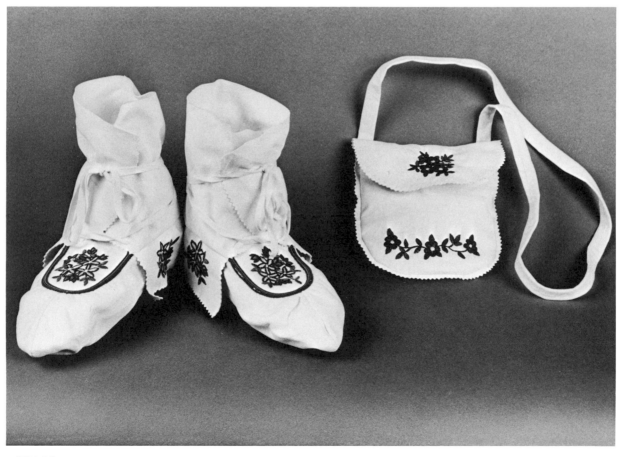

140 A & B

the skeins spread out before her. She was eager to make the moccasins as true to the old way as possible, and would not begin until she had acquired the horsehair, which was not available locally.[2]

Judith described the process of making the moccasins as follows (Buggins, pers. comm. 1987): first she washed the tanned caribou hide in clear water four times, and then hung it outside in the wind. She believes that it is the wind that bleaches it. Next she cut the slipper outline from the hide. In earlier days she used her hand or another object as a measure for the outline, but now, because of poor eyesight, she draws on a paper pattern. Next she embroidered the vamp, or "upper," as she calls it, then tacked it onto the sole at three points, the center and two sides. The edges of

the sole were eased into place with puckering and flattening, and the resulting seam was enhanced with a series of horsehair bundles wrapped with silk thread.

Judith acknowledged that not many native people make this type of slipper any more because it is harder to make well. Also, it is not as popular with customers from the outside as the round-toed style. When the type does appear in a shop, it is usually an older pair being re-sold, and these may number no more than two or three pairs a year.

1 The silk was purchased in China for the Museum, courtesy of Dorothy Nelson.
2 The dyed horse hair was sent to the artist from the Haffenreffer Museum. It had been purchased by Hail and Duncan at an independent trader's store in Fort Providence in 1985.

141

## 141 *Moss Bag*

Slavey, 1980s

Collected by Hail and Duncan, Red Willows Crafts, Fort Providence, Northwest Territories, 1985

L: 49 cm    W: 23 cm

85–651

Black velvet, cotton-print lining; cotton-floss embroidery in floral pattern of dip-petal rose along both sides of front-lacing thongs. Embroidery colors: pink, blue, gold, green.

Among Dene people it is traditional to carry babies in moss bags, so named because they were stuffed with sphagnum moss that was placed between two cloths underneath the baby, or in a specially designed diaper of hide or canvas. The moss is useful because it is extremely absorbent. It is gathered by digging under the surface of a sphagnum clump until the inner, dry moss is reached.

Compare with earlier moss bag for doll, cat. 74.

# Beads

## Bead Embroidery

Bead embroidery is still a woman's art in the Subarctic. Skills and designs are passed down through the generations, from mother to daughter, or within extended families, or are learned through more formal instruction in classes at school or community centers. Designs follow the earlier floral traditions, but motifs tend to be larger and more simplified, in part reflecting the larger size of the glass seed-beads used. The technique used is almost exclusively the overlay or spot stitch, both strung and couched (secured) with thread. By contrast, on the earliest pieces the beads were usually strung on sinew and couched with thread.

The range of bead colors available to contemporary bead workers in the Subarctic is much more varied than that in use in the nineteenth and early twentieth centuries. More vibrant hues, luster, iridescent and pearlized finishes, color-cores, color-linings, and glass beads with various metallic finishes have all become available and are widely used. (For the sake of easy reference, the terms used in catalogue entries follow when possible those on bead cards currently circulated by Elliot Greene & Company, New York.)

## 142 *Mittens*

Western Woods Cree (Swampy), late twentieth century
Made by Marian Bee, Norway House, Manitoba
Collected by Hail and Duncan, Rossville, Norway House, 1985
L: 37 cm   W: 23 cm
85–674

142

Commercially tanned hide, long cuffs trimmed with two bands of rabbit fur; underside of mitts brown hide; upper side hide with white finish; uppers and cuffs embroidered with glass seed-beads, thread-sewn and couched, in stylized floral and geometric motifs; white duffel lining; short fringe on sides of cuffs; bead colors: opaque orange, blues, light green, yellow, red; translucent red, iridescent green, color-core pink, luster blue-violet.

All materials used in these mittens are readily available through "The Bay" store in Rossville, Norway House. Commercial hides and furs are more frequently used by artisans who are making objects for sale as, according to this artist, most purchasers do not wish to spend the amount of money required to pay for the labor of home tanning. The native-tanned hides and home-cured furs are usually saved for personal use and gifts to friends and family (Bee, pers. comm. 1985).

## 143 *Mukluks*

Western Woods Cree (Swampy),
late twentieth century

Made by Marian Bee, Norway House, Manitoba

Collected by Hail and Duncan from Georgina
Albert, Marian Bee's mother, from shop in her
home at Jack River, Norway House, 1985

L: 25 cm    W: 13 cm    H: 44 cm

85–672

143

Commercially tanned hide, yellow-brown and white; T-shaped heel-seam; embroidered with glass seed-beads, thread-strung and couched; remains of paper pattern through which beadwork has been applied; white rabbit fur covers leggings except for front-decorated panel; elastic at tops; machine-stitched, thong ties, rabbit-fur pompons; thong ankle-ties ; duffel lining; hand-pinked leather flap inserted into seam where vamp stitched to sole, folded over to cover seam; bead design of four-petal rose, double buds; leaves outlined in variations of green; spurs on stem; feather wisps emanate from flowers; bead colors: opaque red, orange, yellow, green, iridescent blue and yellow, luster pink and green, translucent red, color-core green.

Mukluks are a form of foot-covering with a long history in the Arctic, where they were made with bearded-seal soles and seal or caribou uppers. In the Subarctic they are of recent use, and are made with tanned hide, duffel, or stroud, decorated with beads, quills, or yarn. When they first became popular they were a luxury item to many native people. According to seventy-five-year-old Harry Sanderson, a Cree-Métis from The Pas, Manitoba, and a former employee of the Hudson's Bay Company, "We children always wore moccasins that our mother made for us. I never owned a pair of mukluks—couldn't afford them. They came in about 1935, for sale to whites" (pers. comm. 1985).

## 144 *Moccasins*

Western Woods Cree (Swampy),
late twentieth century

Made by Geraldine Simpson, Norway House,
Manitoba

Collected by Hail and Duncan, Norway House,
1985

L: 26 cm    W: 13 cm

85–675

144

Soft sole, of commercially tanned hide dyed yellow-orange, T-shaped heel-seam; seams thread-sewn; cuff of black rabbit fur; round toe gathered into vamp, decorated with glass seed-beads, thread-strung and couched, through paper pattern placed on hide, unbeaded sections cut away; bead design stylized floral, bilaterally symmetrical, three-petal flower, stacked buds, leaves in colors of opaque yellow, lavender, blue, red-orange, greens, white, translucent blue and red, and color-core lavender.

For an example of a paper pattern in place, see fig. IV-7.

## 145 *Mittens*

Western Woods Cree (Swampy),
late twentieth century

Made by Esther Chubb

Collected by Hail and Duncan from Esther Chubb
at her home on Tower's Island near Jack River,
Norway House, Manitoba, 1985

L: 28 cm   W: 12 cm

85–676

145

Commercial smoke-tanned hide, seams thread-sewn, black
rabbit fur, glass seed-beads, thread-strung and couched on
upper side of mittens in floral design of six-petal flower,
leaves, buds; bead colors: opaque wine, yellows, orange,
blue, green; translucent and color-core greens.

Esther Chubb, born in Oxford House, Manitoba,
has long been well-known in Manitoba for her skills in
silk-thread embroidery and beadwork. Now in her
eighties, she still accepts commissions for beaded
pieces.

146

## 146 *Vest*

Western Woods Cree, 1975

Made by Sarah Smith, Peter Ballantyne band,
Montreal Lake, Saskatchewan

Collected by William and Michelle Tracy, Prince
Albert, Saskatchewan, 1975

L: 60 cm   W: 46 cm

75–216

Native smoke-tanned moose hide, front zipper; contour-
beaded on front and back with glass seed-beads, thread-sewn
and couched, in floral design of pointed, five-petal flowers,
leaves, stems with spurs; in opaque red, medium blue and
green, orange, white; translucent green. Vest hand-sewn;
two front pockets, edges pinked, short fringing attached
across chest and back; edge-binding of pinked hide; cotton
lining.

Very few large pieces of clothing such as this were
being home-tanned in the Montreal Lake area in 1975.
Sarah Smith was over seventy years old when she
made this vest.

## 147 *Moccasins*

Cree, Cree-Métis, late twentieth century

Collected by Hail and Duncan at Hay River, Northwest Territories, 1985

L: 20 cm   W: 10 cm   H: 11 cm

85–662

147

Soft sole, doubled; rounded toe of commercially tanned, orange-dyed hide; machine stitched; unlined; T-shaped heel-seam; seams thread-sewn. Vamp and stand-up cuff of native-tanned and smoked hide, embroidered and edged with glass seed-beads, thread-strung and couched, in leaf and bud design in colors of opaque blue, green, yellow, red, black, yellow-orange; translucent orange, greens, blues, red, color-core turquoise; pattern pre-drawn in ink on light-weight plastic wrap that has been placed over the hide and embroidered through; cuffs lined with printed fabric.

Since about 1970 many Saskatchewan Cree groups have used thin plastic covering, such as packaged-food wraps or dry-cleaning bags to keep light-colored hide clean while beadwork is in process. The plastic is left on when the object is sold. On this pair of moccasins the beaded areas are more skillfully sewn than is the moccasin itself and are likely the product of a different craftsperson.

A number of Cree and Cree-Métis from Saskatchewan moved to the West Passage area of Hay River in the 1940s in order to find jobs. Germaine Page, an active Cree-Métis beadworker from this community, originally from Sweet Grass, near North Battleford, Saskatchewan, made a pair of moccasins employing the same design as this pair in 1968 and may have also beaded this pair, which was offered for sale at a local shop in 1985.

Compare with moccasins, Germaine Page, Saskatchewan Cree, APM H68.40.1. See also moccasins belonging to Germaine Page (85–10–30, Hail and Duncan field photos).

148

## 148 *Moccasins*

Western Woods Cree (Swampy) or Cree-Métis, late nineteenth century

Collected by Hail and Duncan, The Pas, Manitoba, 1985

L: 29 cm   W: 11 cm   H: 9.5 cm

85–685

Soft sole, doubled; rounded toe, of commercially tanned leather; T-shaped heel-seam; seams thread-sewn; white rabbit-fur cuff, vamp embroidered with glass seed-beads in design of five-petal flower with leaves; beads thread-strung and couched, in translucent orange and blue, luster grey, and opaque green, yellow, and white; double sole; seam attaching vamp to lower covered by hide flap inserted into seam, folded over and sewn down; duffel lining.

The double sole makes these moccasins practical for everyday wear.

## 149 *Mukluks, Child's*

Western Woods Cree (Swampy) or Cree-Métis,
late nineteenth century

Collected by Hail and Duncan, The Pas, Manitoba,
1985

L: 20 cm    W: 10 cm    H: 20 cm

85–665

149

Commercially tanned hide, canvas lining, vamp of white deer hide beaded in stylized floral design; double sole; white rabbit-fur on leg area and pompons; drawstring ties; bead colors: luster pink, lavender, yellow; opaque blue, orange; translucent green.

This type of hide boot, with attached fur-wrapped legging, has become popular throughout the Subarctic among both natives and non-natives. According to the current owner of Kerr's Furs-Rickborn's Ltd. in The Pas, Manitoba, where these mukluks were made, this style was created in 1960 by Ann Liese Rickborn, wife of Bernie Rickborn, the store's founder. She employed many Cree and métis women in making moccasins and other wearing apparel for the store. Because the "Trappers' Festival," held every February in The Pas, attracted visitors from cities farther south who sought to purchase warm native-made footgear, the bead-embroidered, fur-and-hide mukluk became popular.

Other variations of this warm boot, based on Arctic Inuit sealskin footgear (from which the mukluk gets its name), but using materials traditional to the Subarctic, have been made since the 1930s.

These mukluks were made "factory style," in three stages: the vamp was beaded by one person, the leather cut by another, and the object as a whole assembled by a third. Under this system, some craftspeople work at home, while others are employed in the shop.

## 150 *Wristlet*

Western Woods Cree (Swampy) or Cree-Métis,
late twentieth century

Made in Island Lake, Garden Hill, Manitoba

HMA purchase Indian Crafts and Arts Manitoba,
Inc., Winnipeg, 1985

L: 25 cm    W: 9.5 cm

85–668

Commercially tanned hide, button, glass seed-beads, thread-strung and couched; bilaterally symmetrical design of eight-petal flower and buds with stacked lobes, contour-beaded to shape of floral form; white background-beading contoured to shape of wristlet; bead colors: opaque white, medium blue, orange; translucent dark blue, green, dark red.

According to the staff of the native-owned coopera-

tive from which it was purchased, the wristlet's use was both decorative and utilitarian: it held back a man's shirt sleeve from hanging over his wrist.

Both Swampy Cree and Ojibwa (Saulteaux) of the Lake Winnipeg area live in many of the same communities and have long intermarried. Northern Ojibwa and Swampy Cree live in Island Lake, and some Northern Ojibwa prefer to be called Cree (Rogers and Taylor 1981: 241). As with the purse collected by Colcleugh, cat. 20, this wristlet and purse, cat. 151 may reflect a combination of artistic traditions.

Compare with similar bead style of stacked lobes in cat. 151 and in mitten gauntlets of moosehide, Little Grand Rapids band, Lake Winnipeg Saulteaux, Berens River, 1970, UWP E5-346.

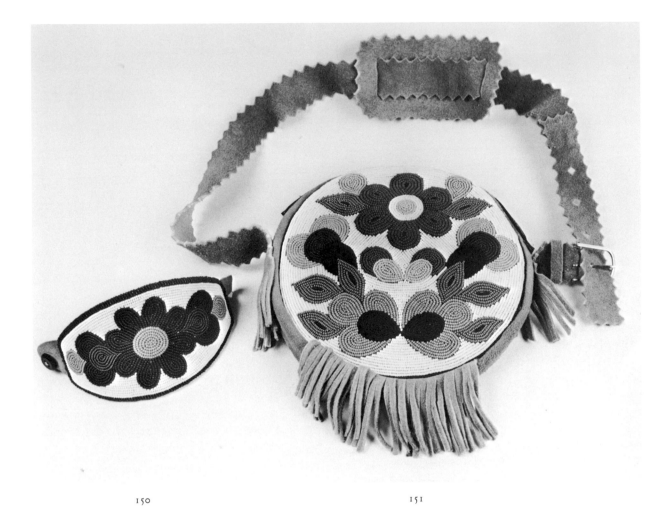

150          151

## 151 *Purse*

Western Woods Cree (Swampy) or Cree-Métis,
late nineteenth century

Collected by Hail and Duncan, The Pas, Manitoba,
1985

D: 23 cm    W: 4 cm

85–666

Circular; smoked moose hide, native tanned, short thick
fringes; pinked shoulder strap, metal buckle, flannel lining
on underside of beaded panel; commercial zipper, machine-
stitched. Fully beaded front, contour beaded, with white
background and bilaterally symmetrical pattern of six-petal
flower, leaves and buds with stacked lobes; bead colors:
opaque white, brown, blues, greens, red, orange, yellow,
luster pink, translucent red.

Kathleen de la Ronde, a Cree-Métis beadwork instructor in The Pas who has often served as a judge at
the native crafts fair which accompanies the town's
annual Trappers' Festival, gave this purse a low rating
because, although the bead embroidery was excellent
in design, color choice, and execution, the purse suf-
fered from an inappropriate mix of traditional and
European techniques and materials; that is, the zipper
and buckle were not consistent with the native smoked
hide.

Round purses were also popular, made-for-sale
items in the mid-1970s among the Western Woods
Cree of Prince Albert, Saskatchewan and the Ojibwa
and Swampy Cree of Red Lake, Ontario (Tracy, pers.
comm. 1985).

## 152 *Baby Belt*

Slavey

Collected by Hail and Duncan, Fort Providence, Northwest Territories, 1985

L: 86 cm + two 40 cm ties   W: 12 cm

85–649

Black velvet, edged with green cotton-bias tape; hide straps; embroidered in design of contiguous five-petal flowers, buds, leaves, along a stem, with glass seed-beads, in translucent silver-lined peach and yellow, opaque light green, silver-lined iridescent green; luster blue; pearlized white.

In earlier days a common method of carrying a baby was to support the infant in a shawl on the back by means of a belt or strap beneath its buttocks. In some areas of the North, especially around Fort McPherson, these belts are still used. In other areas they are made in remembrance of the past. The tapered round-ended belt with ties has been typical of Great Slave Lake Athapaskan groups. Band designs have long been popular for decoration of narrow objects such as belts and garters (see cats. 66 and 73).

Compare with baby belt, TM 1983.36, collected 1982 and cat. 73, collected by Colcleugh in 1894.

The use of the belt among Kutchin mothers of Fort McPherson and Arctic Red River is an example of a continuing tradition. Cree designs have sometimes influenced Athapaskan designs. This baby belt in thread embroidery uses several basic Cree motifs. Courtesy Provincial Archives of Alberta.

152

## 153 *Scissors Case*

Slavey

Made by Jennora Akinneah, Meander River
Reserve, northwestern Alberta

Collected by Hail and Duncan, Edmonton, Alberta,
1985

L: 25 cm    W: 9.5 cm

85–667

153

Smoked moose-hide case, seams sewn with synthetic sinew,
decorated with glass seed-beads, thread-strung and couched,
in floral design of dip-petaled rose and buds, in color-lined
pinks and green, opaque yellow and blue, translucent green;
three-beaded edging in opaque white.

The indentations of the flower petals indicate this to
be a wild rose, or "Alberta rose," as it is called by many
beadworkers of this province. Both Colcleugh and
Elizabeth Taylor, a contemporaneous visitor to the
Mackenzie River area, were surprised at the profusion
of beautiful flowers in the far North. Around Fort Good
Hope, to quote Taylor (1894: 31) "roses were in full
bloom—those beautiful northern roses, fragrant in
flower, stem and leaf—and within a few rods I gathered
twenty-five species of flowers."

The scissors case represents continuity in a type of
functional object that has been made in the Subarctic
from the mid-nineteenth century until the present.
Scissors were an early and valued item in the fur trade,
appreciated especially by the women whose sewing
skills were essential to keeping a family warmly
clothed.

## 154 *Moccasins*

Dogrib

Made by Margaret Lafferty, Rae, Northwest
Territories, 1960s

Collected by Barbara Hail, Yellowknife, 1987

L: 26 cm    W: 11.5 cm    H: 20 cm

87–227

154

Soft sole; smoked moose hide, front seam, pointed toe, puc-
kered around inserted vamp; T-shaped heel-seam; light
smoked caribou-hide ankle wraps, wrap-around thongs;
ankle cuff of two layers pinked stroud, red and white, hand-
sewn with synthetic sinew; vamp and tongue of three layers
moose hide, canvas, stroud; seed-beads in contoured rows
follow edge of vamp in banded pattern of milky white,
opaque blue and iridescent pink; translucent silver-lined red
and color-lined pink; and luster white; thread-strung and
couched.

Pointed-toe moccasins began to be replaced with rounded-toe moccasins in the 1930s. Some women say it is because the rounded-toe ones are easier to make; others because they fit into "moccasin rubbers" which are worn over moccasins to protect them from mud and dirt. Another cause for the change in form was suggested by anthropologist Alanson Skinner. Speaking of the Saulteaux of Island Lake, he said that they preferred "winter" or "mitt" moccasins with no seam over the toe as they provided more room in the toe for extra foot coverings in winter (1911:123). The beads used here are typical of the kind available in Hudson's Bay Company stores in the North today.

## 155 *Moccasins*

Slavey

Made at Sunrise School, Hay River Reserve, Northwest Territories

Collected by Hail and Duncan, Hay River, 1985

L: 27.5 cm   W: 12 cm   H: 8.5 cm

85–648

155

Soft sole, smoked moose hide cut with rounded toe, T-shaped heel-seam; seams sinew-sewn; beaver cuff above red-stroud cut-work lower cuff; vamp of white stroud, decorated in floral design with glass seed-beads, thread-strung and couched, in color-lined pink, opaque reds and yellow, silver-lined yellow and greens.

In recent years fewer women have continued the arduous labor of tanning hides at home. By 1975 the Canadian government subsidized the cost of sending hides out for commercial tanning in order to ensure availability. Commercial tanning processes vary and may affect color and surface texture of hide. Many women do not like working with commercially tanned hide, as its toughness resists the needle. However, shop-keepers have found that a certain percentage of purchasers prefer it to home- or smoke-tanned hide, as they do not like the smoked odor in their closets and drawers. Also, native-tanned moose hide is more expensive because of the time and effort involved in processing it, and so may be priced prohibitively.

156

## 156 *Moccasins*

Slavey

Collected by Hail and Duncan, Hay River, Northwest Territories, 1985

L: 23 cm   W: 12 cm   H: 11 cm

85–644

Soft sole, of smoked moose hide, front seam, pointed toe, T-shaped heel-seam; seams sewn with synthetic sinew; cuff of beaver fur over pinked red-stroud lower cuff; vamp of white stroud, embroidered with thread-strung and couched glass seed-beads in bud and leaf design in color-lined pink, opaque and translucent reds, and silver-lined greens.

## 157 *Moccasins*

Dogrib

Made by Elizabeth Michel, Rae, Northwest
Territories, 1987

Collected by Barbara Hail at Northwest Territories
Native Arts and Crafts Society, Yellowknife, 1987

L: 27 cm   W: 12 cm

87–225

Soft sole, of smoked moose hide, cut in rounded toe; T-
shaped heel-seam; unlined; beaver cuff backed with synthetic
white fabric; seams sewn with synthetic sinew; stroud vamp
and cuff decorated with glass seed-beads, thread-strung and
couched, in stylized floral pattern with translucent blue,
green, red, color-lined pink, silver-lined green on opaque
blue ground. Beads applied through plastic film of which
traces remain.

One blue flower is beaded on the outer side of each
cuff, probably to help the wearer determine the left-
and right-foot moccasin. Some people have found that
although the stiff, fully-beaded lower cuff is handsome,
it is not practical, since the beadwork rubs against the
ground when the moccasin is worn. This wide, double-
cuffed style is made today in several Athapaskan communities, and by the Cree of Norway House, Manitoba.

157

## 158 *Moccasins*

Dogrib

Made by Mary Louise Sangris of Deteh, Northwest
Territories, 1987

Collected by Barbara Hail, Yellowknife, Northwest
Territories, 1987

L: 25.5 cm   W: 11 cm

87–224

Soft sole, of smoked moose hide cut in rounded toe, T-shaped
heel-seam; seams of artificial sinew; beaver cuff over hand-
pinked white stroud; vamp of white stroud covered with
thread-strung and couched seed-beads in geometric pattern
of banded oval rows; colors: opaque white and dark red,
color-lined pink, translucent green, and silver-lined blue.

Although geometric designs are executed by contemporary Subarctic bead artists, they are far outnum-
bered by floral designs. This artist, now in her late
fifties, learned bead embroidery from her mother.

158

## 159 *Slippers*

Chipewyan-Métis

Made in 1986 by Jane Dragon, daughter of Bernadette Mercredi, originally from Fond du Lac, north Saskatchewan, later Fort Chipewyan, Alberta and Fort Smith, Northwest Territories

Collected by Barbara Hail, NWT Native Arts and Crafts Association, Yellowknife, Northwest Territories, 1987

L: 22.5 cm   W: 10 cm

87–229

Sun-bleached white caribou hide, slipper shape with rounded toe, separate sole; seams thread-sewn; white rabbit fur around cuff; cotton-print lining; glass seed-bead embroidery on uppers in floral motif of buds, wisps and dipped, four-petal flowers, in color-lined pink, opaque brown and lime green, translucent green and red, silver-lined green, and luster blue; thread-strung and couched.

These delicate slippers are reminiscent of those collected by Emma Shaw Colcleugh in Fort McMurray, Alberta in 1894 (cat. 18), although embroidered with

159

beads rather than with silk. The two-piece pattern requiring a seam around the foot and up the heel was popular in late nineteenth-century pattern books. Today, as then, such slippers seem to be intended for indoor use.

## 160 *Infant Slippers*

Western Subarctic

Collected by Hail and Duncan, Hay River, Northwest Territories, 1987

L: 12 cm   W: 5.5 cm

85–684

Sun-bleached white caribou hide, rounded toe, separate sole, ankle strap with button, thread-sewn; uppers embroidered with glass seed-beads, thread-strung and couched, in pattern of three-lobed flower and wisps in translucent red and blue, and silver-lined, translucent green; two-beaded edging on ankle strap.

Slippers of this design are not likely to fall off an infant when carried. During the 1950s Kutchin women in Fort Yukon, Alaska, made slippers of this form, basing them on some pictured in a magazine (Duncan and Carney 1988).

160

161

## 161 *Moccasins*

Chipewyan-Cree-Métis

Made by Maria Houle, Fort Chipewyan, Alberta, 1972

Collected by Hail and Duncan, Fort Chipewyan, 1985

L: 28 cm    W: 10.5 cm    H: 14 cm

85–664

Soft sole, of native tanned and smoked moose hide, rounded toe, T-shaped heel-seam, sole attached in a pucker to large vamp, seams sewn with double thread; lined with green cotton twill; elastic across instep. Vamp, upper and lower cuffs solidly contour-beaded on white background, beads thread-strung and couched, in pattern of five dip-petaled flowers, buds emerging from two-color veined leaves; colors: translucent greens, yellow-orange, teal blue, color-lined pink, opaque red and white seed-beads; translucent, wine-colored tubular beads on one flower.

This moccasin appears to be a variation of the higher cuffed "crow boot" popular at Fort Resolution and Fort Chipewyan in the 1980s. Maria spoke of the dipped-petaled flower as the wild rose, or Alberta rose. Understandably proud of this pair, she agreed to part with them only because she wanted her people's work to be represented in a museum and become known to the wider world "that can never get to Fort Chipewyan" (Houle, pers. comm. 1985).

Maria Houle is well known in Alberta as a fine craftswoman. She has been producing crafts since the age of twelve. She was born in 1924. As a child and young woman, she learned her skills while living in the bush with her parents. Even today, she saves porcupine-quill work, which requires concentration and quiet, for her yearly summer visit to her bush camp. Most of the time she works from her home in Fort Chipewyan, often tanning her own hides, but also

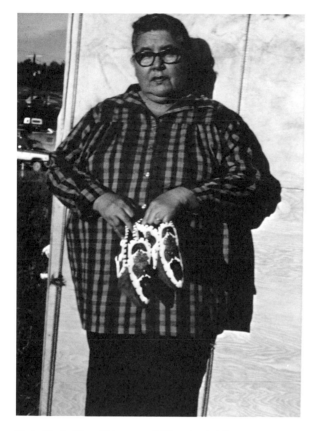

using commercial cow hide and other materials. She has taught craft skills at the local school, and continually instructs young people interested in learning traditional skills through informal sessions in her home.

Because of the flux in ethnicity typical of Fort Chipewyan there are no distinct tribal floral styles in this community. An examination of Maria's ethnic background demonstrates the difficulties encountered in attempting to identify work tribally. Maria Houle grew up with Chipewyan, Cree and French-Métis relations, and she undoubtedly absorbed artistic influences from all of the female members of the family. Because she is married to a Cree, she is currently listed as Cree with the Alberta Vocational Center, Native Arts and Crafts division, through whom she sometimes sells her work. Yet she resides at Fort Chipewyan, a predominantly Athapaskan community, and her mother was Chipewyan.

Maria Houle, Cree-Chipewyan-Métis artist, holding moccasins, (cat. 161) at Fort Chipewyan in 1985 (Hail-Duncan photo).

## 162 *Duffels*

Chipewyan-Cree-Métis

Made by Maria Houle, Fort Chipewyan, Alberta, 1985; commissioned by IIMA.

L: 26 cm    W: 9.5 cm    H: 9 cm

85–893

One piece white wool duffel, hand-sewn; pink acrylic yarn sewn in blanket-stitch as edging and in cross-stitch to cover seams.

Used as liners for mukluks and "crow boots" (cat. 139). The name comes from the fabric. Sold by the Hudson's Bay Company for many years, duffel is a heavy blanket-weight wool available most commonly in white, red, green and navy.

162

# 163 *Mukluks*

Great Slave Lake-Mackenzie River area

Collected by Hail and Duncan, Hay River, Northwest Territories, 1985

L: 30 cm   W: 13.5 cm   H: 34 cm

85–686

Soft sole, body of native tanned and smoked moose hide, T-shaped heel-seam, rounded toe; seams thread-sewn; duffel insertion covers vamp seams; vamp and front leg panel of smoked moose hide embroidered with glass seed-beads in floral pattern, thread-strung and couched, contour-beaded directly on hide, in opaque blues, red, yellow, greens, translucent green and red, clear with blue lining, clear with faceted gold lining; clear with faceted, iridescent blue lining. Beaver fur encircles rest of leg panel; thong drawstring around top; beaver-fur pompons ; synthetic fabric lining.

Clear glass beads with a faceted gold lining are here used where polished iron or brass beads had been placed on earlier work made in this region—that is, at the points of leaves and tendrils and at some base intersections where one motif element underlies another.

The precision and proportions of the beaded motifs, especially of the profile leafed bud, are Cree-like, as is the placement of ornamentation down the center of the leg. Others of the motifs are typical of Athapaskan material. Hay River is a largely Athapaskan speaking community, but a Cree settlement has existed there for close to half a century. One can only speculate as to the history of the maker.

163

## 164 *Mukluks*

Slavey

Made in Wrigley, Northwest Territories

Collected by William and Michelle Tracy in
Churchill, Manitoba, 1975

L: 28 cm   W: 13.5 cm   H: 34.5 cm

75–215

Soft sole, body of native-smoked moose hide, rounded
toe, T-shaped heel; vamp and legging tops of commercially-
tanned moose hide decorated with glass seed-beads in
stylized floral pattern; bead colors: silver-lined teal, dark blue
and yellow with faceted core; opaque yellow, opaque white
with blue lining; thread-strung and couched; long fringing
of light-tan commercial hide, pinked, machine-sewn to leggings below upper cuff; pinked hide border at top; thong
drawstring ties; heavy cotton lining.

Regional or community variations in the method of construction of mukluks may be seen by comparing these with cat.
163 and cat. 149. The faceted cores on the popular silver-lined
teal, blue and yellow beads create a sparkling effect.

164

## 165 *Mukluks*

Chipewyan
Made at Lac Brochet, Manitoba
Collected by William and Michelle Tracy in
Thompson, Manitoba, 1975
L: 23 cm    W: 11 cm    H: 28.5 cm
75-213

Soft sole, native smoke-tanned moose hide, rounded toe, vamp and legging top of home-tanned, bleached caribou hide covered with clear plastic and decorated with glass seed-beads in floral pattern, thread-strung and couched; bead colors: silver-lined teal and yellow with faceted centers, silver-lined green, red and blue with rounded centers, opaque grey and red; beaver-fur trim on top and at ends of thong ties; thick, pinked moose-hide fringing machine-sewn around leggings below upper cuff.

Beading through plastic wrap to keep a light-colored ground clean is common among certain Chipewyan groups. When sold this way, the buyer may decide whether to remove the plastic. According to the Tracys, fancy mukluks such as these were not very

165

common in Lac Brochet during the 1970s, and were worn only on special occasions.

Compare with mukluks, NMM VI-D-88, VI-D-96, collected 1968 by James G. E. Smith at Brochet.

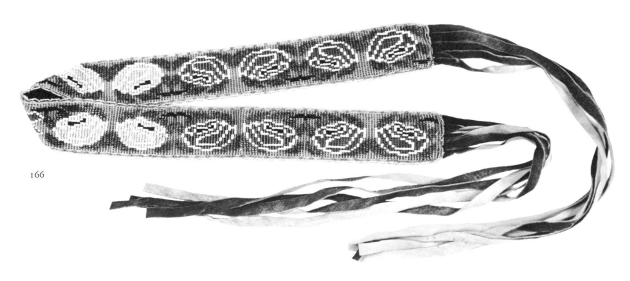

166

## 166 *Belt*

Chipewyan
Made at Nelson House, Manitoba
Collected by William and Michelle Tracy in
Thompson, Manitoba, 1975
L: 70.5 cm + fringe    W: 45 cm
75-212

Strip of native-tanned and smoked moose hide, serves as

backing for loom-beaded glass seed-beads, in stylized rose design, in color-lined pink, translucent blue, red, green, yellow, opaque red, white and black, on translucent silver-lined yellow ground; long hide fringing at both ends; thread warp and weft.

Loomed beadwork has been produced at various times over the years in several Subarctic communities, and many girls did their first loom-work as school projects.

## 167 *Mukluks* (A) *and Liners* (B)

Slavey-Métis

Made by Celine Lafferty, Fort Simpson, Northwest
Territories, 1987

Collected by Barbara Hail, NWT Native Arts &
Crafts Association, Yellowknife, 1987

L: 28 cm    W: 13 cm    H: 37 cm

87–226 A & B

(A)  Soft sole, of smoked moose hide , rounded toe, machine-
stitched to leggings of white and navy stroud; beaver-fur cuff
placed midway on leggings; upper cuff embroidered with
seed-beads in horizontal diamond-chain design; stroud vamp
solidly beaded, thread-strung and couched, in geometric design of banded concentric ovals; bead colors: opaque yellow,
green, red, white, black, orange; translucent luster-greens,
pink; translucent dark blue and green.

(B)  Liners of red duffel with blue yarn cross-stitching on
edges and seams.

Celine "Grandma" Lafferty has been an active arti-

167 B

san for many years. Although raised at the mission
school at Fort Providence early in the century, she
learned to embroider later because, she said, at school
only the best-behaved girls were allowed to do "fancy
work," and she seldom fell into that category (Lafferty,
pers. comm. 1982).

167 A

# Babiche, Hareskin

168

## 168 *Game Bag*

Dogrib
Made by Judy Gon, Rae, Northwest Territories,
1985
Collected by Hail and Duncan, Hay River,
Northwest Territories, 1985
L: 48 cm   W: 6 cm   H: 35 cm
85–650

Smoked moose hide cut into strips, called "babiche," in simple or buttonhole looping crossed left over right, make up
body of bag; made in old style, similar to cat. 90, with wide
strips of moose hide on sides and top edge, in light and dark
tan; three horizontal bands of turquoise-dyed babiche in
loop-and-twist variation, crossed left-over-right, on front of
bag; two horizontal bands babiche, undyed, in loop and twist,

crossed left-over-right on back; commercial wool yarn puffs
in red, pink, green, blue are attached to surface of babiche;
commercial green and blue rickrack machine-sewn around
top; braided moose-hide carrying strap.

This type of bag has a long history of use among
Eastern Athapaskan peoples including the Dogrib (see
cats. 90, 91). Usually it was worn over a hunter's shoulder to carry home freshly killed game, especially birds.
The open netting allowed the blood to drip out and air
to get in, so the game would not spoil. Present-day
babiche bags are made largely for sale. The same simple looping technique is used to make the rabbit-skin
jacket, cat. 169. For terminology and technique, see
Emery, 1980 and Burnham, 1981.

## 169 Jacket

Slavey

Made by Rosa Lie Causa, Fort Providence,
Northwest Territories, 1987; commissioned by HMA

L: 88 cm    W: 65 cm

88–06

Strips of skin, approximately one inch wide, from eighty-five
Varying Hares, woven in looped netting to form long-
sleeved, collarless, fur jacket.

To make the jacket, Rosa Lie cut the hareskin strips
spirally around the pelt in order to get the greatest
length. Next she soaked the strips in water, and twisted
them around a thin rod to bring the fur to the outside.
She left them outside for one day to dry and tighten
up, then pulled them off the rod and joined them with
twine to form long, fur-covered cords that were then
woven in a looped netting technique on an upright
frame.

A piece of twine was attached to a stick at both ends.
The skin cords were then looped around the twine and
attached at the ends. The cords of each subsequent row
were looped through the preceding row until the desired length was achieved. Three rectangular shapes
were laced together to form this jacket. A hood and
long pants are in process and will complete the outfit.

Rosa, who is eighty-five years old, is one of the few
Dene women who still constructs articles of hareskin.
She was born and raised in Fort Providence, and

Women and children of Island Lake, Manitoba, wearing hooded hareskin jackets, at East Deer Lake Camp, 1930s. Photo by Rev. Chapin.
Courtesy Western Canada Pictorial Index, UW.

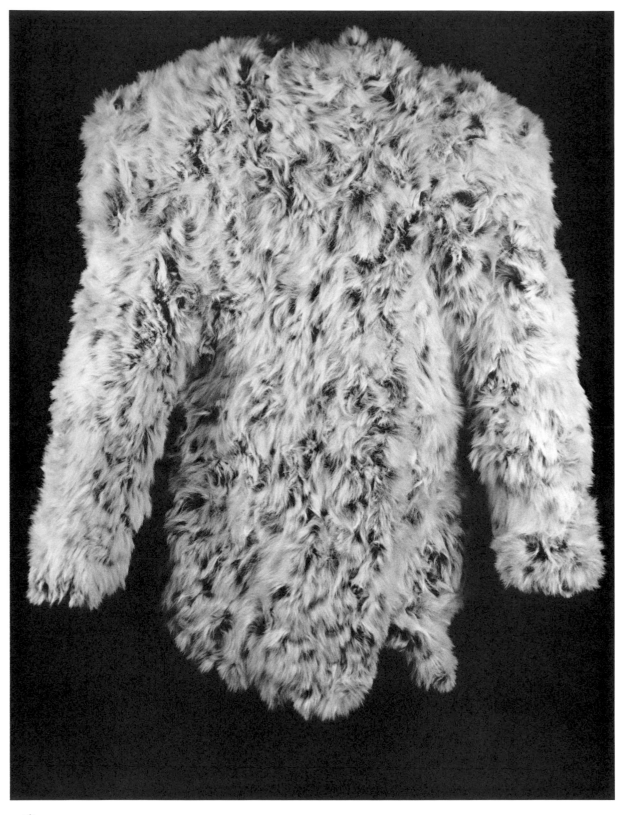

169

learned to do looped netting from her mother. She has made hats, pants and a blanket, as well as jackets. She calls this a "trapper's jacket." Formerly a new jacket was made every year, since the hair tended to rub off with use. Rosa made this jacket from rabbits she and her family had snared during the winter. Rabbits must be skinned between October and February to secure the finest pelts, since they begin to shed their fur in March (Causa, pers. comm. 1988).

In former times, clothing made of rabbit skins was common among native people over a wide area, from Mexico and the Southwest to northern Canada. It provided a light, warm covering, and was made into robes, hooded jackets, coats, blankets, and used as interior liners between two layers of other material to form quilts. In the Subarctic, adult males were the last to wear hareskin clothing; no one wears these jackets any more.

The technique of making hareskin garments is ancient, as described in a Slavey origin tale recorded in the latter nineteenth century by Father Emile Petitot (1976: 26):

> *In the fall, the Wise One's sister*
> *made a hareskin garment.*
> *She cut the garment from a single*
> *skin and she was the first one to do this.*

Compare with man's hooded parka, ROM 959.50.67, circa 1955; robe, GAI AC 147, Dogrib, 1967.

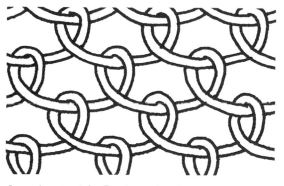

Looped netting (after Burnham 1981: 3)

Boy clad in garments of woven rabbit skin, Moose Factory. East Cree, James Bay. Photo by Alanson Skinner, 1910–1913. Courtesy Museum of the American Indian, Heye Foundation.

# Birch Bark

**Bitten Bark**

The art of bark-pattern biting among hunting peoples of the Northeast and eastern Subarctic seems to reach into antiquity. Historical accounts of the seventeenth, eighteenth and nineteenth century Chippewa, Ojibwa, Beothuk and Micmac have described the practice of biting very thin, folded sections of birch bark with the teeth, thereby creating delicate, unique patterns. In the early twentieth century, elderly women among the Montagnais-Naskapi were biting bark patterns around the evening campfire as a source of family entertainment. Speck noted the admiration accorded to the old women by appreciative audiences of children and others, and considered the art important as a stage in the process of implanting new and fanciful design ideas in the community consciousness (1937: 74–80). Most of the bitten-bark designs were truly ephemeral art, providing pleasure for the moment only, but some of the ideas may have been translated into bark cut-outs or templates for use in decorating bark containers.

In recent years the outstanding bitten-bark artist has been Angelique Merasty, born in 1927, a Western Woods Cree of Cedar Lake, Saskatchewan. She and a very few apprentices have created exciting and highly varied bitten patterns that have been widely circulated through native arts and crafts shops. Examples have been incorporated into museum collections, as their importance as an aboriginal and endangered art form has been recognized.

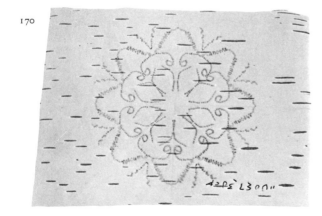

170

## 170 *Bitten Bark*

Western Woods Cree, late twentieth century

Made by Angelique Merasty, Beaver Lake, Saskatchewan

HMA purchase, Flin Flon, Manitoba, 1985

L: 13.3 cm   W: 10 cm

85–898

Very thin, peeled, inner layer of birch bark, with bilaterally symmetrical, stylized pattern of snowflake or flower with possible butterflies on the outer edge. Signed "Angelique" in Cree syllabic.

171

## 171 *Bitten Bark*

Western Woods Cree, late twentieth century

Made by Angelique Merasty, Beaver Lake, Saskatchewan

HMA purchase, Flin Flon, Manitoba, 1985

L: 25 cm    W: 20.5 cm

85–899

Very thin, peeled, inner layer of birch bark, with bilaterally symmetrical, stylized pattern of flower, leaves, birds. Signed "Angelique" in Cree syllabic.

## 172 *Bitten Bark*

Western Woods Cree, late twentieth century

Made by Angelique Merasty, Beaver Lake,
Saskatchewan

HMA purchase, Flin Flon, Manitoba, 1985

L: 25.4 cm    W: 21 cm

85–900

Very thin, peeled, inner layer of birch bark, with bilaterally
symmetrical, stylized design of butterflies around a central
form of either pine cone or flower. Signed "Angelique" in
Cree syllabic.

172

## 173 *Bitten Bark*

Western Woods Cree, late twentieth century

Made by Angelique Merasty, Beaver Lake, Saskatchewan

HMA purchase, Flin Flon, Manitoba, 1985

L: 14.4 cm   W: 14.1 cm

85–897

Very thin, peeled inner layer of birch bark, with bilaterally symmetrical, stylized floral design. Design achieved by folding rectangular piece of bark in half and in half again to make quarter sections, then folding diagonally to make eighths and sixteenths. Artist has bitten through folded sections to create punctate pattern of leaves and nuts. Signed "Angelique" in Cree syllabic.

Compare with collections of bitten-bark pieces by Angelique Merasty and her mother, Susan Ballentine: MMMN, GAI, DAM.

173

## 174 *Bark Box with Lid*

Western Woods Cree, 1985
Made by Hazel Stephens, Red Deer, Manitoba
Collected by Hail and Duncan, The Pas, Manitoba
D: 16.5 cm   H: 10 cm + 4.5 cm handle
85–660 A & B

Round, constructed of birch bark cut in sections, with central part a rolled cylinder; top and bottom cut in tabs, pinked, folded and stitched to cylinder with orange cotton thread; rough, white outer surface of bark forms interior; smooth inner surface of bark forms darker exterior; printed cotton lining sewn in; appliquéd star-shape of bark sewn to top; bark handle sewn on.

The form of this container can be traced to earlier Cree lidded bark boxes with cut-out and appliqué decoration; the tabbed or sawtooth lid edges are also present in cat. 98, collected by Colcleugh near Lake Winnipeg, 1888–1894. This was one of only a few Cree examples seen in 1985 at The Pas and Norway House. Most of the type were covered with shiny red paint or varnish. Fully lined, they are sold primarily for use as sewing baskets.

Compare with lidded bark container, MAI 19-6141, Cree, coll. by Speck at Portage La Loche, Saskatchewan, 1930s; bark container with lid and handle decorated with quill embroidered floral design, LFG 1709, Cree, Pelican Narrows, Saskatchewan, 1959.

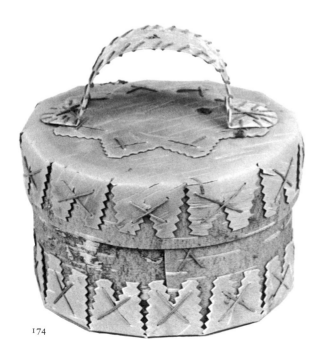

174

## Athapaskan Bark Containers

The center for making bark containers today is a Slavey community in the Fort Liard area. Families work on the baskets in the spring and summer, often while at their trap lines, and distribute them through the native-operated Acho Dene Craft Shop. Both men and women cut, scrape, and sew the containers, but only women apply the quill decoration. Because of the severely cold temperatures in the area, the brittle bark cannot be removed from the trees in winter. When it is taken off, usually in early June, a layer of bark is cut into the desired size, and cold water is applied until the natural dark-orange color is brought up. If the bark is to be decorated by scraping, a design is drawn either on paper or directly onto the bark. A big needle is used to trace the outline of the design onto the bark. While keeping the bark damp, a paring knife is used to scrape away the background. When the design is completed, the bark is warmed so that it will bend easily into the desired shape. The container is then sewn with the evergreen spruce root, which has been dug out of the ground in summer, scraped, boiled, peeled, split in half, and pared to the proper thickness with a small knife. The root is kept in water during the time it is being used, and then stored in a cool place. In addition to the cylindrical bait basket and the berry basket, a third commonly made form is a low bowl, folded at the corners and used as a plate or cup (Hope, pers. comm. 1988).

Floral quill embroidery, or quill insertion, is worked by (1) tracing a design from a pattern or stencil onto the bark with a marker or awl; (2) making a hole in the bark from the underside with the awl and inserting a quill through it; (3) making another hole on the opposite side of the design element, this time from the outer side of the bark, and inserting the quill through it, so that the quill is laid flat on the outer surface, and both ends of the quill are on the underside. Tweezers are needed to pull the quill through the hole. In quill insertion, stitches that resemble the silk embroiderer's satin stitch and running stitch are those most commonly used (Schneider 1972: 216–18).

Quill designs are similar to those of present-day Athapaskan beadwork; the flowers are simple, with primarily gold-colored centers and with some color-splitting of petals. As in beadwork, pink, green and gold are the most frequently used colors.

## 175 *Container with Lid*

Slavey, 1985
Made in Fort Liard area, Northwest Territories
Collected by Hail and Duncan, Hay River, 1985
D: 22.5 cm    H: 28 cm
85–659 A & B

Cylindrical; constructed of double thickness of birch bark, outer side turned in; separate bark bottom and top attached with peeled spruce-root lacings; lid of double thickness, spruce-root stitching around rim, moose-hide thong closure; pinked strip of bark serves as reinforcement over side-seam where ends of cylinder are joined; decorative bark scallop edges top and base, spruce-root stitching; realistic floral pattern of rose, bud, leaf incised in positive (scraping away background to expose pattern) and negative (scraping pattern into bark) techniques on body of container.

This shape of container was traditionally made to carry bait for the trap lines. In its original form it had a round wooden bottom that was pushed into place, and a wooden top with thong handle (Hope, pers. comm. 1988).

## 176 *Container with Lid*

Slavey, 1985
Made in Fort Liard area, Northwest Territories
Collected by Hail and Duncan, Hay River, 1985
D: 20.5 cm lid, 23 cm base    H: 28 cm
85–658 A & B

Round top, square base, constructed from a single piece of birch bark, scored, cut and folded, rounded Y-shaped seams on sides stitched with spruce root; white, outer side of bark turned in; sides and lid decorated by quill-insertion, in design of bilaterally symmetrical five-petal flowers and leaves, in dark and light green, dark and light red, pink, using satin and running stitch; second layer of bark applied under quill-insertion for strength; rim reinforced with pinked, scalloped bark strip sewn on; unscraped interior of bark on outside; thong ties and handle of hide with bark strip.

This kind of container is usually known as a berry basket. Variations of the type were used as pack baskets, storage containers for animal fat, and as water pails. Spruce root seams were sealed with spruce gum to make them watertight (Hope, pers. comm. 1988).

## 177 *Container with Lid*

Slavey, 1985
Made in Fort Liard area, Northwest Territories
Collected by Hail and Duncan, Hay River, 1985
D: 17 cm lid, 20 cm base    H: 23 cm
85–661 A & B

Round top, square base, constructed from a single piece of birch bark, cut and folded, rounded Y-shape seams on sides stitched with spruce root; white, outer side of bark turned in; sides and lid decorated with quill-insertion, in design of one flower superimposed on another; red, pink, yellow, green quills (commercial dyes), using satin and running stitch; second layer of bark applied under quill-insertion for strength; reinforced with scalloped, pinked strip of bark sewn to rim, interior of bark outside, unscraped; thong ties and handle of hide with bark strip.

Both in this example and cat. 176 the scalloped bark strip is probably more decorative than necessary for strength. However, it follows in a long Athapaskan tradition of placing a reinforcing band at the rim of a bark container.

177

"A little Indian girl (mixed Cree and Chipewyan) at the mouth of the Taltson River, with a birch-bark basket of berries. August 16, 1914. Mackenzie District, Northwest Territories." Photo by Francis Harper. Courtesy Smithsonian Institution, National Anthropological Archives.

## 178 *Nest of Four Miniature Baskets*

Athapaskan, Alaska, third quarter twentieth
century

HMA accession 1979

L: 9.5 cm   W: 8 cm   H: 6 cm

79–105

Rectangular base, oval rim; birch bark, white outer surface
on outside, folded at corners, with four separate pieces of
thin bark, inner surface facing out, added as an appliqué; rim
a split red-willow band , sewn with spruce root; the whole
varnished. A second split red-willow band encircles container
reinforcing the sides about 3 cm from rim.

> 79–101 L: 5.5 cm   W: 5.5 cm   H: 4 cm
> 79–102 L: 6.5 cm   W: 6 cm   H: 5 cm
> 79–103 L: 4.5 cm   W: 4 cm   H: 3.5 cm

Rectangular bases, oval rims, inner layer of birch bark,
folded; split red willow sewn on each end and a separate strip
of birch bark sewn on outside below rim, both serving as
reinforcements; sewn with spruce root, open stitching; varnished.

A number of Alaskan Athapaskan people made
corner-folded and appliquéd bark containers. Inland
Eskimo who lived along the Kobuk River have also
long made and used similar folded and appliquéd birch-
bark containers. Interaction between the two groups
was common. It is likely that the Koyukuk Athapaskans taught the Kobuk Eskimos birch-bark construction, since they had a long history of adaptation to the
birch-bark area. There is ample archaeological evidence of the use of birch bark for making containers in
the Kobuk River area. At Onion Portage, remains of a
four-corner folded and sewn birch-bark container dating between A.D. 1000 and 1100 were uncovered (Anderson, pers. comm. 1988). Giddings (1952: 116) cites
the use of birch bark for basketry, snowshoes and other
purposes as characteristic of the Arctic Woodland Culture, and it seems to be a shared trait of Kobuk and
Koyukuk people (Clark 1974b: 133–134).

For construction, see "Birch Bark Baskets" by Sarah Mal-
colm, Han, of Eagle, Alaska (Steinbright 1983: 7–22). Compare with: bark tray with folded corners, MAI 19–6580,
Athapaskan, poss. Ingalik; bark berry-picking basket, HMA
62–687, Inland Alaskan Eskimo, coll. by J. L. Giddings on
Kobuk River, Alaska, 1961.

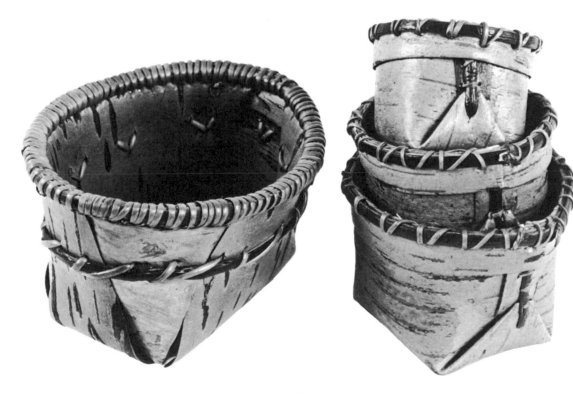

178

# Wood, Hide, Roots

## 179 *Meat Tray*

Naskapi, 1920s
Collected by James Houston 1950–70
L: 46 cm   W: 16 cm   H: 6.5 cm
85–773

Birch, bent in oval shape, rawhide lashings join ends of curved sides and attach wood handles at each end; bottom attached with wooden pegs; red ochre and lampblack paint decoration: on sides, caribou herd, conical and ridgepole lodges, fir trees; on interior bottom, man dressed in decorated clothing beating drum with resonator similar to cat. 180.

This meat tray incorporates both traditional techniques of manufacture and traditional scenes of social activities. According to James Houston, the collector, who has observed the Naskapi method of shaping wood, the birch wood was curved down with a crooked knife, and manually bent into an oval shape using steam and immersion in stone-boiled water. The paint was mixed with a fish-oil binder. The carved handle represents lightning. The painted figure with drum may represent a hunter who, upon return from a successful hunt, is narrating his adventures through song and story to others in the community. He wears a peaked bark hat, legging-moccasins, and a fringed caribou-hide parka, decorated with red and black geometric designs. It is the kind of simple, over-the-shoulder cut garment commonly worn into the 1950s when Houston was in Arctic Quebec. The scene of painted caribou-skin lodges of ridgepole construction represents a dance house in which four tents belonging to part of an extended family have been combined to form a larger family house for feasting, dancing, and celebration. The tray represents the survival of an older type of artifact in the present century.

179

## 180 *Drum* (A) *and Drumstick* (B)

Dogrib

Made by Johnny Tailbone, Rae Lakes, Northwest Territories, 1987

Collected by Barbara Hail, Yellowknife, 1987

Drum Diam: 44.5 cm, head    w: 5cm, frame

Drumstick L: 27 cm    w: 2.5cm

87–230 A & B

(A) Single head, shallow frame; made of caribou rawhide scraped clean and stretched while wet over circular birch frame; thick babiche (cut strands of hide) fastens edge of head to frame in long stitches inserted through frame on both sides of the wood; babiche inserted through frame at four places stretches across inside of head at right angles, meets in center knot forming hand-hold.

(B) Drumstick of carved, sanded birch.

Although not present on this example, Dogrib drums often have resonators formed of two strands of sinew stretched across the outer surface of the head to enhance the sound.

180 A & B

In summer, on the occasion of annual treaty payments, the Dogrib of Rae, Northwest Territories traditionally engaged in drum dances, hand games and communal meals. The excitement of the Dogrib hand game, a hidden object game, is heightened by the vigorous drumming and chanting that accompanies play. Photo (1962) and interpretation courtesy of June Helm.

181

## 181 *Basketry Tray*

Koyukon, twentieth century

Made at Holy Cross Mission, Holy Cross Alaska

Collected by Mary M. Jerome, 1948–53

L: 40.5 cm   W: 33 cm   H: 4.5 cm

83–437

Willow root, single rod coiling, geometric design of red and green-dyed roots on natural background.

Red willow roots collected along river banks in the early fall and peeled of their bark were used for the rods or "ribs." Roots can be stored if covered so that they will not dry out. In preparation, peeled roots are pulled through holes drilled in a piece of bone or wood to assure an even diameter. Any further uneveness is planed or cut away. Each root is then split, usually by holding it in the teeth and pulling a portion away. Roots for wrapping are first split into quarters, then again to make about eight to twelve pieces.

To start a basket, a root is pared thin on one end and wound into a spiral. A split wrapping-root, sharpened to make a needle end, is wound over this rod and inserted near the bottom of the previous coil through a hole punched into it with an awl. Stitches wrap over two coils and new stitches are placed beween those below. The result is a herringbone texture. As the coiling proceeds, stitches are added to increase the rows and enlarge the flat bottom.

Decorative motifs are incorporated using dyed roots. Earlier dyes such as alder, which produced a rust-red color, have been replaced by commercial dyes in the twentieth century. Tray motifs are usually zigzags and triangles. The spacing of coils during the weaving process allows the basket-maker to mark intervals with small pieces of root so that motifs can be evenly spaced.

For a photograph series of willow-root basket-making, see Steinbright (1983: 57–71).

# Abbreviations for Institutions

## United States

| | |
|---|---|
| AMHA | Anchorage Museum of History and Art |
| AMNH | American Museum of Natural History, New York |
| AMF | The Amerind Foundation, Inc., Dragoon, Arizona |
| ASM | Alaska State Museum, Juneau |
| BM | Thomas Burke Memorial Washington State Museum, University of Washington, Seattle |
| DAM | The Denver Art Museum |
| DMNH | Denver Museum of Natural History |
| FMNH | Field Museum of Natural History, Chicago |
| HMA | Haffenreffer Museum of Anthropology, Brown University, Bristol |
| LACM | Los Angeles County Museum |
| LMA | Robert H. Lowie Museum of Anthropology, University of California, Berkeley |
| MAI | Museum of the American Indian, Heye Foundation, New York |
| NMNH | National Museum of Natural History, Smithsonian Institution, Washington, D.C. |
| OHS | Oregon Historical Society, Portland |
| PH | Peabody Museum of Archaeology and Ethnology, Harvard University, Cambridge |
| PS | Peabody Museum of Salem, Massachusetts |
| RHF | Robert Hull Fleming Museum, University of Vermont, Burlington |
| SD | San Diego Museum of Man |
| TM | Taylor Museum of the Colorado Springs Fine Arts Center |
| UI | University of Iowa Museum of Natural History, Iowa City |
| UMP | The University Museum, University of Pennsylvania, Philadelphia |

## Canada

| | |
|---|---|
| APM | Provincial Museum of Alberta, Edmonton |
| BCPM | British Columbia Provincial Museum, Victoria |
| CMC or NMM | Canadian Museum of Civilization/Musée Canadien Des Civilizations (formerly National Museum of Man), Ottawa |
| GAI | Glenbow-Alberta Institute, Calgary |
| HBC | Hudson's Bay Company, Winnipeg |
| LFG | Lower Fort Garry National Historic Park, Selkirk |
| LNM | Sam Waller Little Northern Museum, The Pas |
| McB | MacBride Museum, Whitehorse, Yukon Territory |
| McC | McCord Museum/Musée McCord, McGill University, Montreal |
| MMMN | Manitoba Museum of Man and Nature, Winnipeg |
| MPA | Manitoba Provincial Archives, Winnipeg |
| NLM | Northern Life Museum and National Exhibition Centre, Fort Smith, Northwest Territories |
| NMM | see CMC |
| PWNHC | Prince of Wales Northern Heritage Centre, Yellowknife |
| ROM | Royal Ontario Museum, Toronto |
| UBC | University of British Columbia, Museum of Anthropology, Vancouver |
| UWP | University of Winnipeg |

## Europe

| | |
|---|---|
| BirM | Birmingham Museum and Art Gallery, (Br. Is.) |
| BrM | Museum of Mankind, British Museum, London |
| MH | Musée de l'Homme, Paris |
| NMI | National Museum of Ireland, Dublin |
| PRM | Pitt Rivers Museum, Oxford |
| RSM | Royal Scottish Museum, Edinburgh |

# Bibliography

Anderson, Douglas D.
  1988  Personal communication to Barbara Hail.

Anderson, D. A. and A. M.
  1977  *The Métis People of Canada: A History*. Edmonton: Alberta Federation of Métis Settlement Associations.

Arnheim, Rudolf
  1981  "Style as a Gestalt Problem." *Journal of Aesthetics and Art Criticism*. Vol. 39.
  1974  *Art and Visual Perception: A Psychology of the Creative Eye*. Berkeley: University of California Press.
  1969  *Visual Thinking*. Berkeley: University of California Press.
  1954  *Art and Visual Perception*. Berkeley: University of California Press.

Ballantyne, Robert Michael
  1856  *The Young Fur-Traders*. London. (Reprinted in Doherty).

Barth, Fredrik, ed.
  1969  *Ethnic Groups and Boundaries: The Social Organization of Cultural Difference*. Boston: Little, Brown.

Bee, Marian
  1985  Conversation between Cree bead artist of Norway House, Manitoba and Barbara Hail.

Birket-Smith, Kaj
  1930  "Contributions to Chipewyan Ethnology." *Report of the 5th Thule Expedition 1921–24*. Vol. VI, no. 3. Copenhagen: Glydendalske Boghandel, Nordisk Forlag.

Bloomer, Carolyn M.
  1967  *Principles of Visual Perception*. New York: Van Nostrand.

Brasser, Theodore J.
  1975  "Métis Artisans." In *The Beaver*. Autumn. Winnipeg.
  1976  *"Bo'jou, Neejee!": Profiles of Canadian Indian Art*. Ottawa: National Museum of Canada.
  1985  "In Search of Métis Art." In Peterson and Brown, *The New Peoples: Being and Becoming Métis in North America*. Winnipeg: The University of Manitoba Press.
  1987  Personal communication to Barbara Hail and Kate Duncan.

  1988  "By the Power of Their Dreams." In *The Spirit Sings: Artistic Traditions of Canada's First Peoples*. Calgary: Glenbow Museum.

Brown, Jennifer S. H.
  1980  *Strangers in Blood: Fur Trade Company Families in Indian Country*. Vancouver: University of British Columbia.

Buggins, Judith
  1987  Personal communication to Barbara Hail from Chipewyan silk embroiderer, Yellowknife.

Burnham, Dorothy
  1981  *The Comfortable Arts. Traditional Spinning and Weaving in Canada*. Ottawa: National Museums of Canada.

Butler, Eva L., and Wendell S. Hadlock
  1957  *Uses of Birch-Bark in the Northeast*. Bulletin VII. Bar Harbor: The Robert Abbe Museum.

Cardinal, Harold
  1977  *The Rebirth of Canada's Indians*. Edmonton: Hurtig.

Carney, Eunice
  1984  Personal communication to Kate Duncan.
  1986  Correspondence with Barbara Hail.

Causa, Rosa Lie
  1988  Correspondence via Ruth Philipp, Fort Providence, Northwest Territories, with Barbara Hail, 1/16/88.

Chalmers, J. W.
  1972  "Inland Journey." Pp. 53–59 in *The Beaver*. Autumn. Winnipeg.

Charette, Guillaume
  1976  *Vanishing Spaces: Memoirs of a Prairie Métis*. Winnipeg: Editions Bois-Brules.

Clark, Annette McFadyen
  1974a  *The Athapaskans: Strangers of the North*. Ottawa: National Museums of Canada.
  1974b  *Koyukuk River Culture*. NMM Mercury Series. Canadian Anthology Service no. 18. Ottawa.

Clark, Donald W.
  1981  "Prehistory of the Western Subarctic." Pp. 107–129 in *Handbook of North American Indians*. Vol. 6: *Subarctic*. June Helm, ed. Washington, D.C.: Smithsonian Institution.

Coe, Ralph T.
1986 *Lost and Found Traditions: Native American Art 1965–1985*. New York: The American Federation of Arts.

Cohen, Robin
1977 "Contemporary Native Art of Canada—the Western Subarctic. Porcupine Quillwork-Moose Hair Tufting." *Exhibition Gallery Guide.* Jan.-Mar. Toronto: Royal Ontario Museum.

Colcleugh, Emma Shaw
n.d. *Alaskan Gleanings.*
1906 *Worldwide Wisdom Words.*
1932 "I Saw These Things," [Providence] *Evening Bulletin*, Aug. 30 – Sept. 31, 1932. ESC I-XIX.

Conn, Richard
1979 *Native American Art in the Denver Art Museum.* Denver.
1980 "Native American Cloth Appliqué and Ribbonwork: Their Origin and Diffusion in the Plains." Pp. 9–23 in *Native American Ribbonwork: A Rainbow Tradition.* Cody: Buffalo Bill Historical Center.
1982 *Circles of the World.* Denver: Denver Art Museum.

Corbett, Rev. G. O.
1967 *Notes on Rupert's America.* Toronto: The Bibliographical Society of Canada. (Facsimile of 1868 edition).

Cornsweet, Tom
1970 *Visual Perception.* New York: Academic Press.

Coues, Elliott, ed.
1897 *The Manuscript Journals of Alexander Henry, Fur Trader of the Northwest Company, and of David Thompson, Official Geographer and Explorer of the Same Company, 1799–1814.* Vols. I-III. New York: Frances P. Harper

Crowe, Keith J.
1974 *A History of the Original Peoples of Northern Canada.* Arctic Institute of North America. Montreal and London: McGill-Queen's University Press.

Dept. of Culture and Communications
1985 *The Heritage of the Northwest Territories.* Yellowknife: Northwest Territories Information.

Dept. of Indian Affairs
1886 *Annual Report for the Year Ended 31st December, 1886.* Ottawa.

Dept. of Indian Affairs and Northern Development
1980 *Linguistic and Cultural Affiliations of Canadian Indian Bands.* Ottawa.

Dept. of Indian and Northern Affairs
1974 *Central Cree and Ojibway Crafts.* Nos. 1–9. Ottawa.

Doherty, Helen
1984 *Red River Settlement.* Winnipeg. (Includes Ross, Alexander, *The Red River Settlement; its Rise, Progress, and Present State* [q.v.] and Ballantyne, Robert Michael, *The Young Fur-Traders* [q.v.]).

Donaldson, Pat
1975–76 "Moosehair Tufting." Pp. 20–25 in *Canadian Golden West.* Winter.

Duncan, Kate
1980 "The Far Northern Plains Tradition: Eastern Athapaskan Appliqué." *In Native American Ribbonwork: A Rainbow Tradition.* Cody, Wyoming: Buffalo Bill Historical Center.
1981 "The Métis and Production of Embroidery in the Subarctic." Pp. 1–8, *The Museum of the Fur Trade Quarterly.* Vol. 17, no. 3. Fall. Charles Hanson, Jr., ed. Chadron, Nebraska.
1982 Field notes based on research of Kate Duncan and Eunice Carney, Kutchin, from Old Crow, Yukon Territory, among Athapaskan artists of bead, quill and silk embroidery in Alaska and the Northwest Territories, using techniques of interview and photo-elicitation.
1984 *Some Warmer Tone: Alaska Athabaskan Bead Embroidery.* Fairbanks: University of Alaska Museum.
1987 "Yukon River Athapaskan Costume in the 1860s: Contributions of the Ethnographic Illustrations of William Dall." In *Faces, Voices and Dreams: A Celebration of the Centennial of the Sheldon Jackson Museum.* Sitka, Alaska: Sheldon Jackson Museum.
1989 *Northern Athapaskan Art: A Beadwork Tradition.* Seattle: University of Washington Press.

Duncan, Kate C., and Eunice Carney
1988 *A Special Gift: the Kutchin Beadwork Tradition.* Seattle: University of Washington Press.

Ellis, Willis
1939 *A Source Book of Gestalt Psychology.* London: Kegan Paul, Trench and Trubner & Co.

Emery, Irene
1980 *The Primary Structure of Fabrics.* Washington, D.C.: Textile Museum.

ESC
See Colcleugh, Emma Shaw.

Feder, Norman
1984 "The Side-Fold Dress." Pp. 48–55 in *American Indian Art Magazine.* Vol. 10, no. 1.

Feest, Christian F.
1980 *Native Arts of North America.* London: Thames & Hudson Ltd.
1987 "Some 18th Century Specimens from Eastern North America in Collections in the German Democratic Republic." Band XXXVI: 281–301. Leipzig: *Jahrbuch des Museums für Volkerkunde.*

Francis, Daniel, and Toby Morantz
　　1983　*Partners in Furs. A History of the Fur Trade in Eastern James Bay 1600–1870.* Kingston and Montreal: McGill-Queens University Press.

Francis, Peter
　　1988　*The Glass Trade Beads of Europe: Their Manufacture, Their History, and Their Identification.* Vol. 8. Lake Placid: The Center for Bead Research.

Franklin, Sir John
　　1824　*Narrative of a Journey to the Shores of the Polar Sea in the Years 1819-20-21-22.* Second edition. Two vols. London: John Murray.
　　c. 1859　*Thirty Years in the Arctic Regions: A Narrative of The Explorations and Adventures of Sir John Franklin.* New York: United States Book Company.

Garbutt, Dorothy
　　1985　Personal communication to Barbara Hail, Aug. 5. Dorothy Garbutt was a first cousin of Ramona Sinclair, and a cousin-by-marriage of Emma Shaw Colcleugh.

Gardner, James S.
　　1981　"General Environment." Pp. 5–14 in *Handbook of North American Indians.* Vol. 6: *Subarctic.* June Helm, ed. Washington, D.C.: Smithsonian Institution.

Giddings, J. L. Jr.
　　1952　*The Arctic Woodland Culture of the Kobuk River.* The University Museum. Philadelphia: University of Pennsylvania.

Gilman, Carolyn
　　1982　*Where Two Worlds Meet: The Great Lakes Fur Trade.* St. Paul: Minnesota Historical Society.

Glenbow Museum
　　1988　*The Spirit Sings: Artistic Traditions of Canada's First Peoples.* Vol. I, Essays; Vol. II, Catalogue. Calgary: Glenbow Museum.

Goddard, Ives
　　1989　Conversation with Barbara Hail, April.

Gombrich, Ernst
　　1979　*The Sense of Order.* Ithaca: Cornell University Press.
　　1961　*Art and Illusion.* Princeton: Princeton University Press.

Graham, Andrew
　　1969　*Andrew Graham's Observations on Hudson's Bay, 1767–1791.* Glyndwr Williams, ed. London: Hudson's Bay Record Society.

Hail, Barbara A.
　　1987　Field notes from research among Ojibwa, Cree, Athapaskan and métis artists of bead, quill and silk embroidery in Selkirk, Manitoba, Yellowknife and Rae, Northwest Territories, using techniques of interview and photo-elicitation.

Hail, Barbara A., and Kate C. Duncan
　　1985　Field notes from research among Cree, Ojibwa, Athapaskan and Métis artists of bead, quill and silk embroidery in Lake Winnipeg area (Norway House, The Pas), Manitoba; Edmonton and Fort Chipewyan, Alberta; Fort Smith, Hay River and Fort Providence, Northwest Territories, using techniques of interview and photo-elicitation.

Hallowell, A. Irving
　　1930　"Notes on the Material Culture of the Island Lake Saulteaux." Archives, Museum of the American Indian, Heye Foundation, Box V-1, no. 2. (Unpublished.)

Harbor Springs [Michigan] Historical Commission
　　1983　*Ottawa Quillwork on Birchbark.* Harbor Springs.

Harriot, Thomas
　　1972　*A Brief and True Report of the New Found Land of Virginia.* The Complete 1590 Theodor de Bry edition. (Reprint.) New York: Dover.

Harrison, Julia D.
　　1985　*Métis: People Between Two Worlds.* Vancouver/Toronto: The Glenbow-Alberta Institute and Douglas & McIntyre.

Healy, W. J.
　　1923　*Women of Red River.* Winnipeg: Peguis.

Helm, June, et al.
　　1975　"The Contact History of the Subarctic Athapaskans: An Overview." In Proceedings: Northern Athapaskan Conference, 1971. Ottawa: Canadian Ethnology Service Paper 27 (1): 302–349.

　　1981　*Handbook of North American Indians.* Vol. 6: *Subarctic.* Washington, D.C.: Smithsonian Institution.

Helm, June, and Eleanor Burke Leacock
　　1971　"The Hunting Tribes of Subarctic Canada." Pp. 343–374 in *North American Indians in Historical Perspective.* E. L. Leacock and N. O. Lurie, eds. New York: Random House.

Helm, June, and Nancy O. Lurie
　　1961　*The Subsistence Economy of the Dogrib Indians of Lac la Martre in the Mackenzie District of the Northwest Territories.* Ottawa: Northern Coordination and Research Centre, Department of Northern Affairs and National Resources. NCRC-61-3.

Helm, June, Edward S. Rogers and James G. E. Smith
　　1981　"Intercultural Relations and Cultural Change in the Shield and Mackenzie Borderlands." Pp. 146–157 in *Handbook of North American Indians.* Vol. 6: *Subarctic.* June Helm, ed. Washington, D.C.: Smithsonian Institution.

Honigmann, John
  1981    "Expressive Aspects of Subarctic Indian Culture." Pp. 718–738 in *Handbook of North American Indians*. Vol. 6: *Subarctic*. June Helm, ed. Washington, D.C.: Smithsonian Institution.

Hope, Eva
  1988    Personal communication to Barbara Hail from Slavey bark specialist: Acho Dene Craft Shop, Fort Liard, Northwest Territories, August 15.

Horse Capture, George P., ed.
  1980    *Native American Ribbonwork: A Rainbow Tradition*, Cody: Buffalo Bill Historical Center.

Hosley, Edward H.
  1981    "Intercultural Relations and Cultural Change in the Alaska Plateau." Pp. 546–555 in *Handbook of North American Indians*. Vol. 6: *Subarctic*. June Helm, ed. Washington, D.C.: Smithsonian Institution.

Houle, Maria
  1985    Personal communication to Barbara Hail. Houle is a Cree-Chipewyan-Métis craftswoman from Fort Chipewyan.

Hurlich, Marshall G.
  1983    "Historical and Recent Demography of the Algonkians of Northern Ontario." Pp. 143–199 in *Boreal Forest Adaptations: The Northern Algonkians*. A. T. Steegmann, ed. New York: Plenum Press.

Innis, H. A.
  1930    *Peter Pond, Fur Trader and Adventurer*. Toronto: Irwin & Gordon, Ltd.

Isham, James
  1949    *Observations on Hudson's Bay, 1743*, and *Notes and Observations on a Book Entitled A Voyage to Hudson's Bay in the Dobbs Galley, 1749*. E. E. Rich, ed. (Reprint.) Toronto: Champlain Society.

Joseph, Marjory L.
  1981    *Introductory Textile Science*. New York: Holt, Rinehart and Winston.

Kaufman, Lloyd
  1974    *Sight and Mind: an Introduction to Visual Perception*. New York: Oxford University Press.

Kemp, H. Douglas
  1954    "Land Grants Under the Manitoba Act: the Half-Breed Land Grant." Pp. 33–52 in *Papers of the Historical and Scientific Society of Manitoba*. Series III, no. 9. Winnipeg.

Koffka, Kurt
  1935    *Principles of Gestalt Psychology*. New York: Harcourt Brace.

Kohler, Wolfgang
  1947    *Gestalt Psychology*. New York: Liveright.

Krause, Mary
  1982    Interview with Kate Duncan; Krause is a Slavey craftswoman from Little Doctor Lake.

Krech, Shepard, III
  1978    "On the Aboriginal Population of the Kutchin." Pp. 89–104 in *Arctic Anthropology*. Vol. XV, no. 1. Madison: University of Wisconsin.

  1984    Ed., *The Subarctic Fur Trade: Native Social and Economic Adaptations*. Vancouver: University of British Columbia.

  1986    *Native Canadian Anthropology and History: A Selected Bibliography*. Rupert's Land Research Centre, University of Winnipeg.

  1987    "The Early Fur Trade in the Northwestern Subarctic: The Kutchin and the Trade in Beads." In *Le Castor Fait Tout*. Fifth North American Fur Trade Conference. Montreal: Lake St. Louis Historical Society.

  1988    "The Hudson's Bay Company and Dependence Among Subarctic Tribes Before 1900." Pp. 62–70 in *Overcoming Economic Dependency*, no. 9, Occasional Papers in Curriculum Series. Chicago: The Newberry Library, D'Arcy McNickle Center for the History of the American Indian.

  1989    *A Victorian Earl in the Arctic: The Travels and Collections of the 5th Earl of Lonsdale, 1888–9*. London: British Museum Publications.

Kroeber, Alfred L.
  1939    *Cultural and Natural Areas of Native North America*. No. 38, University of California Publications in American Archaeology and Ethnology, Berkeley.

Laferte, Joe
  1982    Interview with Kate Duncan at Fort Simpson.

Lafferty, Celine
  1982    Interview with Kate Duncan at Fort Simpson.

Lamb, W. Kaye, ed.
  1970    *The Journals and Letters of Sir Alexander Mackenzie*. Cambridge: Cambridge University Press.

Larsen, Helge, and Froelich Rainey
  1948    *Ipiutak and the Arctic Whale Hunting Culture*. Vol. 42, Anthropological Papers of the American Museum of Natural History. New York.

Leduc, Sister Beatrice
  1925–63    "Moose-Hair Work in the North West Territories." (Unpublished.) Files, Department of Ethnology, Alberta Provincial Museum. Edmonton.

Leeuwenburg, E.L.J., and H. F. Buffart
  1978    *Formal Theories of Visual Perception*. Chichester: John Wiley & Sons.

Leishman, Margaret
  1985    Interview with Barbara Hail at Kakisa Lake, Northwest Territories.

Lemire, Marie, S. G. M.
  1986    Correspondence with Barbara Hail.

Marriott, Alice
  1958    "Ribbon Appliqué Work of North American Indians," part I. Pp. 49–59 in *Oklahoma Anthropological Society Bulletin*, no. 6. Oklahoma City.

Mason, J. Alden
  1946    *Notes on the Indians of the Great Slave Lake Area.* Yale University Publications in Anthropology, no. 34. New Haven.

Mason, Leonard
  1967    *The Swampy Cree: A Study in Acculturation.* Anthropology Papers, National Museum of Canada. No. 13. January. Ottawa.

Mayer, Frank B.
  1851    F. B. Mayer Sketchbook, Edward Everett Ayer Collection, Newberry Library, Chicago.

McClellan, Catharine
  1981    "Tutchone." In *Handbook of North American Indians*. Vol. 6: *Subarctic*. June Helm, ed. Washington, D.C.: Smithsonian Institution.

McClellan, Catharine, and Glenda Denniston
  1981    "Environment and Culture in the Cordillera." Pp. 372–386 in *Handbook of North American Indians*. Vol. 6: *Subarctic*. June Helm, ed. Washington, D.C.: Smithsonian Institution.

Mercredi, Louis
  1982    *Interview with Kate Duncan.*

Mooney, James
  1928    *The Aboriginal Population of America North of Mexico.* Smithsonian Miscellaneous Collections. Vol. 80, no. 7. Washington, D.C.

Morantz, Toby
  1980    "The Fur Trade and the Cree of James Bay." Pp. 39–58 in *Old Trails and New Directions*, C. M. Judd and A. J. Ray, eds. Toronto: University of Toronto Press.

Morier, Jan
  1979    "Métis Decorative Art and its Inspiration." Dawson and Hind. Vol. 8, no. 1.

Morisset, Jean, and Rose-Marie Pelletier
  1986    *Ted Trindell: Métis Witness to the North.* Vancouver: Tillacum Library.

Morse, Eric W.
  1969    *Fur Trade Canoe Routes of Canada: Then and Now.* Ottawa: Queen's Printer.

Nelson, Richard K.
  1973    *Hunters of the Northern Forest. Designs for Survival Among the Alaskan Kutchin.* Chicago: University of Chicago Press.

Neumier, Sister Anna
  1985    Interview with Barbara Hail and Kate Duncan, Fort Providence, August 10.

Nicks, Trudy
  1982    *The Creative Tradition: Indian Handicrafts and Tourist Art.* Edmonton: Provincial Museums of Alberta.
  1985    "Mary Anne's Dilemma: The Ethnohistory of an Ambivalent Identity." Pp. 103–114 in *Canadian Ethnic Studies*. Vol. 17, no. 2.

Orchard, William C.
  1971    *The Technique of Porcupine Quill Decoration Among the North American Indians.* Contributions from the Museum of the American Indian, Heye Foundation. Vol. IV, no. 1. Second Edition. New York.
  1975    *Beads and Beadwork of the American Indians. A Study based on Specimens in the Museum of the American Indian, Heye Foundation.* Contributions from The Museum of the American Indian, Heye Foundation, Vol. XI. Second Edition. New York.

Osgood, Cornelius
  1931    "The Ethnography of the Great Bear Lake Indians." Pp. 31–92 in *Bulletin no. 70 of the Canadian Department of Mines, National Museum of Canada, Ottawa.*
  1971    *The Han Indians.* No. 74, Yale University Publications in Anthropology. New Haven.

Oswalt, Wendell H.
  1980    *Kolmakovsky Redoubt: The Ethnoarchaeology of a Russian Fort in Alaska.* Monumenta Archaeologica 8, The Institute of Archaeology. Los Angeles: The University of California.

Overvold (burger), Joanne, ed.
  1976    *Our Métis Heritage: A Portrayal*, The Métis Association of the Northwest Territories.

Peel, Bruce
  1964    "First Steamboats on the Saskatchewan." Pp. 16–21 in *The Beaver*. Autumn. Winnipeg.

Peterson, Jacqueline, and Jennifer S. H. Brown
  1985    *The New Peoples. Being and Becoming Métis in North America.* Winnipeg: The University of Manitoba Press.

Petitot, Emile
  1970    *The Amerindians of the Canadian North-west in the 19th Century, as Seen by Emile Petitot.* Vol. 2: *The Loucheux Indians.* (Reprint.) Donat Savoie, ed. Mackenzie Delta Research Project. Ottawa: Dept. of Indian Affairs & Northern Development.
  1976    *The Book of Dene.* Programme Development Division. (Reprint.) Yellowknife: Dept. of Education.

Phillips, Ruth
  1984   *Patterns of Power.* Kleinburg: The McMichael Canadian Collection.
  1988   "Like a Star I Shine: Northern Woodlands Artistic Traditions." In *The Spirit Sings: Artistic Traditions of Canada's First Peoples.* Calgary: Glenbow Museum.

Pierson, Sister Flore
  1985   Personal communication with Barbara Hail and Kate Duncan at Fort Providence, Northwest Territories.

Pritchett, John Perry
  1942   *The Red River Valley 1811–1849: A Regional Study.* New Haven: Yale University Press.

Rae, John
  1882   *On the Conditions and Characteristics of Some of the Native Tribes of the Hudson's Bay Company Territories.* Pp. 483–499 in *Journal of the Society of Arts.* Vol. 30. No. 1. London.

Ray, Arthur J., and Donald B. Freeman
  1978   *Give Us Good Measure. An Economic Analysis of Relations Between the Indians and the Hudson's Bay Company Before 1763.* Toronto: University of Toronto Press.

Red Willows Crafts
     "Moose Hair Tufting." Fort Providence, Northwest Territories.

Reid, Elizabeth
  1987   "Fiber Identification of Floss Embroidered Objects in the Subarctic Collection of the Haffenreffer Museum of Anthropology, Brown University." Laboratory report.

Rhodes, Richard A. and Evelyn M. Todd
  1981   "Subarctic Algonquian Languages." Pp. 52–66 in *Handbook of North American Indians.* Vol. 6: *Subarctic.* June Helm, ed. Washington, D.C.: Smithsonian Institution.

Richardson, Sir John
  1851   *Arctic Searching Expedition: A Journal of a Boat-Voyage Through Rupert's Land and the Arctic Sea, in Search of the Discovery of Ships Under Command of Sir John Franklin with an Appendix on the Physical Geography of North America.* 2 vols. London: Longman, Brown, Green and Longmans.

Robinson, H. M.
  1879   *The Great Fur Land or Sketches of Life in the Hudson's Bay Territory.* New York: G. P. Putnam's Sons.

Rogers, Edward S.
  1969   "The Naskapi." In *The Beaver.* Winter. Winnipeg.
  1970   *Indians of the Subarctic.* Toronto: Royal Ontario Museum.

Rogers, Edward S., and Eleanor Burke Leacock
  1981   "Montagnais-Naskapi." Pp. 168–89 in *Handbook of North American Indians.* Vol. 6: *Subarctic.* June Helm, ed. Washington, D.C.: Smithsonian Institution.

Rogers, Edward S., and James G.E. Smith
  1981   "Environment and Culture in the Shield and Mackenzie Borderlands." Pp. 130–145 in *Handbook of North American Indians.* Vol. 6: *Subarctic.* June Helm, ed. Washington, D.C.: Smithsonian Institution.

Rogers, Edward S., and J. Garth Taylor
  1981   "Northern Ojibwa." Pp. 231–243 in *Handbook of North American Indians.* Vol. 6: *Subarctic.* June Helm, ed. Washington, D.C.: Smithsonian Institution.

de la Ronde, Kathleen
  1985   Interview with Barbara Hail and Kate Duncan, The Pas, August.

Ross, Alexander
  1856   *The Red River Settlement: its Rise, Progress, and Present State.* London. (Reprinted in Doherty.)

Ross, Bernard R.
  1862   Unpublished collection notes. Royal Scottish Museum, Edinburgh.

Ross, Hugh Mackay
  1986   *The Apprentice's Tale.* Winnipeg: Watson & Dwyer.

Russell, Frank
  1898   *Explorations in the Far North.* Iowa City: University of Iowa.

Sanderson, Harry
  1985   Interview with Kate Duncan and Barbara Hail, The Pas, Manitoba. August.

Schneider, Richard C.
  1972   *Crafts of the North American Indians.* New York: Van Nostrand Reinhold.

Sealey, D. Bruce, and Antoine S. Lussier
  1983   *The Métis: Canada's Forgotten People.* Winnipeg: Pemmican Publications.

Siemens, Dennis G.
  1979   *On The Banks of the Slave: A History of the Community of Fort Smith, Northwest Territories.* Education Programs and Evaluation Division, Department of Education, Northwest Territories.

Simeone, William E., and James W. VanStone
  1986   *And He Was Beautiful: Contemporary Athapaskan Material Culture in the Collections of the Field Museum of Natural History.* Fieldiana, Anthropology, New Series, no. 10. Chicago: Field Museum of Natural History.

Skinner, Alanson B.

1911    Notes on the Eastern Cree and Northern Saulteaux." Pp. 1–177 in *Anthropological Papers of the American Museum of Natural History*. Vol. 9, pt. I. New York.

Slavey Research Project

1987    *Nahecho Keh: Our Elders*. Dept. of Culture and Communications, Dept. of Education, Govt. of the Northwest Territories. Fort Providence.

Slobodin, Richard

1966    *Métis of the Mackenzie District*. Centre for Research for Anthropology. Ottawa: University of St. Paul.

1981    "Subarctic Métis." Pp. 361–371 in *Handbook of North American Indians*. Vol. 6: *Subarctic*. June Helm, ed. Washington, D.C.: Smithsonian Institution.

Smith, James G. E.

1978    "The Emergence of the Micro-Urban Village Among the Caribou-Eater Chipewyan." Pp. 38–49 in *Human Organization*, Vol. 37, no. 1. Spring.

Snow, Chief John

1977    *These Mountains Are Our Sacred Places. The Story of the Stoney People*. Toronto: University of Toronto Press.

Speck, Frank G.

1925    "Montagnais-Naskapi Tales from the Labrador Peninsula." Pp. 6–8 in *Journal of American Folklore*. Vol. 38, no.147. Washington, D. C.

1935    *Naskapi. The Savage Hunters of the Labrador Peninsula*. Norman: University of Oklahoma Press.

1937    *Montagnais Art in Birch-bark, a Circumpolar Trait*. Indian Notes and Monographs. Vol. XI, no. 2. New York: Museum of the American Indian, Heye Foundation.

Sprague, D. N., and R. P. Frye

1983    *The Genealogy of the First Métis Nation: The Development and Dispersal of the Red River Settlement 1820–1900*. Winnipeg: Pemmican Publications.

Steegman, A. Theodore Jr., ed.

1983    *Boreal Forest Adaptations. The Northern Algonkians*. New York: Plenum Press.

Steinbright, Jan, ed.

1983    *From Skins, Trees, Quills and Beads: The Work of Nine Athapaskans*. Fairbanks, Alaska: Institute of Alaska Native Arts, Dept. of Community and Regional Affairs.

Stocking, George W. Jr.

1985    *Objects and Others: Essays on Museums and Material Culture*. History of Anthropology, Vol. 3. Madison: University of Wisconsin.

Stubbs, Roy St. George

1967    *Four Recorders of Rupert's Land. A Brief Survey of the Hudson's Bay Company Courts of Rupert's Land*. Winnipeg: Peguis.

Sutherland, Mary Agnes, S. G. M., ed.

1984    *Souvenir Album, Bishop Paul Piché, O. M. I.*, Diocese of Mackenzie, Fort Smith, Northwest Territories.

Taylor, Elizabeth

1894    "A Woman in the Mackenzie Delta." In *Outing*. Vol. 12, nos. 1–4.

Teit, James

1909    "Notes on the Chilcotin Indians." Pp. 759–789 in *The Shuswap*. Memoirs of the American Museum of Natural History. Vol. 4, no. 7. New York.

Thayer, Burton

1942    "Some Examples of 'Red River Half-Breed' Art." *Minnesota Archaeologist*. Vol. 8. St. Paul.

Thompson, Judy

1983    "Turn-of-the-Century Métis Decorative Art From The Frederick Bell Collection." Pp. 36–45 in *American Indian Art Magazine*. Vol. 8, no. 4. Autumn.

1988    "No Little Variety of Ornament: Northern Athapaskan Artistic Tradition." In *The Spirit Sings: Artistic Traditions of Canada's First Peoples*. Calgary: Glenbow Museum.

Tobey, Margaret L.

1981    "Carrier." Pp. 413–432 in *Handbook of North American Indians*. Vol. 6: *Subarctic*. June Helm, ed. Washington, D. C.: Smithsonian Institution.

Tracy, William

1985    Personal communication to Barbara Hail.

Turner, Geoffrey

1955    *Hair Embroidery in Siberia and North America*. Occasional Papers on Technology. Vol. 7. Pitt Rivers Museum. Oxford: University Press.

Usher, Peter J.

1971    *Fur Trade Posts of the Northwest Territories 1870–1970*. Ottawa: Northern Science Research Group, Dept. of Indian Affairs and Northern Development.

Van Kirk, Sylvia

1980    *Many Tender Ties: Women in Fur-Trade Society, 1670–1870*. Norman: University of Oklahoma.

VanStone, James W.

1974    *Athapaskan Adaptations. Hunters and Fishermen of the Subarctic Forests*. Worlds of Man, Studies in Cultural Ecology. W. Goldschmidt, ed. Illinois: AHM Publishing Corp.

1981    *Athapaskan Clothing and Related Objects in the Collection of Field Museum of Natural History.* Fieldiana, Anthropology, New Series, no. 4. Chicago: Field Museum of Natural History.

1985    *Material Culture of the Davis Inlet and Barren Ground Naskapi: The William Duncan Strong Collection.* Fieldiana, Anthropology, New Series, no. 7. Chicago: Field Museum of Natural History.

Webber, Alika
    1978    "Wigwamatew, Old Birch Bark Containers." Pp. 57–61 in *American Indian Art Magazine.* Winter.

West, George A.
    1970    *Tobacco, Pipes and Smoking Customs of the American Indians.* Parts I, II. Westport, CT: Greenwood Press.

West, John
    1966    *The Substance of a Journal During a Residence at The Red River Colony. 1824.* Johnson Reprint Corporation.

White, Elmer
    1985    Interview with Barbara Hail in Thompson, CT.

Whiteford, Andrew Hunter
    1977    "Fibre Bags of the Great Lakes Indians." Part II. Pp. 40–47, 90 in *American Indian Art Magazine.* Vol. 3, no. 1. Winter.

    1986    "The Origins of Great Lakes Bandolier Bags." Pp. 32–43 in *American Indian Art Magazine.* Vol. 11, no. 3. Summer.

    1988    Correspondence with Barbara Hail.

Whitney, Caspar
    1896    *On Snow-shoes to the Barren Grounds.* London: Osgood, McIlvaine & Co.

Willey, Gordon R.
    1966    *An Introduction to American Archaeology. Volume One: North and Middle America.* Englewood Cliffs, NJ: Prentice-Hall.

Wilson, James
    1982    *Canada's Indians.* Minority Rights Group, Report No. 21, revised. London.

Wobst, H. Martin
    1977    "Stylistic Behavior and Information Exchange." Pp. 317–342 in *Anthropological Papers.* No. 61. Ann Arbor: Museum of Anthropology, University of Michigan.

Wright, James V.
    1981    "Prehistory of the Canadian Shield." Pp. 86–96 in *Handbook of North American Indians.* Vol. 6: *Subarctic.* June Helm, ed. Washington, D.C.: Smithsonian Institution.

Young, Egerton Ryerson
    1893    *Stories from Indian Wigwams and Northern Campfires.* London: Charles H. Kelly.

Zusne, Leonard
    1970    *Visual Perception of Form.* New York: Academic Press.

COMPOSITION, PRINTING, AND BINDING · MERIDEN-STINEHOUR PRESS

TEXT TYPESETTING IN LINOTRONIC FOURNIER · DISPLAY TYPE IN PILGRIM

PAPER · MOHAWK SUPERFINE HIGH FINISH

DESIGN · KIT KUNTZE